Confessions of a
Real Estate Mini-Mogul

HOW TO SUCCEED IN REAL ESTATE INVESTING DESPITE GHOSTS, PITBULLS, ANNOYING TENANTS, AND THE GOVERNMENT

JAMES S. POCKROSS

Samson Publishing, Inc.
Chicago, Illinois

CONFESSIONS OF A REAL ESTATE MINI-MOGUL

*How to Succeed in Real Estate Investing
Despite Ghosts, Pitbulls, Annonying Tenants,
and the Government*

by James S. Pockross

Samson Publishing, Inc.
PO Box 59695
Chicago, IL 60659
847-256-2399
www.samsonpub.com
samsonpublishing@comcast.net

Interior illustrations by Marlene K. Goodman
Cover design by One-On-One Book Production, West Hills, CA
Interior editing, design, and typesetting by Creative Editorial Services

ISBN-13: 978-0-9796951-0-0

Library of Congress Control Number: 2008903135

Printed in the United States of America

FIRST EDITION

TABLE OF CONTENTS

Part I – My Story

Part II – Lessons from the Street

Part III – Ruminations from the Mind of a Mini-Mogul

DEDICATION

This book is dedicated to my father,
Raymond L. Pockross

May you rest in peace.

Jim

DISCLAIMER

This book is designed to provide information on real estate investing. It is sold with the understanding that the publisher and author are not engaged in rendering legal, accounting, or other professional services. If legal or other expert assistance is required, the services of a competent professional should be sought.

It is not the purpose of this book to reprint all the information that is otherwise available to investors, but instead to complement, amplify, and supplement them. Readers are urged to read any available material, learn as much as possible about real estate investing, and tailor the information to their individual needs. For more information, recommended resources are listed in the Appendix.

Real estate investing is not a get rich quick scheme. Anyone who decides to pursue this path must expect to invest a lot of time and energy.

Every effort has been made to make this book as complete and accurate as possible. However, there may be mistakes, both typographical and content-related. Therefore, this text should be used only as a general guide and not as the ultimate source of real estate investing information. Furthermore, this book contains information on real estate investing that is current only up to the printing date.

The purpose of this book is to educate and to entertain. The author and Samson Publishing shall have neither liability nor responsibility to any person or entity with respect to any loss or damage caused, or alleged to have been caused, directly or indirectly, by the information contained in this book.

If you do not wish to be bound by the above, you may return this book to the publisher for a full refund.

PART I

MY STORY

1

Do You Have
What It Takes?

This story ends with my having a net worth of millions of dollars, an annual income in the hundreds of thousands of dollars, and the liberty to do what I want when I want. When this story began twenty plus years ago, I had nothing but fear and low self-esteem on which to build a future. Doubts plagued me. I worried about pleasing my boss and keeping my job.

So how did an ordinary guy like me end up with a portfolio consisting of hundreds of rental units and a cash flow that's more like a cash torrent? How did I become a mini-mogul, enjoying freedom and self-confidence? I would love to share the details with you, because I believe you too can accomplish what I did.

Making money as a real estate investor is not unusual. Thousands of people representing all the diversity humanity has to offer have done well in real estate. My lessons came from the streets. My motivation was strong: I yearned to escape the poverty my parents had suffered. I made a commitment to be independent of other people's decisions, especially those that could affect my financial well-being.

To become a mini-mogul and beyond, you have to believe you can attain the real estate dream and then take action. I'll show you *what* action, so you won't waste time and money with missteps and miscalculations.

My goal is to touch you from my soul and equip you to be a street-smart, hugely successful real estate investor.

Does that sound inviting to you? Good! Let's get started. Our first step is a simple self-evaluation. Having been a real estate investor for over two decades, I've observed the actions of many people engaged in the same activity and wondered what, if anything, they and I have in common. The pot of gold sits at the end of the rainbow, but not everyone gets to haul it home. Some succeed, some fail, and most never even try.

DO YOU HAVE WHAT IT TAKES?

TRAIT #1: DETERMINATION

Most of us have set goals for ourselves: losing weight, getting in shape, watching less television, or setting aside enough savings to take an annual vacation. Do you have the necessary *focus* and *determination* to succeed in real estate? Are you able to set your mind on a goal and remain focused on that goal until you achieve it? Are you capable of intense focus? Are you likely to be so intent upon a project that you lose track of time or forget to eat?

On a separate sheet of paper, list three recent objectives you have set for yourself. How would you rate the success you've experienced with them?

In my early days as an MMM (Mini-Mogul-in-the-Making), a successful friend told me, "Jim, if you want to succeed in the real estate game – or in anything else, for that matter – you'll need grim resolve."

Grim resolve? I thought, as a distressing image came to mind: I was wearing a Puritan's wide white collar, black coat and short pants, and white stockings, and I was about to give myself a rhinoplasty on a grindstone.

The idea did not go over well with me. I wanted to work, sure, but I wanted life to be fun. I loved to laugh and make jokes. A puritanical work ethic had never appealed to me. As I thought further about my friend's advice, though, it made sense. I replaced the phrase "grim resolve" with the words "focus" and "determination," neither of which implied a life without fun.

If your goal is to own or control one thousand rental units, then you are always focused on building your portfolio and being alert for new opportunities. Along the way you may suffer setbacks, but they won't lessen your intention to achieve your goal. Becoming a mogul or mini-mogul is a high priority in your life, and you are willing to make the sacrifices and climb over the hurdles necessary to get there.

What sacrifices have *I* made? I am a rabid sports fan. Every year I look forward to watching the NCAA basketball tournament on television in March ... which is also the peak rental season in Chicago, where I live and work. Would I rather watch college basketball from my nice, comfortable recliner or get into a frigid car and drive thirty minutes to unlock a vacant apartment for a prospective tenant who may or may not show up for the appointment?

Duh... But part of the deal in my success is the sacrifice. Yes, I miss a lot of tournament games, but I am willing to do whatever is necessary – and legal and ethical – to ensure my investments' success.

TRAIT #2: ENERGY

Everyone has a different level of energy to expend on physical activities. Real estate mogulism demands so much running around, I get tired just thinking about it. Investors search for property, negotiate offers, check on malfunctions and make repairs or arrange to have them done while supervising, pay bills, deal with lawyers, bankers, and contractors. Do you have the *energy* and *stamina* to be a mini-mogul?

Are you able to move around without debilitating pain? Can you go up and down stairs without feeling winded or dizzy? Can you work a successive number of hours to complete errands? Are you a procrastinator?

I love the idea of snoozing in my recliner while money rolls in. I would recognize an "armchair investment" immediately and buy it right away. Although I have looked hard, one has yet to show up.

My industrious neighbor Mr. Hayes once said, "The hardest part of doing any job is thinking about it, Jim. Just do it." This is particularly crucial with rental investments. A tiny discoloration in the corner of the ceiling could mean a leaking roof or pipe. Unless someone investigates why the white ceiling has a yellow stain, a small leak can turn into a huge, expensive roof repair or rotting wood inside a wall.

TRAIT #3: PERSISTENCE

Sir Winston Churchill, the British prime minister during World War II and the secretary of the navy before that, was the commencement speaker at the Harrow School in October 1941. Churchill was no stranger to the campus; he had flunked out of Harrow three times. Despite his spotty academic performance, Churchill was a brilliant man. Aside from his illustrious political career, he was an accomplished writer and public speaker. His address at Harrow was among his most memorable. He stood at the podium, eyed his audience, and said, "Never give up!"

He paused, examined the gathering again, and repeated: "Never give up!" He paused again, slowly looked at every graduate, and told them, "Never give up!" He then returned to his seat.

Property investors must be persistent to be successful, and if they have chosen a particular Realtor to represent them in a transaction, that real estate professional must persevere in the investor's behalf. People who give up never get the deal.

Are you *persistent?* Are you aware of the importance of patience?

Can you draw the line between being persistent and making a nuisance of yourself?

My friend Suzanne saw a gem of a downtown property in a small southern city. She immediately submitted a full-price offer through her agent. The sellers – three siblings and a bank trustee – decided to take the property off the market. It had been listed for one hour.

Suzanne's viewing was its first and only.

Every week for a year thereafter, Suzanne's realtor placed a call to the bank trustee and to the siblings' Realtor, asking if they had changed their minds about selling the property and reminding them that an offer was on the table. The bank and two siblings were eager to sell; one sibling held out. Finally she changed her mind. The property was not listed again for the general public. Because of her Realtor's persistence and the offer she had submitted, Suzanne was invited to adjust her offer to compensate for the property's appreciation. She did so and closed the deal.

The fine little investment she purchased for $230,000 in 1998 she sold for over $1 million in 2004.

TRAIT #4: PEOPLE SKILLS

Real estate is a people business that requires *good interpersonal skills*. Property owners and investors deal constantly with tenants, employees, bankers, attorneys, accountants, vendors, and other owners. Each individual plays an important role in the operation of a real estate business. Their desire to work hard for you and their loyalty are key to your success. To get what you need from these people, you must make them feel comfortable and confident when dealing with you.

What are good interpersonal skills? I believe they include the following attributes:

- the ability to listen and understand accurately what the other person has to say

13

- the ability to express yourself clearly and concisely, to make certain the other individual understands your communication in the way you intended it

- the ability to look at a situation from another person's perspective

- the ability to exert self-control and remain calm when you are about to act angrily or impulsively

I also believe good interpersonal skills means that you are honest, reasonable, consistent, and fair, and that you will keep your word. In general, how do you get along with other people? Are you sociable? Do people seek you out for friendship? Do you have any long-lasting relationships? None of us is perfect, but we must be willing to work on improving those areas where we fall short.

TRAIT #5: DECISIVENESS

Real estate requires *decisiveness*. You must be able to weigh your options and select which one is the best among them. That's only half the process, though. Once you've made a decision, you must have the courage to move forward with it. When you purchase a property, you have to decide you want that one from among the various places you've considered. Next, you have to decide how much to offer for it. Once an offer is on the table, negotiations begin, and you must make multiple decisions on the way to a deal.

When the property is yours, the decisions are endless: how you plan to manage the property; determining the correct rent; how you will upgrade a property; when you should sell and at what price; and, perhaps most importantly, where to have the employee holiday party. Do you believe you can make a series of quick, good decisions and enjoy the process?

Some people are afraid to make decisions and take action. If you know yourself to be indecisive or a procrastinator, then active real estate investing is not for you.

TRAIT #6: OPTIMISM

One of my friends, Karen, dabbles in real estate. She bought her own home and a four-unit building, but she never expanded beyond that. She recently confided to me how much she envied my strongest and most unforgettable trait: my *optimism*.

I was shocked. I'm actually a full-fledged pessimist. My wife calls me Mr. Glass Is Half-Empty. Either Karen saw something in me I didn't know was there, or I had done an excellent job of fooling her. I thought about her comment and realized that, although I am usually a pessimist, I am a big-time optimist when it comes to real estate investing.

Historically, real estate values increase over time. Given the right location, both cash flow and property value will increase. I believe real estate works.

Whatever you believe will happen will indeed happen. You create self-fulfilling prophecies with your every thought, whether or not you are aware of what you are doing.

When you think of your personal future, do you feel good about it? Do you envision yourself living in abundant security, or do you see yourself struggling and living in confusion? Or are you not able to visualize your future at all?

When you think of becoming a real estate investor, does a small voice inside your head cheer you on, or does it jeer at you for being so stupid as to believe you could succeed in such an endeavor?

How about the future of civilization? Do you think humanity's basic goodness will bring the world to peaceful coexistence, or do you have a bleaker view of the future? Are you an optimist or a pessimist?

I have yet to find a real estate investor who believes his or her new investment is ready to tank. When thinking of what the future will bring, I'd rather be on the side of the optimists.

TRAIT #7: KNOWLEDGE

Knowledge is power. Knowledge of what you are doing in real estate enables you to make lots of money. Whatever your specialty in real estate investing, the more you know about it, the better your decisions will be and the more money you will make.

For example, if your niche is apartment-building acquisition and rehabilitation, you need to know how to:

- project income and expenses

- secure real estate financing

- arrange for competent management

You will also need to research your local demographics and its housing needs and determine which cost-effective improvements to make on your property.

Much of the information you'll need is available in books, magazines, newspaper articles, and television programs. You can also learn from seminars, helpful people, and experience. Are you a life-long learner? Do you enjoy gathering research? Can you remember what you read and hear, and then apply it to yourself? Can you build time into your schedule to gather the information you will need?

Lack of knowledge should never be used as an excuse to refrain from real estate investments. The knowledge you need is truly accessible.

TRAIT #8: SELF-CONFIDENCE

Self-confidence is key to success in life. Real estate investors must believe in themselves and have the courage to act confidently based on that belief. Some people exude self-confidence in certain areas but appear timid in others. For example, when I am inspecting a new investment, I am in full command. Call me Field General Pockross! In another, less familiar situation, such as a hike down the Bright Angel Trail of the Grand Canyon, I would have to crawl to the chasm's floor.

Self-confidence means in part that you look to yourself for approval for a job well done, rather than waiting for someone else to commend you. If you are self-confident, you will not depend upon someone else to tell you how you look, how you should wear your hair, or how you should dress.

Does this describe who you are? Are you self-empowered? Do you operate the steering wheel of your life? Or do you feel you need someone else's permission to be alive? Do you have a sense where your self ends and other people's begin? Do you know who you are?

The good news is that self-confidence can be developed, and real estate is a wonderful arena to accomplish exactly that. Each successful small step you take in real estate builds on the previous one, to the point where you feel confident to make upcoming decisions and take subsequent actions.

TRAIT #9: MECHANICAL APTITUDE

Mechanical aptitude must be passed down in families through the genes. I'm convinced the mind either "sees" systems in three dimensions and understands intuitively how they function and fit together, or it does not. Mine does not. I wish it did.

I am worse than a mechanical idiot. The U.S. Army Mechanical Aptitude Test had, at the time I took it, twenty-five multiple-choice questions. A monkey randomly selecting one of the four possible answers would get six correct. I managed to get four right, and I promise I tried my best. (I suppose that's how I ended up being a clerk-typist.)

17

Somehow I've survived my mechanical-aptitude deficit, but I have made a point of understanding the basics of carpentry; plumbing, heating, electrical systems; and construction methods and code compliance.

Do you have a natural mechanical aptitude? As a child, did you take things apart to see how they worked? (Putting them back together is another conversation.) Do machinery and tools fascinate you? Are you attracted to do-it-yourself books, television programs, and Web sites? When you go to a home-improvement store, do you lose track of time just wandering around, looking at the various kinds of merchandise?

The best-case scenario is when a property owner knows how to do his or her own repairs and enjoys the activity, because do-it-yourself investors save money on every job.

The operative word here is *knows*. If you don't know how to do plumbing work, for example, don't attempt it. Hire a plumber to

Hey! Quit trying to cheat!

do the job and watch carefully as the repairs are made. Ask questions along the way. Your plumber may not be overjoyed about offering a tutorial, but you'll pick up valuable information.

At the very least, a real estate investor must know how each job should be done, approximately how long it will take – for example, a stopped-up toilet shouldn't take two days to fix – what materials and tools are necessary, if any equipment needs to be rented, and how much everything will cost. This helps to keep your contractors in line. And if I could learn this, anyone can.

TRAIT #10: PASSION

Someone once said, "If you love what you do, you will never work another day in your life." I envy and respect people who have a *passion* for what they do. I think if they love their field, they'll do an excellent job. And yet, surveys indicate that a high percentage of people are unhappy with their jobs. I see evidence of this in people all around me. The exception seems to be real estate investors. Many of them really like what they do. I believe an important ingredient for success is that *you like to play the real estate game.*

Not everyone enjoys every aspect of property investment. Some investors love to bargain and get the best deal they can. Some like to be detectives who track down opportunities. Others satisfy their ego by building a huge real estate empire. Still others love to rehab buildings, thereby increasing their value. Some people simply love to count their money. Most investors like controlling their own destiny rather than punching a time clock (or wanting to punch their boss).

Do you have a passion for real estate? Ask yourself:

- Do I really like to search for properties?

- Do I enjoy negotiating deals and managing assets?

- Do I like to pore over books about real estate investments?

19

- Do I read, without fail, the real estate section and ads in my local paper?

- Do I enjoy talking about real estate with friends?

- Do I like to attend open houses?

- Do I drive around neighborhoods I like, just to see what's on the market?

Feeling passionate about real estate is helpful, but if that's not how you feel, it's not a deal breaker. I don't have great enthusiasm for real estate per se, but investing in property has proved an excellent way to reach my goals of financial and personal freedom, and I feel great zeal for them. I like some parts of being a real estate investor, of course, but I was not born to be a real estate investor and I can't say it's my calling.

If you like *most* of what you do, you will enjoy doing the tasks that appeal to you, and you'll feel more positive about completing the aspects you don't enjoy as well.

TRAIT #11: INTEGRITY

If you are to succeed in real estate, you must govern your every action with *integrity*. I define *integrity* as consistency in word and deed. If you say you are going to do something by a specific time, you deliver. Your reputation precedes you, and acting with integrity keeps doors and opportunities open to you. If you have a reputation for being dishonest and a cheat, it will catch up with you.

If you are trying to buy a property and you have a bad reputation, the sellers will be skeptical of any offer you make, no matter how fair it might be. If you are trying to fill a vacancy but a group of angry tenants has created a Web site to list your many failures to follow through, then you're in trouble.

I belong to many real estate investor groups, where we trade information we believe will be helpful to one another. At some point the discussion will turn to group members who are absent. The comments might include something along the lines of, "Joe Doe is an unfair negotiator," or "James Able cheats his contractors."

How do *you* conduct business? Do you set high standards for yourself? If your every move in the business arena were publicized on the front page of your local newspaper, would you feel proud of yourself, or would you be mortified?

Do you know the difference between what is moral, immoral, or amoral? Do you know the difference between ethical and unethical actions? Do you think telling the truth is a choice, determined by circumstances? I personally don't do business with people I don't trust, and obviously I am not the only individual who feels that way. If your record does not make you feel proud or good, then I'd suggest you turn yourself around and recreate yourself before becoming an investor.

TRAIT #12: THE ABILITY TO ADD, SUBTRACT, MULTIPLY, AND DIVIDE

I've always viewed real estate investing as "doing the numbers." To be successful, you must be able to *add, subtract, multiply, and divide.* Beyond basic arithmetic, you will need to understand certain concepts well enough to complete the calculations. This means plugging in the numeric data in the correct places in an equation.

For those of you who are arithmetically challenged, manufacturers such as Texas Instruments or Hewlett Packard offer affordable, simple-to-use handheld calculators specifically designed for real estate professionals. These handheld calculators are programmed to amortize loans, figure net present and future values, and calculate internal rates of return. In addition, PC-compatible software programs will provide you with spreadsheet analyses.

Are you a math whiz or math challenged? Are you willing to learn the concepts necessary to run your own calculations and use the results to make decisions? Are you willing to arrange for tutoring or to enroll in a math class – or even a real estate class that includes math in the curriculum – to fill this need in your education?

I have a friend who never did well in math in school, and she took her last math class as a tenth-grader in 1964. Forty years went by. She purchased a handheld calculator for real estate professionals and signed up for an appraisers class. She was so nervous about failing the exam, she made herself sick. But she concentrated on the work and did very well on the exam. The moral? Concepts that may have been too difficult for the school-age brain might be easy for your more-developed, sophisticated, adult gray matter.

So remember Trait #6 and approach your learning with optimism!

TRAIT #13: COURAGE

Owning or controlling real estate means taking risks. While risk can't be avoided, it can be intelligently controlled by way of good decision-making and sufficient knowledge of your intentions. As an investor, you will need the *courage to take risks* and face the consequences of your actions. You have to understand that you could lose money or even go bankrupt.

Are you able to feel some understandable anxiety about undertaking this new (and costly) enterprise and yet move forward with your plans? Can you tell the difference between a calculated risk and a foolish one? Have you attempted new ventures in the past? How did they work out for you? What did you learn from them that you can apply to your real estate investments?

If you are in a long-term relationship or have a spouse, does your significant other encourage you to move ahead with your intentions? If your investment doesn't work out and you lose money, do you have a fallback plan? Are you willing to do whatever is necessary (and legal, of course) to get back on your feet?

Some anxiety is natural when you are first starting out. Buying property is not like picking up a pair of jeans at the discount store; you are committing yourself to a lot of responsibility – financial and otherwise. If you felt no trepidation, I might wonder if you truly grasped what real estate investment was all about.

The courage I refer to here isn't in the same category as the kind you need in a foxhole in the middle of a war zone. Entrepreneurial courage simply needs to override paralyzing fear.

TRAIT #14: SELF CONTROL

Has anyone told you that real estate investing is uninterrupted delight? They were kidding. Some of the challenges and annoyances and aggravations you will face require *emotional maturity* and *self-control*. I'd like to share a few of the less than delightful challenges you may experience (like I have):

- You work very hard on a deal for several months, and it falls through.

- Needing to rent out an apartment, you wait for an hour in subzero weather, and the prospect does not show up.

- Your tenant has made it his/her life's mission to drive you crazy with unreasonable, pointless requests and loves to threaten and scream at you.

Will you be able to absorb these aggravating events and move ahead? Will you be able to keep your emotions out of the business?

If a deal falls apart, can you believe that this is for the best and look for the next deal? If your unit isn't renting or selling, can you remain relaxed and able to focus on new solutions? How about taking a look at what your competition is doing? If you have unreasonable, demanding tenants, can you dream up ways to improve your relationship with them and reduce your stress level?

The world of real estate investing is not perfect, and some days won't be much fun.

(This is an understatement.)

TRAIT #15: THE DESIRE TO IMPROVE YOUR LIFE

I grew up fairly poor, as did many of the investors I know. Much of our motivation to enter real estate investment was *a strong desire to make our lives better*. We didn't want to perpetuate the lifestyle of poverty and worry that our parents suffered as adults and we endured as children. We wanted to improve our situation. We wanted to live a life of prosperity and control our own destiny, and we were willing to work very, very hard to make that happen.

What is your motivation for entering real estate investment? Are you committed to making your life better? What reason is behind that commitment? Is the reason core enough to fuel your hard work and long hours? Is it strong enough that you will keep going and refuse to fail?

This strong desire has motivated me to become a mini-mogul. I have succeeded in reaching my goals, as have many of my colleagues. The key is to have the determination to do real estate investing.

These are the fifteen key characteristics I consider important to becoming a successful real estate investor. Most of us are strong in some areas and have room for improvement in others. Fortunately, many of the traits can be developed or learned. Do you have what it takes? I hope so. I would like to see you succeed.

Let's move ahead. I'll now share with you my journey, starting with my first investment in 1982.

2

FEAR VS DESIRE:
BUYING MY FIRST BUILDING

According to most of the real estate books I read, the ideal investment property is a newer house or apartment building in need of some cosmetic repairs (new landscaping, paint, carpeting, or general cleaning up). Conversely, it should not require major structural work (new foundation, boiler, or roof). The rents should be low, even though the property is situated in a good or an up-and-coming neighborhood. Lastly, the owner should be eager to unload the property. When the seller is motivated, he or she will be open to negotiating the price and other terms of the sale, such as the amount of the down payment, the closing date, and, if the seller is financing the deal, the interest rate.

(In the decades since I walked into my first showing, I've probably considered over one thousand properties. Very few qualified as "ideal," but I did not realize at the time that by following the popular wisdom, I was setting an almost impossible goal for myself.)

I decided to purchase a small apartment building – in the range of four to ten apartments – which would provide a better chance for a positive cash flow than, let's say, a duplex.

As my search began, two opposing emotions dominated my brain: fear and desire. As to fear, I didn't know what I was doing. I had no idea how to find investment property. I didn't feel street-smart. All of my employment history had been with the government or in the not-for-profit sector, and I had never ventured into the for-profit arena. I felt like a lamb who had to deal with wolves.

My most recent job as an assistant hospital administrator in Pittsburgh had ended with me essentially being fired. The prospect of losing another job and starving to death concerned me.

In general, I was a fearful person.

While I had read several books on the subject of real estate investment, my knowledge was basically theoretical. Now I had to face the real world. I had to force myself to evaluate buildings, tenants, and even real estate agents who cared more about earning a commission than about finding me the best deal.

Virtually all the books I had read advocated using a good real estate agent who could find me fantastic deals and would therefore be worth his/her weight in gold. I did not know even one real estate agent, so I struck out on my own. I really got an education.

Every Sunday I scanned the *Chicago Tribune* real estate section. Almost all the For Sale ads read the same way:

Great Location. Priced to sell. Motivated seller. Don't pass this one up!

(Unfortunately, I could find very little useful information about the property itself.)

I could not have entered the market at a more extraordinary – or shall I say "bizarre?" – time. The interest rates were so high, few people could afford monthly mortgage payments. The lowest **adjustable mortgage** rates at financial institutions were 15%. The **prime interest rate** exceeded 20% (as opposed to 8% and rising at the time of this writing). By today's standards, real estate prices and rents were low, but that did not offset the shock of a double-digit mortgage interest rate. No one guessed that commercial or home mortgage rates might return to the 5% to 6% range. The thought of single digit mortgage rates was inconceivable.

Almost daily the real estate ads in the newspaper or the MLS book read in boldface type:

BELOW-MARKET SELLER
FINANCING AVAILABLE!

Even so, very little incentive existed to push people toward real estate investment. Investors were content to put their cash into money market funds, which were paying over 18%.

All this added to my general anxiety about my new venture. Counteracting the fear, however, was desire. After my lousy experience in hospital administration, my mantra became, "I will never depend upon a job for my financial security." Never again did I want to subject myself to the insecurity of a job. Never again would I allow myself to be in that position. I wanted to control my own destiny.

All my life I had a rebellious streak in my nature, which led to my belief that I could control my fate through my actions. I had grown up poor and didn't want to live that way. My desire proved to be stronger than my fear, and so the journey began and the search was on.

I'd call the agent named in an ad and obtain some preliminary information on the building: address, projected rents, some of the projected expenses, and the price and terms. Then I'd drive to the location, park my car, walk around the property, check the mailboxes for vacancies, and so on. If the property looked interesting, I'd make an appointment to see the interior.

I felt very uncomfortable doing these inspections. I had no idea what I was doing. I could not tell a good investment from one just short of displaying a **BUYER BEWARE!** sign on the front door.

Going by the advice in the books I had studied, I would pull out my "Apartment Inspection Checklist" and insist on looking at every room, including closets, in every apartment.

A typical inspection of a four- to six-unit building would take me two hours. (To put this in perspective, once I became experienced, I could conduct a ten-minute inspection on a sixty-unit-building and purchase it on the spot.)

As hungry as real estate agents were for commissions at this crazy time, and even though the majority of them had plenty of free time, many refused to work with me a second time. They despaired of my ever making a purchase. They were wrong.

After driving by about a hundred buildings and inspecting twenty of them, I made an offer on an eight-unit building with an asking price of $135,000. The seller and I agreed on the price and terms. My agent mailed a standard contract to him at his winter home in Arkansas, with a few blanks filled in based on our agreement.

All the seller had to do was sign it, date it, have it witnessed, and return it. That never happened. About six months later I learned that the seller sold the building to someone else for the same price and terms as ours, about three months after he and I had struck a deal. To this day, I don't know what happened. Suddenly I was back to square one.

I continued to search. One day I received a call from an agent who had shown me one of her listings. She wanted to tell me that a six-unit building in a good area with low rents was being offered for a low price. I knew the area; at one time I had lived a quarter of a mile east of there.

I drove by and asked for a showing. The seller's agent scheduled an open house on the Saturday before Christmas – the first time the property would be shown. Ten people showed up, which was a good turnout, considering the market was slow and the holiday fast approaching.

I liked what I saw: the apartments were large and well designed. But I didn't know what I was doing and was nervous about making an offer on the building. Fortunately I had a little help. I had brought two friends with me to the open house. Michele, whom I had just started dating, found my new venture interesting, and she proved to have an intuitive sense about real estate. Fletcher, someone I knew through work, had a Harvard law degree and was a law professor in the Chicago area. He, too, was fascinated with real estate.

The asking price was $85,000. The seller wanted $25,000 down and was offering 13% financing. As far as I could make out, the seller was retiring and planning on moving out of state. He wanted to liquidate this asset, his only real estate investment, before moving from Chicago.

My friends' input made my decision easy. Fletcher stated simply, "If you don't buy it, I will."

"You'd be a fool to pass it up," Michele told me. "If you don't buy it, our relationship is over." (Three years later I married her.)

I told the agent I'd put in an offer. We drove to her office to draw it up. She agreed the building was a good deal and warned me that several other offers would be coming in from other people at the open house. She persuaded me to offer more than the asking price, to maximize the odds of my offer being accepted. I offered $85,700 with $25,000 as a down payment.

As a first-time investor, I was very cautious. I asked my agent to include certain conditions, known as *contingencies*, in the offer, so I would be protected against unseen problems, should the seller accept my proposal. These contingencies had to be met to my satisfaction before I would finalize the purchase. My conditions were:

- My attorney would review and approve the contract.

- A professional building inspector would examine the overall condition of the property and give me a report of his findings.

29

- The seller would give me access to the building's financial records for the previous two years.

The inspection proved very enlightening. The electrical system was ancient, installed around the turn of the last century, before hair dryers, microwaves, and air conditioners existed.

The whole building could handle only thirty amperes of electricity, which meant that if three window air conditioners operated simultaneously, the electrical system would be overloaded.

We could find no storm windows in the basement, so I would have to purchase the energy-savers for the entire building. The paint protecting the wood window frames needed scraping and painting.

The plumbing was fine, except none of the apartments had shut-off valves. This meant if I had to do even the simplest repair – such as replace a leaking faucet – I would be forced to shut off the water supply to the entire building. Otherwise, when I removed the leaking faucet, a geyser of water would spew everywhere in the room. Obviously being able to turn off the water supply under every sink and commode is the way to go.

The steam boiler heating system was functional, but according to the inspector, too small for a building with the square footage of mine. The building had a very thick stone foundation. The brick walls bowed inward.

Fortunately, the owner had completed structural repairs to make sure this would not develop into a long-term problem. The last item on the inspection was the flat roof; it would need replacement in about three years.

The inspector estimated the cost of repairs, then said, "The building would work out if you follow my suggestions for improvements." He handed me his invoice. "I've owned some buildings myself, and to be honest, management is the dregs."

**"Good luck if you buy this, but remember that
management is the dregs."**

As I wrote out his check, I chuckled and asked, "Are you trying
to scare me off?"

"Nah. It just wasn't for me. You might like it fine."

At this point I had three choices: I could back out of the purchase agreement because of the cost of the repairs; I could request,
through our agent, that the seller look over the inspection report
and the repair estimates and adjust his asking price down; or I
could approve the inspection contingency. I chose option three.
Here's why:

1) Everything was cosmetic, except for upgrading the
   electrical service.

2) My agent had been right about other offers coming

in. Three were presented three days before Christmas, and the seller chose ours because of the extra $700. Three offers in a lousy market indicated that I was getting a good property at a good price. I did not want to risk losing this building to one of the other prospective buyers by giving the owner an opportunity to back out by asking him to lower the purchase price.

One condition satisfied, two to go. The seller provided his income tax records for the prior two years along with copies of his electric and gas bills because he included those utilities with the rent. While some of the expenses seemed unusually high, his explanations satisfied me. Of course the gas bill would be high if the place lacked storm windows during Chicago's winter season. Besides, I already had plans to raise the tenants' rent by 25%.

My attorney approved the boilerplate contract. I was on the road to becoming a mogul. I had only one small problem: I didn't have $25,000. But my cousin had $15,000 to be added to my $10,000, and he and I became partners.

The seller was to finance the purchase at 13% interest for five years. That was good for him; he would have income from me at a hefty rate, and if I failed to pay in a timely manner, the building would be his to sell again, and I would forfeit my down payment and whatever payments I had made up to that point. The deal was also good for me: 13% was a lot cheaper than if I had borrowed from a bank or credit union.

After five years, I either had to get a new loan and pay him off, or he could reclaim the building. (In real estate lingo, it was a *land contract with a five-year balloon.*) I thought this was a good gamble. I did not believe the very high cost of borrowing money would last forever. I figured Ronald Reagan would whip inflation. Surely in five years I would be able to get a more favorable rate than even the 13% the seller offered.

The *closing*, the finalization of a purchase, was scheduled, and reality slowly sank in. I would soon be the owner of an apartment building, with total management responsibility.

My cousin had agreed to provide the bulk of the down payment and a small contribution toward the storm windows and the upgrade of the electrical system. Knowing that the rest of the money would come from my pocket, I envisioned worst-case scenarios: rent strikes, phone calls at all hours of the day and night, and devastation by fire. My greatest fear was being exposed as an incompetent manager who would create unacceptable living conditions and lose tenants as a result.

Aspiring moguls must move forward, however. To calm myself, I read several books on real estate management. (Remember Trait #7, Knowledge and Trait #13, Courage?)

I was sure managing a building would be a piece of cake.

We closed on March 8, 1982. I didn't attend the closing. I had previously bought a home in Pittsburgh as my private residence and had attended that closing. My investment hadn't worked out, and after I moved back to Chicago, I decided never to attend closings. My superstition must have some basis, because every subsequent investment has done well for me.

Once I took possession of the property, I met with the seller to learn how to operate the mechanicals. (If you are not mechanically inclined, you may want to bring along your handyman to this meeting and at the very least take notes of the instructions.)

"This building has been good for me," the seller told me. Then he added a remark that struck me to the core: *I only wish I had bought more buildings like this one.*

I only wish I had bought more buildings like this.

I immediately passed around a notice of new ownership and met with all the tenants. I dreaded informing them of the rent increase but was hopeful the improvements I had already begun to implement would show, in part, what they would be getting for their money.

Events unfolded just as I had hoped: to my shock and relief, they all agreed to pay the increase – including the seller's sister-in-law, who had the best unit in the building and was paying $190 per month. I raised her unit to $260.

The residents appreciated that I was upgrading the electrical system and had installed an intercom system between their apartment and the lobby. New landscaping spruced the place up in the summer, and triple-track storm windows would add to the renters' comfort in the winter.

In general, though, I still felt very insecure about making decisions on electrical wiring, purchasing a certain brand and type of storm windows, and fixing leaky faucets. One Sunday I spent four hours installing one dead bolt lock. But I survived the trauma, and so did the tenant.

If I had been holding my breath because of anxiety, the oxygen deprivation lasted only thirty days. The building had a positive cash flow by the second month, and it steadily increased in value.

The investment worked out so well, in fact, I quickly felt I was ready for my second building.

3

Buying Building Number 2: Why Is This So Much Work? Is the Effort Worth the Reward?

I continued to educate myself about real estate. I read countless books, bought seminar tapes, and attended monthly meetings of a wealth builders' group in Chicago.

In addition to my real estate education, I took a strong interest in self-improvement. I started reading books by W. Clement Stone, Zig Ziglar, Denis Waitley, and Napoleon Hill. I also began seeing a psychotherapist to help me in my efforts to grow as a human being.

In the spring of 1982, I moved to an apartment not far from Wrigley Field and befriended the landlord, John Corboy. As a fellow landlord, he took an interest in me and introduced me to a group of landlords who called themselves the Lakeview Developers Association. The group, which met twice a month, consisted of apartment building owners with property near Wrigley Field. Many of the members were active rehabbers, experienced in buying and upgrading buildings. Some owned as many as four hundred rental units.

Meetings typically had a speaker who spoke on a subject of interest to the group. Topics included roofing, replacement windows, landlord/tenant laws, paint, landscaping, estate planning, energy conservation, and so forth. The speaker did not charge a fee for the presentation, but was happy to get future business.

The meetings were an excellent forum in which to share information and get feedback from others who were in the same situation. Members would discuss rent levels, changing neighborhoods, and were a great resource when I needed help.

Within me, things were changing. I had begun to question what I was doing on my job at the Chicago Hospital Council. Real estate was exciting, while my job seemed meaningless. I didn't think I had any impact on local hospitals, on patients' welfare, or on the politicians and decision-makers we were trying to influence. On the other hand, I needed a job for the income and benefits it provided me, as well as for the employment reference when I applied for real estate loans. One or two hundred dollars of positive cash flow wasn't going to put a roof over my head or food on the table. A semimonthly paycheck would.

My spiritual and romantic pursuits were evolving as well. Spiritually, I had chosen to follow the path of Zen Buddhism in 1974. The teachings of Buddhism seemed closer to my inner core of beliefs than any of the major Western religions. (I actually view Buddhism as a healthy way to live, rather than as a religion.)

To share what I was doing with like-minded people, I joined a Buddhist meditation group. I attended meditation sessions lasting two hours each, two evenings a week and on Sunday mornings. Sometimes I'd meditate at group sessions for entire weekends or even longer. I reaped many benefits from this practice, such as greater alertness, awareness, and peacefulness. In any case, it took up a lot of time and energy.

Romantically, my first date with Michele was on September 11, 1981, when I was just beginning the search for my first building. By the second date, my intuition told me Michele was the right person for me.

While I quickly concluded Michele was the one for me, she took longer to come to the same conclusion. I had to woo her for about three years to get her to say yes. Actually, her response to my proposal was "I think so." Much of my free time was devoted to pursuing her.

Overall, I was going in four different directions at once : holding a professional job; doing real estate – managing the building and looking for a new acquisition, etc.; ardently practicing Zen Buddhism; and romancing Michele.

I am not a person of limitless energy. My dissatisfaction with my job was growing. I hated going to work each day. My job performance declined, and my performance review was only fair, with a warning that I needed to improve. My heart really wasn't in it. My inner drive was pushing me to make another real estate acquisition.

I had mixed feelings about proceeding with a new acquisition, though. Finding the first building had been a lot of hard work. Only through an extra push from Michele and Fletcher did I finally decide to buy it. Now I had to make the decision on my own.

I had also been attending meetings with recent graduates of the "how to get rich" weekend seminars. Most of the investors who attended were newbies who were purchasing single family homes and renting them out. I wondered whether this was a better strategy than buying multiunit buildings.

The chart on the following page shows how analytical I can get regarding which direction to follow:

INVESTING IN SINGLE FAMILY HOMES

PROS	CONS
• There are more of them than multiunits; therefore there are many more motivated sellers	• It's either 100% occupied or 0% occupied. A vacancy is brutal on cash flow.
• Financing is easier to obtain	• Multiunits usually offer a better chance for a positive cash flow. Many houses are negative cash flows.
• If need be, you can live in it.	
• Value increases based on market conditions, not on the building's income and expenses.	
• Sellers are less sophisticated.	• Multiunits are more cost efficient – a new roof on a four-unit doesn't cost four times a roof on a house.
• It's easier to get creative financing, such as lease with option to purchase.	
• There are many more unsophisticated buyers.	• One bad tenant in a house can really hurt.
• You can fix it up cheaply and raise the value.	
• It's easier to manage.	• Houses rent to families (plus pets), This can increase maintenance expenses.
• It may be subject to fewer government building inspections and regulations.	
• You don't have to mediate tenant disputes.	• Houses are more likely to have children, which increases the liability risk.
• Tenants stay longer, because they tend to be families who take pride in their homes.	
• You can often get in with a lower down payment.	• An empty house is more likely to be vandalized than an empty apartment in a multiunit.
• It's easier to geographically diversify your economic risk (it's better to own six houses with one in a deteriorating neighborhood than to own a six-unit in a deteriorating neighborhood)	• Houses cost more per unit.
• If you sell, there are many more buyers of houses than multiunits.	• Cosmetic improvements and better management can have a greater impact on the value and cash flow of a multiunit vs a house.
• There are government-funded programs to help home buyers, such as low interest and forgivable loans.	• FNMA lending limit on houses.
• Property insurance is more available for houses than for multiunits.	
• Utility costs can more easily be passed on to the tenant in a house.	

After mulling over the pros and cons for several hours, I decided to look into multiunit properties. I felt they offered me a better chance for a positive cash flow.

So, in the summer of 1983 I began the search for my next building. Rather than spread myself out in different directions, I decided to work with a local real estate agent who had been recommended by some of the Lakeview Developers. The realtor would pay attention to the listings that came up, and I would visit his office weekly.

I really had no money, as I was diverting my job income to upgrading Building Number 1. Also, with my job in a precarious position, I was saving whatever I could for an emergency cushion. If I bought anything, I would have to do a "no money down" acquisition.

In November 1983, the realtor called me and said he had just listed a four-unit building a little west of De Paul University, on the north side of Chicago. The neighborhood had some rough elements but was slowly gentrifying.

I drove by and arranged an inspection. My inspection went much faster than with my first building. I no longer used a checklist for every room and closet. I'd walk through an apartment to get a feel for how a tenant would view it – size, layout, light, and amenities. I'd check the kitchen and bathroom and the closets. I'd look for electrical outlets and inspect for water damage, peeling paint, and so forth. I'd also examine the major mechanical components of the building: roof, foundation, exterior appearance, plumbing, heating, and electrical. Being mechanically challenged, I still didn't know what I was looking at, but figured an inspector would tell me. I signed the contract that included having an inspection contingency.

The four-unit had little curb appeal. It was a frame building with ugly gray asphalt siding. I believe it was originally a two-unit building that had been converted to four apartments.

"Cut-up" is a term used for this in the business. The configuration of the units was weird. The first floor front unit had a large living room and kitchen and a very small bedroom. The bathroom was really small. It had a sink tinier than any I had ever seen – even smaller than one on an airplane. If it ever had to be replaced, I'd have no idea where to find another like it. The other bathrooms didn't even have sinks. The tenants used the kitchen sink to wash up and brush their teeth.

The building was heated by individual space heaters dating back to the turn of the century. I later learned these contraptions were vented into the walls, as opposed to the chimney. The first floor front unit was duplexed into the front part of the basement below. This could be used as a second bedroom. The area was quite unattractive, with a floor of poured concrete over dirt. Water would seep in during heavy rains. In total, the apartment had about a thousand square feet.

The second floor front unit was what sold me on the building. It too was a duplex. The second floor was similar to the first floor unit in terms of layout. However, it had a staircase that led up to the attic, which was somewhat habitable. It had a huge bedroom at the front of the building and a huge bedroom in the back. Between the front bedroom and back bedroom, there were a few "mystery" rooms which tenants could use as they chose. The upstairs was so large, it was possible to house five bedrooms in it. I later learned that the Milwaukee Road Railroad had a big office building across the street and many of the railroad workers would rent rooms in the attic of the apartment. This apartment was about twenty-one hundred square feet – larger than many houses.

The building also had two smaller units in the rear. Neither was a duplex. They had large kitchens and living rooms and very small bedrooms. Closet space was limited. And, of course, the bathrooms didn't have sinks. In the back of the structure was a small, weed-infested yard and a dilapidated garage.

The asking price was $79,500, and the owner was willing to provide some financing as long as the purchaser could get a conventional first mortgage from a bank. Based on my financial analysis, I expected a $450 per month positive cash flow from the property. I figured the total rents to be about $1150 per month, and expenses including mortgages, taxes, insurance, and so forth to be about $700 per month, based on existing information. I offered $79,000. I would get a first mortgage of $71,000. At the closing, I would put $8000 down that I borrowed against stock I owned. After the closing, the seller would give me a certified check for $14,000. This would pay off my $8000 loan and leave me an extra $6000.

That money would pay for an exterior stair system so tenants on the second floor would have two ways of exiting the building in case of fire. I would owe the bank $71,000 and the seller $8000. The $71,000 was secured by the building and me. The $8000 was secured by the stock I owned. The loan from the seller was a "secret second," since the bank wouldn't know about it.

The terms of the note to the seller were as follows: no payment for the first ninety days, then 8% simple interest for five years (about $53 per month), and after that, I'd have to pay him back the $8000. The 8% interest was well below the going rate of 12% at the time.

The seller accepted my offer. It was now time to do my "diligence." Since I was not in the best financial position, I decided to economize and use my good friend's brother to inspect the building. He had taken a couple of years of architectural courses in college. Having paid for a new electrical service once before, I didn't want to go through that again. I inquired about the roof and also about the heating, as the space heaters had to be at least thirty years old. I was told everything was fine.

My attorney approved the contract and told me to go to City Hall to check if there were any building-code violations on record and to see if the water bill and property taxes were paid to date. According to the folks at City Hall, there weren't any code violations or delinquent payments. The financial records for the building were basically nonexistent, so I thought I'd gamble on the numbers. The sellers claimed they didn't maintain any records.

Lastly, I was to get a loan (first mortgage) for 90% of the purchase price of the property. To get a 90% loan, I was to state that I intended to move into the building. The bank wanted the property to be "owner occupied."

After shopping around for a mortgage (more on this in a later chapter), I selected a bank and applied for the loan. The terms of the loan were 12% interest for five years and then annual adjustments every year thereafter.

To qualify for the loan, I needed a good employment history and credit report. I had these. Fortunately, the bank only wanted my employer to verify that I worked there. They did not inquire about my future prospects. In addition, the bank would send one of its employees out to appraise the building.

Being an opportunist, I phoned him beforehand and told him that I was very concerned about the purchase price. I said that in retrospect I felt I had grossly overpaid, and that the property was worth about $70,000, not $79,000. I was really hoping that he'd come back with a low appraisal so I could go to the seller and shave more off the purchase price. I must admit, my projections for the market value of the building were actually $90,000 by December 1984; $100,000 by December 1985; and $110,000 by December 1986, based on the neighborhood upgrade.

Unfortunately, the appraiser did not do as I wanted. He valued the building at $80,000, and the bank approved the loan. The closing was set for December 28.

In general, this was a tough time for me. I was under pressure to perform on the job. Every little thing I did wrong was brought to my attention. Fearing unemployment, I remember looking through the "Help Wanted" ads a few days before Christmas and not finding one job that either interested me, or that I felt I could do. I feared I could do nothing and that I might starve to death.

To make matters worse, the weather turned severely cold. While I love Chicago and think it's a great city, I don't like the winters here. An extreme cold spell hit the area on Christmas weekend as temperatures dipped to windchills of eighty degrees below zero Fahrenheit. I felt trapped indoors with a severe case of cabin fever. When I went to visit Michele the Friday before Christmas, my car wouldn't start again after I got there. Neither would hers.

The closing on the property was scheduled for ten in the morning on the 28th of December. As noted previously, I don't attend closings. At ten o'clock, just when the closing had begun, my boss called me into the conference room. My services were no longer viewed as useful. I'd be kept on until the end of February, in light of my past contributions to the organization. After that, I would have to clean out my office and go.

Following the conference, my attorney called to congratulate me on my new acquisition. I had mixed feelings, having just been fired. All in all, I was feeling lousy. I pondered some difficult questions: Was I capable of doing anything right? What if the new building didn't work out? Why would Michele have any interest in marrying me – who wants to marry someone you have to support? If I didn't have a job, where would I live when my lease expired in April? No landlord wants an unemployed person. (I couldn't even meet my own rental requirements as a tenant.) I was afraid of what the future might bring.

I took over managing the property upon closing. My attorney promptly informed me that the tenant in the lower front apartment had unexpectedly moved. Now I had to fill a vacancy in the heart of winter. This did not bode well.

January was rent collection time. This was a neighborhood in the beginning stages of gentrification. I learned later that I was "pioneering" with my new acquisition. The tenants were very different from those in my first building. None had checking accounts. They all paid their rent in cash, but at least they paid. Fearing I'd be clubbed over the head on my way out, I'd always conceal the money in my sock and run to the nearby bus stop as soon as the collections were complete. The tellers at the bank would gaze in wonder at me when I took off my shoe and sock to make the deposit. At least I offered a diversion from their standard customer deposit.

Money doesn't always grow on trees

As I had feared, management of the building initially went poorly, though I did get the vacant apartment rented to three communists. In March, an attorney from the bank telephoned, inquiring why I had not moved into the building and more importantly, what I was planning to do to correct all the building-code violations.

Apparently the Department of Buildings had mailed me notices about these at the property. When the notices came back saying "no such person at this address," they contacted the mortgage lender. The code violations had been cited before my acquisition. I'll never know why the clerk at the Department of Buildings couldn't find them when I checked before buying the property. While I could certainly go after the seller legally for nondisclosure, my immediate concern was my pending court date for noncompliance. I didn't know what to do.

As I had suspected, my tenants turned out to be real gems. Early one Sunday morning, I got a call from the police, asking what kind of people I had in my building. They had just arrested one of the tenants running down Southport Avenue, wearing nothing but a negligee. When they caught her, she was wielding a huge machete, and was chasing a young man clad only in his underpants.

Then there was a murder in a park about an eighth of a mile from the property. Within a day the police had a suspect – the tenant in the second-floor unit. They carted him off for interrogation, while the other tenants complained that I was harboring murderers. Fortunately, he turned out to be innocent, or I would have lost more tenants.

The lowest point in my quest to become a real estate mogul occurred one pleasant spring day in April. I got a call from my communist tenants that there was a puddle of water on the basement floor and they didn't have any hot water. Being unemployed and soon to become homeless, I went over myself to check on the hot water heater. While I am a mechanical dunce, it didn't take much to figure out that the tenants needed a new hot water heater.

I drove to the local plumbing supply place and purchased a thirty-gallon hot water heater. When they gave me the price for installation and removal of the old one, it was $130. One of the other "customers" overheard my dilemma and offered to install the new heater, with my help, for $35. The deal was made.

My installer did not look like your typical plumber. He was about sixty-five years old and had long, straggly, unkempt white hair. His smile was memorable, as his front teeth were missing. But he told me he was a handyman and had installed numerous hot water heaters. It sounded good to me – especially the price. When the plumbing supplier dropped off the new heater, our work began.

The first task was to drain the now kaput old hot water heater. This is when I discovered that the previous owner had cemented over the only drain in the basement in order to make a bedroom down there. I found a little pail outside and emptied the water one pail at a time in the backyard. It took an hour and a half to empty the tank. We then unhooked it and dragged it out of the way. I never knew how heavy hot water heaters were.

We eventually installed the new heater and ignited it. Fortunately it worked. The handyman did know what he was doing. I paid him and then proceeded to lug the old heater to the alley for garbage pickup. It took me an hour to get it out there.

I sat down upon the hot water heater to reflect on the day and on my situation in general. I was jobless and soon to be homeless – I couldn't get an apartment because I had no job or predictable source of income. I couldn't live in one of my own units because I couldn't afford my own rent. I was uncertain Michele would want to be with such a loser anymore, and saw little promise for the future. Well, at least I had my health. Or, as it turned out, I had it for about the next five minutes.

As I got up to leave, a stray dog that had been menacing my tenants and other neighbors wandered over. The animal had no ownership tags. "Rover" was medium-sized with filthy, matted, light brown hair. The dog attacked me unrestrainedly. It went straight for my ankle, biting me and drawing blood.

Now I had a moral dilemma: as a vegetarian who chose vegetarianism as an expression of compassion towards animals, do I let the

Maybe you can fix the broken water heater?

dog do its thing, or as a human being under attack, do I defend myself? I chose the latter. I picked up a rake that was lying nearby and whacked the animal several times. After about ten whacks, the dog stared at me and I stared right back into its eyes. It ran away, and my tenants were never bothered by it again.

Since I didn't have medical insurance, I hoped the dog did not have rabies. I'd gotten a tetanus shot a little over ten years before; I thought I'd push my luck, figuring that maybe tetanus shots were good for a little more than ten years.

As I walked to my car, I was feeling dejected. If self-esteem was measurable on a scale of one (low) to ten (high), mine was in the negative numbers. I felt I was a total fool, and that I had been stupid enough to buy a real lemon.

Remarkably, one of my fellow landlords from the Lakeview Developers Association drove by, as I moped my way to my car. He commented that I looked depressed and inquired whether perhaps my mother or Michele had just died. He gave me a pep talk, and drove off.

I made it to my apartment and went to bed at six p.m. The day had been bad enough, and I didn't want anything else to happen.

In this difficult period of unemployment, I found myself with little choice – I could either sit in a morass of anguish and give up, or I could look for a way to bring in income. I didn't have nearly enough property to count on real estate income. I never gave up, though. I continued to look for income-generating possibilities, including a regular (ugh!) job.

The building's situation didn't improve in the months that followed. There were constant vacancies and much deferred maintenance. I wasn't even breaking even and had to use part of my unemployment check to cover the negative cash flow.

My own landlord, John Corboy, was very compassionate. When my lease expired on April 30, he let me store my few possessions in the basement, and allowed me to stay rent-free in an apartment he was rehabbing in another building, so long as I only slept there.

On the job front, I didn't know what kind of work I wanted. Actually, I wanted a salaried position in real estate, but I couldn't find one. In retrospect, hospital administration had not turned out to be my calling. I thought maybe I could drive a limousine or cab if that's what I had to do.

I got married August 12, 1984. It was a beautiful day. Even the Chicago Cubs won that day. Unlike most people, who dream of a happy future with their new spouse on their wedding night, I worried about how I was going to bring in money.

My fortunes changed immediately upon my return from my honeymoon. I landed a job in the City of Chicago benefits management office. I was essentially the assistant benefits manager. I also got to move in with Michele, since we were now married. My homelessness and joblessness had ended.

The new job was demanding. Under the purview of Mayor Harold Washington, the city was completely revamping its benefit programs to bring them into line with what the private sector had long been doing: controlling costs. I became an integral part of the change and actually loved that job. Nineteen eighty-four had started out so bleakly for me, and yet it ended on an upswing.

With little free time, I decided to hire a manager for the four-unit building. I continued to manage the six-unit, as there wasn't much to do there. With my new salary, I was able to set aside money to correct some of the building-code violations. (The key to keeping the city building inspector off my case was showing that progress was being made.)

The situation came to a head when the code violations were all corrected. The city wanted me to give up either the attic or the basement, so I would lose one of my duplexed apartments. I had an attorney who specialized in building-code matters, who told me this was the deal he worked out with the city attorney. As a point of information, no one representing the city knew I was a city employee.

On the appointed court date for the final hearing, my attorney forgot to come. My heart sank when the court clerk called my name. My property manager and I asked if the judge could call us later, in the hope that my attorney would appear. The attorney never showed.

When all the other cases were finished, I was called to the bench again. The judge looked at my worried face, and I explained that my attorney had failed to show up to represent me. To my total shock, the judge asked the building inspector if the work at the building had been done in a workmanlike manner. The inspector said yes. The judge then kindly suggested to the building inspector and the city attorney that the case be dismissed, since I had complied with the law and had put forth an earnest effort. They agreed, and the case was dismissed. I got to keep the attic and basement as habitable space. In the end, it was a good thing my attorney was a no-show.

My second great joy that day was when I called the attorney that afternoon. It was with total gladness that I heard him exclaim, "Oh shit!" after I said my name. It's the only time anyone has so expressed himself at the sound of my voice. I calmly explained how I had shown up in court that morning and waited for him. His apology was quick in coming. When I told him that the judge had dismissed the case, he was in disbelief. He asked me to send him the court papers so he could see for himself (Faxes were few and far between in 1985). I sent him the papers. I never heard from him again – nor did I get a bill.

After the court date, I noticed that some of the other buildings in the neighborhood were being rehabbed. My manager suggested I rehab one of my apartments and see what happened. I would pay for the rehab from the income from my job.

I figured that the apartment in question could be improved by trading some of the space in the very large kitchen for a bedroom which could handle a bed *and* a dresser, that a heating system better than an ancient space heater would be good, and that something other than a concrete floor which had water seepage whenever it rained was needed. Through my manager, I hired a general contractor to do the work. Six months and $10,000 later, the rehab was complete. I raised the rent from $375 to $550 and brought in some good tenants.

With the success of this first rehab, the idea crossed my mind to do the other three units. I did not, however, have the money and wasn't excited about funding this from my salary again. My wife was getting tired of hearing that money was being diverted from my paycheck to the rehab.

By 1985, interest rates were falling. An adjustable mortgage at 12% was high. I decided to refinance the property and hoped that the appraisal would come back high enough so that I could pull some money out for subsequent rehabs.

I shopped the mortgage market and selected Avondale Federal, who offered a loan that was like a checking account. You could write checks as needed, so long as the amount owed never exceeded 80% of the appraised value. I only had to pay the interest (the prime rate) that was due.

I applied for the loan and made an appointment with the appraiser. When I went to the property with the appraiser, I pointed out all the nice features of the remodeled unit. He did not appear very impressed with the old space heaters or sinkless bathrooms in the other units. I was hoping the appraisal would come in between $100,000 and $110,000 so I'd have some rehab funds. The lending officer called me a few weeks later and told me the appraisal had come back and the bank was ready to close. I meekly asked what the appraiser had set as the property's value. He responded, "$237,000." I asked if he had the right appraisal, and he verified that the address was indeed that of my building.

I was in total shock. Things like that didn't happen to me. I couldn't reconcile this with my self-image. I felt like I could hardly work. I couldn't even talk. I went home and asked my wife to leave me alone for a while. Then I cried for about two hours.

I had finally done something right (besides marrying my wife). The building I had feared was a lemon, wasn't. My view of myself was changing. Building Number 1 was working, the second building had changed to $160,000 of equity, I was happily married, and I even had a job I liked. The equity in the building ($237,000 appraisal value less $77,000 owed equaled $160,000) was incomprehensible to me. I had never had that kind of money or net worth.

I continued with the rehab and finished the other three units. I got the building reappraised. This time the appraisal came in at over $300,000. Since I owed around $110,000, I had the capability to write a good check for $100,000. The words of Seller Number 1 echoed in my mind, "I wish I had bought more buildings." It was time to move ahead.

REAL ESTATE
MISADVENTURES IN THE CITY
OF LIGHTS — AURORA, ILLINOIS

With two buildings under my belt, I felt ready for another acquisition. I focused on the north side of Chicago. Unfortunately, the appraisal of $237,000 I had received on the second building wasn't a random, lucky event. Real estate prices had increased sharply during the mid-1980s and little was available for under $200,000. With the help of some Realtors, I combed the multiple listing ads weekly for new opportunities. But the numbers never worked out.

In the fall of 1986, after a year of searching, I found a six-unit building for sale by owner in an up-and-coming neighborhood called Roscoe Village. The seller was asking $85,000 for a frame building with two structures: a three-unit in the front of the lot and a three-unit coach house in the back. For you non-Chicagoans, a coach house was where the owner kept the coach in the old days. When coaches became passé, many coach houses were converted into residences, to bring in some extra income for the owner. Coach houses tend to be small and cozy. This one, however, was exceptional. The first floor unit was the smallest I had ever seen. The monthly rent was $85 in 1986. I estimated the square footage at one hundred.

Recognizing that the building was underpriced, I offered full price – $85,000. The seller accepted and referred the contract to her attorney for review and approval. The attorney told the seller she was giving the building away, and he wouldn't approve the contract. The seller listed the property for $120,000 the next day, and it was under contract within twenty-four hours. I always wondered if that attorney was acting within the scope of his license by advising the seller as to price. I was angry, but I had to move on.

As I had found in the past, jobs are not a source of economic security. In the spring of 1985, there was a shift in management at my office when a risk manager was hired. The risk manager was responsible for both the health benefits management of the city as well as the property and casualty insurance programs. The risk manager had philosophical differences with the benefits manager to whom I reported, and within six months he fired her. I feared I was next in line.

The risk manager was a risk taker and confided in me one day that he had recently bought a two-unit building in Aurora, Illinois for about $25,000. The monthly rents were around $800. He thought Aurora was "Bargain City," and suggested that I expand my search there.

Consequently, one crisp autumn Saturday I drove forty miles west of downtown Chicago to Aurora to see for myself what the city was like. It looked clean, with numerous frame buildings, many of which had been converted from single-family homes into multiunit properties.

When I talked to the city planning department, I was told that Aurora was the fastest growing city in Illinois and would soon become the second largest city in the state. Many major companies were relocating to Aurora, as the property taxes were low and it was right in the path of U.S. Interstate 88, known as the High Tech Corridor.

Aurora, the shining city that was home to Wayne and Garth in the movie *Wayne's World*, was a river town divided into two sides – East Aurora and West Aurora – by the Fox River. It was known as the City of Lights because it was the first city in the world to have its streetlights powered by electricity, in 1881.

As I drove around, I concluded that Aurora was really two cities. One was a central core that had existed for over a century and which was essentially blue-collar. The buildings were old, typically built in the 1910s and 1920s. The second city consisted of new housing developments outside the inner core.

Chicago had been great, but it was getting too expensive, and I decided that Aurora looked promising.

About two weeks later, I confidently strode into one of the local real estate offices, asked for the agent who listed and sold small multiunit buildings, and said, "Here I am – what great opportunity does Aurora have for me?" The agent ran off the appropriate section of the multiple listing book. I reviewed it and did some drive-bys. Everything worthwhile seemed within a mile of downtown Aurora. I arranged inspections of a few properties for the next Sunday.

After going through the properties, I decided that one stood out. It was a six-unit building about a mile west of the Fox River. The asking price was $68,000 and the seller was offering to be the lender at 12% seller-financed interest – about the same as the local banks. The property was a dumpy-looking gray building with four one-bedroom apartments and two two-bedroom units. I estimated the square footage of the one-bedrooms at 450 each and the two-bedrooms at 650. The rents were $225 for the smaller units and $275 for the larger ones. All utilities except water and sewer were the tenants' responsibility. The units were equipped with space heaters. In addition, a vacant lot next door was part of the purchase.

I offered $52,000 at 8% interest. I was not interested in the vacant lot. I didn't want to build on it and didn't really want to pay the property taxes or insurance for it. The seller and I compromised. We agreed to $60,000 at 10% interest with the vacant lot included. I made a down payment of $20,000, which I borrowed against the line of equity from one of my Chicago buildings. We consummated the sale in January 1988.

Since I was busy with my job, I hired a management company to manage the property – the same one my boss had used. I eagerly awaited what I anticipated would be a $500 per month positive cash flow.

My anticipatory mood was short-lived. I soon received a call from the management company that one of the tenants in the smaller apartments had abandoned the apartment without paying the rent. It was February, a tough rental period because people don't like to move in the winter. Nevertheless, we were able to rent the apartment to a family of four within a few days.

All went well for about two weeks. Then the manager mailed me a list of building-code violations. Unbeknownst to me, the city of Aurora held mandatory annual inspections of all apartments buildings with more than two units. Most of the items on the list were minor, but two items stood out. My new tenants had multiplied rapidly. I got cited for housing ten people in the 450 square-foot unit, instead of the four I originally rented it to. The extra people exceeded the occupancy limit. In addition, the city wanted certification from an approved heating and ventilation contractor that the space heaters were in good condition.

The following Saturday, I drove to Aurora to see for myself how ten human beings could fit into 450 square feet. The kitchen contained two double bunk beds, as did the living room. I could only imagine what the water bills were going to look like. The management company began the eviction process. My hope was that this would proceed more quickly than the one eviction I'd had in Chicago, where the tenant filed under Chapter

13 bankruptcy protection and got free use of my apartment for six months.

An approved heating contractor inspected all the space heaters and informed my manager that all of them were defective. Three of them had cracked heat exchangers and were emitting carbon monoxide into the units. The contractor commented that one of the units had two of the space heaters with cracked exchangers, and the only thing that was saving my tenant from serious, if not deadly, carbon monoxide poisoning was the poor insulation in the unit, which allowed air drafts to come in and carbon monoxide to escape through the walls. His report indicated that the unit should be vacated immediately because it was a health hazard. Or, for about $2500 he could remove the space heaters and put in a new, efficient forced-air unit and a chimney liner. I wasn't happy, but I authorized the work. There went five months of positive cash flow.

I had time to bid out the other five units. I found a competent heating contractor desperate for work who did the other units for $4100. There went another eight months of positive cash flow.

Upon the completion of the work, the city inspector approved all the units and even thought I was a decent landlord. I eventually put a total of $40,000 into that building to upgrade it, and raised the rents substantially. In 1993, the city of Aurora awarded me its annual Mayor's Award for Excellence in Property Improvement. This was an honor, as the city gave out only one award per year from the several hundred buildings in that size category.

The property was cash-flowing nicely when disaster struck. A curious four-year-old fascinated by matches set the building on fire. No one was hurt, but the damages exceeded $100,000. Fortunately, I had been prudent enough to upgrade the insurance policy substantially after rehabbing the property. I had assumed the existing insurance policy when I purchased the building, but after plowing $40,000 into the place, I reviewed that policy and realized the property was woefully underinsured. Had I kept the original policy, the fire would have cost me $70,000.

The city of Aurora deemed the building to be less than 50% damaged. It was classified as having "legal nonconforming" zoning. What this meant was that if the fire had destroyed more than 50% of the building, I could only have four units, not six. With under 50% damage, I was able to keep the six units.

I immediately hired a general contractor. We pulled building permits and the work commenced. Although I had substantially upgraded my insurance, I did not include a provision known as "building ordinance and increased cost of construction." If you have these coverages, the insurance company will cover the necessary upgrade repairs due to new building ordinances one is required to meet in the case of a fire. In my case, the city wanted me to put in new electrical wiring, including increased electrical service coming into the building and circuit breakers accessible in every unit. My policy would have covered replacing the existing screw-in fuses, but not the new requirements. This cost me about $10,000 over and above what the policy paid.

The repairs took around six months, after which the building was operational again. I re-rented the apartments, and the building ran well. In general, after a rocky start this property had moderate appreciation and cash flow.

As previously noted, I had determined in 1979 never to count on a job for financial independence. The wisdom of this decision was reinforced in late 1987, when I had to resign from the city of Chicago position. One of the requirements of that job was that I actually reside within the city boundaries. When I applied for the job I was a city resident, but I moved to the suburbs after I had been hired. Someone tipped off the Office of Municipal Investigations, and they spent a year following me.

I was less despondent this time than I had been when previous jobs had terminated. The success of the first few buildings helped raise my self-confidence, and I no longer dreaded the future.

My wife had often told me that things always work out for the best. The equity gain in less than three years on the second building (about $160,000) more than doubled the amount of money I would have made had I stayed in my job at the Chicago Hospital Council, not even counting tax and Social Security withholdings. Of course, in fairness, real estate equity does not put bread on the table – only cash flow does that.

In any case, I did not attempt to look for another job. I would never again work as an employee. My situation was helped by my wife's having a good job with health benefits. And I did some consulting work for about a year after I left my job with the city.

Most importantly, I continued to pursue real estate acquisitions. The source of my funding was the equity in the four-unit building and the six-unit building in Chicago.

While I was doing consulting, I identified two more properties with potential. The first was a five-unit building located just west of the Fox River in Aurora, brought to my attention by the owner of the management company. The asking price was $75,000. When I inquired about the financing, the agent told me it had an existing first mortgage of about $41,000. The interest rate was 0%. Stated differently, all the money that went to pay the mortgage paid off principal. In addition, the seller was willing to hold a second mortgage.

I learned that the seller was in an unfortunate position. The building had been profitable for him, but he had incurred a substantial hospital bill for one of his children and he did not have health insurance. He got tired of bill collectors hounding him, and decided to sell the property. The key thing for him was to get a $10,000 down payment so he could pay off the hospital. He didn't really want to sell.

He and I agreed to a purchase price of $70,000. The seller would carry a second mortgage at 0% interest for six months, and 10% thereafter. He also agreed to manage the building for a monthly fee. The monthly payment helped him, and having him as manager helped me.

Recalling the fiasco of Building Number 2's prepurchase inspection, this time I hired a professional inspector. The property was in very good condition. Inspecting the place was a rather odd experience, as one of the tenants had gotten married the night before, and the owner, inspector, and I cheerily woke the newlyweds up at 8:00 a.m. after their evening of matrimonial bliss. They were not exactly thrilled.

I took in an investor – a cousin through marriage. We closed, and the building ran well.

The other building was a four-unit property located on the east side of Aurora, about a mile north of downtown. Two of the units had two bedrooms, and two had one bedroom. The asking price was $59,000. The seller was the owner of another management company. He had bought the property in foreclosure for $35,000, and put in approximately $10,000 to restore the building. He was cashing out his investment. From my perspective, the numbers made economic sense and offered an acceptable return on investment – 15%. Financing was available from the existing lender, although we had to be approved to assume the loan. The seller basically wanted his existing equity in a cash down payment. Since I had cash available from the four-unit building and my cousin wanted to invest in another building, we bought this one too. The seller agreed to a price of $56,000 and agreed to manage the property at no charge for a year, and to do so thereafter for $50 per month.

The building was brought to my attention by the real estate agent who had sold me the six-unit building in Aurora. Both the seller and I liked and trusted this agent. Sadly, just one week before the closing was scheduled, the agent suffered a massive heart attack and passed away. The seller and I, working in good faith, pieced together the various elements and completed the transaction. We made sure the agent's widow got the commission.

The new building was predictably profitable. With the positive cash flow, I was able to pay off extra principal every month. The property ran well for several years, until I had another fire at a different building. After the second fire, the city's Inspection Department was on my case.

One of their inspectors cited several violations and proved to be a quite difficult person to please. My cause was not helped by the tenants in the lower rear unit, who decided to conduct training classes for pit bulls in the basement. The inspector was far from

The building inspector's welcoming committee.

happy when the pit bulls attacked him. He barely escaped with his life – literally. Neither my property manager nor I was aware of the dog situation until the inspection. We evicted the tenants and their dogs, and $10,000 later the code violations were satisfied.

The last of my Aurora purchases was a three-unit building located in the east side historic district. Many homeowners in the area were proudly restoring their houses. Values were slowly appreciating.

The three-unit building was half brick and half frame. Each apartment had two bedrooms and measured 1500 square feet. Beautifully crafted woodwork punctuated all the units. The building had belonged to a judge around the turn of the last century.

Through one of my property managers, I had become friendly with the owner. He had mentioned at lunch one day that he was tired of dealing with the Aurora building inspectors and the city government, and was selling all his Aurora properties. He wanted $85,000 for the building.

My analysis of the numbers showed that it should be profitable, and the seller and I agreed on a price of $75,000. I pulled $30,000 out of one of my buildings in Chicago (the six-unit in the Lakeview neighborhood) and used it for a down payment.

In general, Building Number 6 was a disappointment. The tenants on the third floor unexpectedly moved out a week before the closing. After that, there always seemed to be a vacant apartment in the building, usually on the third floor. Without the $525 in monthly rent from the apartment, the property lost money. I was not happy.

One day I got a phone call from the second-floor tenant. She was a very good tenant who kept her apartment immaculate, paid her rent on time, and was invariably reasonable.

She told me she'd had an argument with her live-in boyfriend and had gone upstairs to the third-floor apartment to get away

If you won't leave I'm going to put a No-Haunt clause in your lease.

Hah! Try and collect rent!

from the situation. As usual, the third-floor apartment was vacant.

While she was up there resting, she claimed a ghost appeared and told her to get out of the apartment immediately. She gave me a physical description of the ghost. She said she'd felt scared, and so she called me. This woman was a very religious person and quite honest, so I didn't want to make a judgment as to the veracity of the ghost story. I simply suggested that she not use that apartment as a place to rest, since in any case it was not her apartment.

About two weeks later, I received a call from the first-floor tenants. It seemed they had decided to use the empty third-floor apartment as a neat spot to cap off their work week and have a few beers. After they'd had a few drinks, they said the ghost appeared to them and scared them into leaving. Their description of the ghost matched the other tenant's. I told them to stay off the third floor, too.

I knew none of the tenants was trying to use the ghost as a ploy to move out since they had no intention of leaving and always paid the rent on time. I don't know whether the various tenants talked about it with each other. I was beginning to wonder if I had bought a haunted apartment building.

Concerned, I called the seller and reported the ghost sightings. To my shock, he confessed that he too had seen the ghost. He explained that it was the spirit of a former tenant who had lived in that apartment. The woman had committed a felony and been sent to prison, where she died in a fight. I imagine she liked the apartment and wanted it to be her home forever.

I decided I wasn't about to give the ghost an eternal estate in the apartment, however, and rented it out again. Once more, the renters bogeyed on me, and I had to re-rent the place.

The coup de grace came one cold Saturday morning in December 1993. The tenant on the second floor called me at 7:15 and informed me that the building had burned down.

While I knew her to be honest, I could not believe the building had actually burned without anyone calling me about it. Nevertheless, I immediately called an insurance adjuster and told him of the call. He suggested I not call the insurance company right away, but check out the situation for myself. If there had been a fire, he wanted to talk to the insurance company adjuster on Monday.

I sped off to Aurora – about an hour's drive – and, to my shock, saw that the building had indeed burned down. The roof had collapsed into the structure, and the place had major water damage from the firefighters' hoses. The tenants were all waiting for me to get their security deposits back. Fortunately, the Red Cross was able to find them temporary housing and no one was seriously injured, although two firefighters suffered minor smoke inhalation. I felt especially bad for the tenant on the second floor, as she had once lost a child in an apartment fire, and this experience of course brought back painful memories.

The building was up for sale at the time. I was asking $85,000, since I wanted to use the equity elsewhere. The police and fire department conducted a major investigation about the fire's source and origin. So did the insurance company. I was not at all surprised to learn the fire had started on the third floor. Somebody "had it in for" the tenants there and had poured an accelerant, probably gasoline, on the third-floor landing and back door, thrown a match on it, and disappeared into the night. It happened around midnight. After questioning me thoroughly about the fire, the police, fire department, and insurance company figured out that I had nothing to do with it. The arsonist never was caught.

My insurance adjuster did a good job, and the insurance company paid around $154,000 as the settlement. The cost of replacement far exceeded the market value of the building, which is why I got more than the $85,000 asking price. At this point, I had $154,000 less $54,000 to pay off the mortgage, and a shell of a building. I wanted to sell the fire-damaged building, but the city of Aurora wanted me to tear it down. After about six months of battling over the matter, I prevailed. I ended up selling the shell of the property to a rehabber for $25,000. My buyer had put about $40,000 into repairs when the city offered him $110,000 for the place.

After paying that ridiculous price for it, the city then tore the building down, filled the foundation in with dirt and grass seed, and at the time of this writing, they have a nice-looking lot there.

I made a decision shortly after that fire to sell all my Aurora properties, because someone in Aurora evidently had thought nothing of setting a fire that could have killed ten sleeping residents. Aurora had a record number of homicides that year, as well. Lastly, my good standing with the head of the Department of Inspectional Services had diminished when I challenged him regarding the tear-down issue. The thought of Aurora building inspectors annually surveying every room in every apartment concerned me.

In the end, though, Aurora proved a useful learning experience. With the exception of the last building, the properties I bought there produced a positive cash flow and appreciated about 5% per year in value. Overall, I had done well. My confidence grew.

Over the next two years, I sold the four buildings in Aurora, paid the capital gains tax, and used the proceeds to buy property in Milwaukee, Wisconsin.

In the case of the three-unit burn-out, I used the remaining funds as a down payment on an eighteen-unit building in Milwaukee. The Internal Revenue Service code allows for a Section 1033 Exchange, or an "Involuntary Conversion." (This differs from the typical 1031 or Starker Exchange.) I was able to defer paying capital gains taxes on the money from the insurance and sale by following the I.R.S. rules and reinvesting the money in a similar property (details about this will be discussed in a later chapter). It was time to move ahead.

After my city job was finished and my consulting assignments were completed, I faced the prospect of being unemployed. Stated more positively, I had a lot of free time to do what I wanted. I already owned five buildings, and with the support of my wife, I decided to do something I had always been eager to try – become a full-time real estate investor.

I look back with real fondness on the days after I left my last (and final) job. Many days I would walk the streets of Chicago or Aurora, looking for property that might be profitable to purchase. I loved exploring. Other days I would sit home (especially in the winter) and read self-improvement books. I also read about spiritual practice, money, health, and of course, real estate.

I would try to take an hour a day simply to think. Then I'd write down my thoughts on various questions. At times it was difficult to be honest with myself, but I did achieve some insights.

Among the topics I covered during my "thinking" periods were:

- What are my lifetime goals?

- What is my mission in life?

- What holds me back?

- What are my strengths?

- What are my weaknesses?

- How do I want to expand in real estate?

- How can I improve myself?

- What are my passions?

- How can I be more loving toward my wife?

- Who is the best possible Jim Pockross?

I tried many different approaches to find bargain real estate:

- I went to the county tax records in Chicago and Aurora to identify taxpayers of record (most likely the owners) of properties in my target areas. I then wrote the taxpayers, inquiring about their interest in selling.

• With the help of Realtors, I checked the multiple listing book each week for all buildings for sale. I asked the realtors to call me right away if a listing looked promising, and I then investigated the property.

• In Aurora, my agent reluctantly agreed to contact every seller of a multiunit building and offer a letter of intent to purchase the building at 25% less than the listing price. Unfortunately, none of the sellers responded.

• I ran ads in the *Chicago Tribune* stating that I was a motivated buyer of real estate.

• I attended public and private real estate auctions. These included sheriff's sales as well as brokerage office sales.

• I followed foreclosure notices to see if any properties could be purchased below market value.

• I contacted several banks to ascertain if they had foreclosed on any REO (Real Estate Owned by the lending institution) properties and wanted to sell.

• I made a pest of myself at the county offices where probate records of deceased real estate owners were kept. I truly believe the clerks began to dread seeing me show up, as I requested hundreds of files that had to be pulled and refiled later. I then contacted the attorney for the owners' estates to see what real estate was owned, and if it was for sale.

- I talked to several funeral directors to see if they knew of any estate property that was available.

- I spent days walking through up-and-coming neighborhoods on a block-by-block basis, looking for run-down buildings that could be upgraded for increased property value. I'd write down an address, find the taxpayer of record through the tax records, and contact the person.

In retrospect, it was an exhilarating, though at times frustrating and time-consuming, process. I really enjoyed prospecting for property. I loved attending auctions, digging through public records, and searching for the elusive gem. The thought of finding a small gold mine that would spout positive cash in the future and help in my efforts to be financially independent excited me and gave me hope.

5

HITTIING IT BIG
IN MILWAUKEE

I learned about opportunities in Milwaukee from Mary, my building manager for the Chicago four-unit. She was a Milwaukee transplant whose heart was always in that city.

Mary called me one day when I was still working for the city of Chicago and said she was interested in buying a two-unit building in Milwaukee. She asked if I would look at it with her and advise her if it was a worthwhile purchase, as well as help her negotiate the contract and arrange financing. She offered to pay me a consulting fee, which I refused. I didn't want to get paid as a consultant for helping a friend.

The property was not in the best of areas. Of course, it didn't have the highest asking price; it was listed for about $28,000. It was a house with a coach house in the rear. We figured the rents would be about $400 per month per unit. I encouraged her to buy the building and helped her with the contract negotiations and the financing. That property worked out well for her.

About six months later, she called to tell me of a three-unit (really a two-unit building in front with a single family home in the rear) located down the street. It was for sale in a Department of Housing and Urban Development (HUD) closed bid auction.

The asking price was $7000. For that price, one would not expect the Taj Mahal. The buildings were in fact boarded up. They also had no electrical, gas, or water service. Thus the experience of inspecting the property proved unique. On a frigid February day in 1989, Mary and I got out our battery-powered flashlights and traipsed through the property. It is an eerie feeling to go through a building that is pitch dark inside and freezing cold. We felt like we were scuba diving our way through the wreckage of the *Titanic*.

For a boarded-up property, it was in decent condition. Most of the rooms were intact. The bare bones of the plumbing were there (piping, sinks, toilets, etc.). The boilers were not functional and would need replacing. The electric was serviceable. The roofs were questionable. The windows and doors were intact. The building appeared structurally sound.

Mary asked if I wanted to be her partner. She would take over as general contractor for the rehab of the property as well as manage it when the work was completed. I would basically be the money person. We'd be fifty-fifty partners, and for her share she would put out some money and be credited with her time as general contractor. I told her I'd think it over.

After inspecting the property, Mary and I stopped by the City of Milwaukee Housing Development and Rehabilitation Division. The section head told us the property was located in a "target area" where the city would lend us federal money – 50% of the estimated and approved cost of rehab. If we kept the place up to HUD standards, the city would forgive 20% of the loan each year, including interest. In essence, if we met HUD standards for five years after the rehab was complete, all the debt would be forgiven. We'd obviously have to buy the property and apply for and guarantee the loan. The section head also mentioned that Wisconsin had a program where investors in low-income and senior housing could get substantial tax credits on their personal income tax returns.

We would have to rent to tenants who qualified as low income.

The tax credit would be 45% of the estimated rehab cost for the building. We could take 4.5% of the rehab cost off our tax bill each year for ten years. At the time the tax credit was granted, we'd have to commit to renting to low-income tenants for fifteen years. (Since then, the program has increased that fifteen-year obligation to thirty years.)

This program could be piggybacked with the forgivable loan. Analyzing the deal proved not too difficult. We'd buy the property for all cash, and eventually the city and state governments would provide 95% of the rehab costs (50% from the city for the forgivable rehab loan and 45% from the state for the low-income housing tax credits over a ten-year period). This would be a moneymaker.

At Mary's urging, we submitted a bid for $8100, so no one would outbid us. We were the winning bidder, and my adventures as a Milwaukee investor began in April 1989.

After the closing, we applied for both a rehab loan from the city and low-income housing credits from the Wisconsin Housing and Economic Development Authority (WHEDA). The city approved a loan of $24,000 (one half of the $48,000 they estimated the total rehab would cost), and WHEDA approved a low-income housing credit of $21,600 to be taken in installments of $2160 annually over a ten-year period.

The rehab took about a year and a half at a cost of $60,000. Upon completion, we rented out the property within a few months to low-income tenants.

To date, the project has not worked. Virtually all the tenants had several children and didn't maintain the property the way the adults had in my Chicago buildings. In addition, the tenants frequently were unable to pay their rent and had to be evicted. With rents collected lower than expected and maintenance expenses higher than anticipated, the building lost money.

Mary had some financial reverses and I ended up buying her

out in 1996. My dream of money coming in with no work on my part was an illusion. I ended up both managing the property and carrying it.

Despite our difficulties, I believe we did provide well-maintained housing to our tenants. I hope our efforts improved the lives of some of the tenants. I even offered to teach classes to them on basic money management and investment, at no cost. I hoped this would be of assistance to the tenants. No one was interested.

I began exploring other areas closer to downtown Milwaukee and to Lake Michigan, ones that attracted a more affluent tenant. The area that best matched my parameters was the east side of Milwaukee, where deluxe high-rise apartments and condominiums overlooked the lake. This was the place to be.

When I investigated the rent levels and building price levels, I found that both were much lower than in comparable areas of Chicago. I concluded that I could get better deals for my money in Milwaukee. If I put down 33% on a building in Chicago, maybe I'd break even. In Milwaukee I could make a positive cash flow with a 20% down payment.

A second factor influenced my search for new buildings. I had nine years of experience managing smaller properties. In my view, the cash flow in smaller properties didn't compare to the potential of larger properties. I felt I'd paid my dues as a real estate investor in smaller buildings and wanted to move up to larger acquisitions. The thirty-one units I controlled (ten were really owned by my investors as their share of the investment – I myself owned twenty-one) would not get me to financial independence for another twenty years.

It is one thing to set parameters on a type of building to buy, but quite another to find one. I've always felt the most difficult part of real estate investing is finding worthwhile property. As expected, I initially searched to little avail. The multiple listing book did not have much. The same held true for the major newspaper, the *Milwaukee Journal Sentinel.* I lacked the network of contacts I had developed in Chicago and Aurora.

My big breakthrough finally came from a cousin who was one of my investors. He too was eager to move up to a larger property, and suggested I contact Mr. Wheeler Dealer (hereafter Mr. W.D.) in Milwaukee. He knew Mr. W.D. because they worked together on a national drive for a charitable cause.

I telephoned Mr. W.D. and set a time to meet with him in at his office in early December 1991. Mr. W.D. turned out to be a major real estate player in the Milwaukee market. We hit it off well, as our philosophies in investing were very similar. Mr. W.D. drove me around the east side, pointing out many buildings he owned.

When we got back to his office, he offered me a deal. He had a contract to purchase a twenty-unit building for $350,000. For $50,000, I could buy his contract. In essence, he offered me the building for $400,000. I responded that I couldn't agree to buy something without seeing it or investigating it further.

I made arrangements to walk through the property. It was a two-story brick building that had been built around 1960. All the units were one-bedroom with hardwood floors. In Mr. W.D.'s view, the units and building as a whole were showing their age, and the property was prime for cosmetic renovation. (Cosmetic renovation translates into inexpensive improvements that make a building look good to a prospective tenant.) In this case, it meant new landscaping, recarpeting the hallways, putting in up-to-date lighting fixtures, cleaning the building, and painting the apartments. Afterwards, the rents could be raised about 20%. Mr. W.D. said part of the deal would include managing the building for 4% of the gross revenue monthly fee. He would oversee all the improvements at no additional management charge.

When I analyzed this proposal, many things looked right. At

the higher rents, the building would produce an acceptable investment return. It was located in my target area – the east side. It offered the opportunity to move into what I'll call the minor leagues – up from a mom-and-pop situation. Lastly, I wouldn't have to manage the property myself.

On the negative side, there was more risk. I had never paid more than $85,700 for a building, and the negative cash flow for a larger property has the potential to be great.

I decided it was worth the risk, and agreed to buy the property. The source of the $80,000 down payment was the equity of the original six-unit building in Chicago. Like my four-unit near De Paul, it had increased in value substantially.

I checked with several local banks on the financing, and chose Marquette Savings Bank. To no one's surprise, the property was appraised at $400,000. The purchase was finalized in January 1991. My cousin/partner and I were excited. We liked the idea of renovating and getting higher rents.

I wish I could say that the property operated according to expectations. It did not. When the tenants learned that the building was going to be sold and the rents raised, several left. I had anticipated a 100% occupied building, and was very disappointed to learn there were five vacancies out of twenty units at closing, with another couple of tenants on notice to move out by February 1. Our new cash machine quickly turned into a cash drain.

The cosmetic rehab proceeded on schedule, but renting apartments proved difficult. As a general rule, warmer weather months in the north are better rental months than January or February. A tenant has to be motivated to move in the snow and cold. Typically, phone calls from prospective tenants start to increase in mid-March and grow as April and May arrive. Until we filled the building, we were "feeding an alligator" (a real estate expression for having a negative cash flow).

Within six months, the rehab was complete and we were able

to fill most of the building. In an average month, we had one to three vacancies there. The building produced some positive cash flow, which we used to make extra principal payments to reduce our interest cost.

After about a year, Mr. W.D. found managing the property to be burdensome and asked me to take over the management. He had enough to take care of with his own buildings.

Needless to say, his 4% fee would disappear. I reluctantly took the reins. Two of the tenants occupying the same unit had actually been the resident managers. They lived in the building rent-free. They were responsible for the janitorial services, showing apartments, and minor repairs. They agreed to continue on as resident managers. I would make the big decisions, such as how much and when to raise rents, approving or rejecting applications, what capital improvements to make, selecting contractors, and paying the bills.

This arrangement worked out well for everybody. We always had vacancies, but the property was kept clean and well-maintained. It made a respectable cash flow. We sold that building in 1995 for $440,000. We made $40,000 over our purchase price, and were able to reduce the mortgage by $80,000 in the four years of ownership. We sold it because an opportunity developed at a nearby building (more on this later).

By mid-1991, my empire had fifty-one apartment units – ten in Chicago, eighteen in Aurora, and twenty-three in Milwaukee. Some of the buildings I managed directly. Managers or apartment management companies handled the rest.

Mr. W.D. called me in September 1991 with another opportunity. He had just purchased a thirty-nine-unit building on the east side. It was in a good location, with expensive townhouses and condominiums sprouting up all around it. He explained that he had paid $550,000 for the property and had made a down payment of $50,000. He was in possession of the building.

He offered it to me for $650,000. Apparently he needed cash at the time. The building had existing financing on it. Mr. W.D. had bought it from one of his buddies, affectionately known in Milwaukee as Moneybags. Moneybags was getting up in years and had decided to liquidate his sizable real estate portfolio. Mr. W.D. was the first in line. The financing included an interest rate of 9% and, according to the loan payment schedule, the building would actually be paid off within a ten-year period (to use a technical term, it would *amortize* over ten years).

The thirty-nine units were small, furnished efficiencies or studio apartments. Rents ranged from $240 to $260 per month. The building had been constructed around 1950 and was built like a fortress. I would call it a California-style building. It had four floors, each with an exterior walkway. Each apartment unit was accessible from the outdoor walkway.

While I viewed the building as structurally solid, I was concerned about the structural integrity of the exterior walkway. It was exposed to our wonderful northern weather, including heat, cold, snow, rain, and ice. I reluctantly hired a structural engineer to inspect the property. His review was positive. He gave me a few recommendations on how to strengthen the walkways.

Acquiring the building meant moving into risky territory. I had never run a property with furnished apartments. It also had thirty-nine units – nearly double anything I had ever owned.

When I analyzed the revenues and expenses, the arithmetic appeared favorable. I'd be able to make the mortgage payments with a 4% vacancy factor, and build a reserve. I factored in the structural upgrade for the walkways.

So I called Mr. W.D. and made the deal. The purchase price was to be $625,000. In addition, Mr. W.D. agreed to replace the very dilapidated roof. Figuring I would need about $200,000 in cash to close, I contacted some relatives (one was an investor in Aurora), who would each put in $70,000 for a one-third interest in the property. I would put in $58,000 for my third.

The holder of the note, Moneybags, had to approve the note assumption. Upon reviewing our background, he approved it. He nevertheless still wanted Mr. W.D. to be held liable in case we didn't meet the mortgage payment schedule. Mr. W.D. agreed.

We closed on the building in October 1991. The property operated as expected for four months. Then one of the tenants noticed a gas odor in his apartment and called the gas company. They sent an inspector who checked out that apartment for gas, as well as the heater itself. The inspector then decided to check all the other thirty-seven apartments' gas-fired wall heaters. (One apartment had electric baseboard heat; the original owner who built the property had a mistress who didn't like gas-fired wall heaters.)

The gas company concluded that about twenty of the wall units were seriously defective and could not be used. They shut off the defective heaters and put red tape on them, indicating that if anyone turned on the heater they could be charged with a crime. I had twenty tenants with no heat in the middle of February.

I immediately bought twenty electric space heaters. Fortunately, the units were small enough that one space heater was adequate to heat them on a short-term basis. (I offered to pay the additional electric bill for each of the tenants.) My goal was not to lose any tenants over this, and I succeeded.

I then had to find a heating contractor who could procure the necessary wall heaters and install them as soon as possible, and at a reasonable cost. It was the heart of the busy season for them. Nevertheless, I did find a contractor, and within two weeks twenty apartments had new, energy-efficient wall heaters. Fortunately, we had the necessary funds in reserve to meet this expense. We eventually ended up replacing the other wall heaters as well.

Since then, the building has operated as expected. When commercial interest rates dropped under 8% in the late 1990s, I refinanced the property with a local bank, as Moneybags was unwilling to lower the interest rate from 9%.

On a glorious July day in 2000, an historic event occurred – I actually paid off the mortgage note on a building. It was a special day for me. I called the bank president two days before and alerted him that I was planning to pay the principal balance off on Thursday. He gave me the payoff figure and had the necessary paperwork prepared.

For the first time in my real estate career, I actually put on a suit. I marched into the bank, delivered the check, and after eighteen-plus years of real estate investing, I had a free and clear building (as did the other investors). The building was paid off ahead of schedule – eight years and eight months. The investors were delighted. Thereafter, each of us drew two thousand dollars a month from that building.

One other important event occurred in early 1991, before I finalized the purchase of the twenty-unit building. My supportive and devoted wife mentioned one day that she had worked full-time ever since she had graduated from college, and was, in general, getting tired of working. She informed me that she had made a unilateral decision. She planned to retire by the age of fifty, and there had better be enough money coming in to provide for her in the lifestyle TO WHICH SHE HAD BECOME ACCUSTOMED.

This didn't set well with me. Unilateral decisions are fine when I'm the decision-maker, but not when the decision made is about me. I tried to negotiate, but I might as well have been talking to one of our cats – they've never listened to me either.

I assessed our situation. Of the thirty-one units at the time, about twenty were ours. When I factored in the additional payments I'd make with the projected payoff dates for the buildings, I found a major disparity between the money needed to support the lifestyle my wife was accustomed to and the anticipated positive cash flow.

How would I develop the necessary cash flow? Because of the buildings, I couldn't commit to a normal job. Besides, the thought of working full-time for someone else was abhorrent. A second option was healthcare consulting. However, I didn't like consulting. In the past, as a self-employed consultant, I had to work tirelessly to find consulting engagements. Once I found them, it meant twelve-hour days with deadlines. Then as soon as an assignment was completed, I had to start looking for the next one.

I actually had a strong itch to try selling health insurance to small employers and individuals. I had a background in healthcare; I had worked for both providers of services and for a major purchaser of healthcare. I mentioned this to some key people, such as my career counselor and a sales training expert who knew me well, and they all told me I'd never make it as a salesperson. Even my mother took Michele aside and urged her to torpedo my plans to sell insurance. I am basically a shy person – about as different from a "born salesman" as you can get. My wife told my mother to "butt out," saying, "Jim could do anything he sets his mind to." She believed in me.

My mother's lack of encouragement was all I needed to spur me to move forward with my plans. I passed the required State of Illinois insurance exam in October 1991. "James S. Pockross and Associates" was born. Other than our cat Claudius, I didn't have any associates at the time.

On a very cold January morning in 1992, I donned a suit, drove out to a nearby industrial/commercial area, and began knocking on doors. To no one's surprise, I had very little business in the beginning, but instead of prospecting for real estate investments, I was prospecting for insurance clients. I really enjoyed cold-calling on businesses to see if they would let me quote on their insurance. I love to search and find. Eventually the business blossomed into a major cash flow generator, and it has worked out well.

As the insurance business grew, more of my time was devoted to finding new insurance prospects and keeping my current clients happy. I had less time to spend on finding new properties. In a sense, the decision was one of choosing to have cash flow in the present versus the future. Some of my full-time real estate investment buddies questioned my sanity. Why sell insurance when you have so many buildings? I simply told them I was crazy and they should enjoy my craziness. The bottom line is that this became my strategy to meet a deadline my wife had set.

My efforts to attain financial independence through real estate investing continued. As I had learned so well in 1979, you can never count on a job for financial security.

6

MORE ADVENTURES IN MILWAUKEE

After acquiring the thirty-nine-unit building in October 1991, I had control and responsibility for ninety units – ten in Chicago, eighteen in Aurora, and sixty-two in Milwaukee.

Starting in January 1992, I began prospecting for insurance clients when I wasn't involved in managing the buildings. Consequently, I did not acquire anything in 1992 or 1993.

Mr. W.D. gave me a call in the autumn of 1993. He had just purchased five buildings as part of a package. Three were on the east side of Milwaukee and two were in west Milwaukee.

Like me, Mr. W.D. was focused on the east side. He didn't really want the two buildings on the west side, but he'd had to buy them as part of the package. The buildings showed very good potential cash flow. He asked if I wanted to buy them from him at his cost ($410,000 apiece).

I told him I'd have to investigate. I had very little money available for a down payment of 20%, but I could bring in investors and get a piece of the action and a monthly management fee. Two issues concerned me:

1) What was the future of the neighborhood in west Milwaukee?
2) Were the buildings good investments that would yield the return I desired?

I decided to conduct a survey of the neighborhood. I went door-to-door, asking residents their views. I also interviewed merchants, the local police, the mailman, and the assigned planner with the Milwaukee Planning Department. Lastly, I contacted commercial appraisers who had done appraisals for me in the past. I figured they owed me a free piece of knowledge. In general, people were very informative. I suppose people love to tell you how much they know and what they think, if given the chance.

Some of the locals weren't too thrilled with me, though. They must have thought I was a burglar casing out the neighborhood. Once, two squad cars drove up and the officers came out to arrest me. After they checked me out for my nonexistent criminal background, I explained what I was doing and interviewed them. I took it as a good sign that the neighbors would call the police when someone as scary-looking as me was prowling around their neighborhood.

My overall view of the area was that it was a stable, working-class neighborhood. The homes were mostly frame and were in the $50,000 to $80,000 range. The properties might not have the long-term potential of the east side, but they would probably be moneymakers.

The buildings were brick eighteen-units. One was built around 1950, and the other was built around 1910 and was what in Chicago we call a "vintage" property. All the apartments had hardwood floors. There was beautiful oak woodwork in its original state throughout the older building, and several beautiful stained-glass windows. The building had mostly studio or efficiency apartments, with six one-bedroom units. The 1950s-era building was larger and had mainly one-bedroom units.

Both buildings had good curb appeal. In general, the properties appeared in fine condition. The electric was modern, with circuit breakers and several circuits per apartment. The boilers were fairly new. The buildings appeared structurally sound. The flat roofs were in fair condition.

The plumbing was questionable, in that the piping I could see (horizontal pipes in the basement) was old and had clamps where leaks had been discovered. I figured that some of the pipes known as risers, which fed up to the apartments, were not in the best condition. I knew that replacing risers is expensive.

Having shopped the financing market before inspecting the buildings, I knew most lenders were going to require a structural engineer's report before approving a loan.

The review of the cash-flow analysis looked promising. I figured the buildings would produce a 15 to 20% cash on cash return. I decided purchasing the buildings was worth the risk. At $410,000 apiece, there wasn't much of a downside. The bank appraisals were higher for both properties.

My plan to fund the down payment was different for each building. On one of the eighteen-unit properties, I would raise $126,000 as the down payment and working capital. I established ten shares worth $14,000 each. I would receive one share for putting the deal together. Nine shares at $14,000 each is $126,000. I put in $14,000 and other investors put in $112,000 and owned 80% of the building.

The plan for the second property was less definite. Since the three-unit building in Aurora wasn't working out, I decided to sell it. I hoped to pull $20,000 out of that property which could be used as part of the $82,000 down payment. I would raise the other $62,000 for the down payment. I was essentially redeploying the equity from Aurora to west Milwaukee – in my view, buying a better location.

I reached an agreement with Mr. W.D. Since he wasn't under any great pressure to sell, we agreed that I'd buy the buildings when I was ready. After I made the deal, I contacted the current investors and a close friend to see if they'd want to fund the first property. Within two days, they had all agreed.

I then performed my "due diligence." The structural engineer found little wrong with the buildings. He wanted the parapet walls repaired in one of them, and he wanted the garages repaired in the other. Other needed repairs were very minor.

The purchase of the first building proceeded smoothly. As for the other property, it was contingent on the sale of the three-unit building in Aurora. I had the property listed for $85,000. My partner and I owed $55,000. I figured we'd net $20,000 to $25,000 after selling the building.

The property was put on the market in November 1993. In December, the fire mentioned in Chapter 4 occurred and the building was deemed a total loss by the insurance company. They ended up compensating us $154,000. After paying expenses, we had more than the $82,000 (20% of $410,000) required by the bank as a down payment. I purchased the second eighteen-unit building in June 1994 and have now operated the two properties for over a decade. Because the resident managers of the buildings had done such a fine job, the properties performed better than expected. The first building was paid off in eight-and a-half years, and the investors very much enjoy receiving their monthly income distributions. The annual income is about 35% of their investment. The property has also appreciated in value.

The second building would have been paid off, but was refinanced in 1998 to raise part of a down payment for a larger building on the east side. We pulled out $180,000 (compared to our $82,000 down payment.) In effect, we reallocated most of the equity to the east side. This property, too, has operated very well.

With the acquisition of the two eighteen-unit buildings and the fire sale of the three-unit property, the total number of units under my control increased to one hundred twenty-three.

As described earlier, Moneybags was selling off his inventory of buildings. I'd had my eye on one of these buildings on Prospect Avenue in Milwaukee for over a year. This was a seventy-seven-unit property. The building was constructed around 1950, and contained studios and one-bedrooms. What I really liked about it was that it was on Prospect Avenue, one of the best addresses in Milwaukee. My twenty-unit property was only about three hundred feet away, on Farwell Avenue. Farwell, while in a desirable location on the east side of Milwaukee, was not as prestigious as Prospect. Prospect runs parallel to Lake Michigan. I really wanted to liquidate the twenty-unit building and move up to the best location I could. I had developed a very good relationship with Moneybags since I had assumed his loan on the thirty-nine-unit building. We were quite similar in investment philosophy. A couple of differences did exist, though: he did not upgrade his buildings, which I was willing to do, and, owning many free and clear buildings, he could properly be called Moneybags. In my case, my lenders could be called Moneybags and I could be called the filler of the Moneybags.

Moneybags also had a very strong relationship with Mr. W.D. When the time came for him to sell the seventy-seven-unit property, he called Mr. W.D. first. Unfortunately for me, Mr. W.D. purchased the building. After the sale was completed, Moneybags called me and apologized. He told me he knew I wanted that property and would have offered it to me had Mr. W.D. declined. He didn't want to start a bidding war between us or hurt our relationship.

I was disappointed, as I really had wanted the seventy-seven-unit building, but I had to move ahead. I approached Mr. W.D. about selling the building, but he wasn't interested.

Mr. W.D. proceeded to upgrade the building and increase the rents. (I kept my eye on the property throughout the process, in the hope it might become available.) Around two years after he bought the building, I got a call from Mr. W.D. Along with two other investors, he had committed to the purchase of a real estate package that included six hundred-plus rental units, as well as retail space. His share of the down payment was about $2 million. As part of his efforts to raise his down payment, he asked if I wanted to buy the seventy-seven-unit.

I was absolutely interested. We agreed to a price, and it was in my court to conduct the due diligence. The overall condition of the property was satisfactory, other than about one-third of the units not having been remodeled. The financial figures were difficult to analyze because the property had above average vacancy due to the rehab. Thus, the income was lower than expected. The expenses were higher than anticipated because of the rehab. In short, figures from the past weren't very helpful in projecting how much money the building would make. All I could really do was to project income and expenses after all the units were rehabbed. After calculating the rents less vacancy and credit loss (tenants who don't pay the rent), and making projections/guesses on the expenses, it appeared to be a marginal investment. I did like the property because it was in an excellent location, and the thought of owning a building in a prime location twenty or thirty years into the future appealed to me. However, because it was on an eleven-year note, the property would break even or possibly be a negative cash flow. And I was concerned about the vacancies and the unrehabbed units.

In terms of financing, Moneybags offered 9% financing, which was assumable. The original note called for the building to be paid off over a thirteen-year period. I could assume it with eleven years left. As noted earlier, with a short-term amortization, the monthly payments were close to $16,000. The total rent if fully occupied was about $33,000. During the rehab, the monthly income collected fluctuated between $25,000 and $30,000. If expenses ran on the high side, cash flow could be a problem.

In terms of the funding for the property, my plan was to make a down payment of about $800,000. I intended to sell the twenty-unit building that I had purchased in 1991. This would provide around $200,000. I would then raise the remaining $600,000 from investors, including myself. I had some money left over from some of the sales in Aurora. I was also able to borrow against my house from a line of equity that my wife and I had established. Michele was supportive and agreed to let me do this.

After adding the down payment and the principal balance on the existing loan, I would still be about $300,000 short of the purchase price. One of my banks agreed to grant me a $325,000 business loan with a three-year balloon. (A balloon payment meant I'd have to pay the bank $325,000 at the end of three years, no matter what.) The interest rate was 9.75%, payable over ten years. If I made my loan payments on a timely basis, they would renew the loan for up to seven more years. Their loan was not a second mortgage, as the bank would not place a second mortgage lien against the building. It was strictly a business loan, and the bank was counting on the investors to pay it back.

With the financing in place, it was time for me to make a decision. Mr. W.D. needed to sell to make his trade, and had a back-up buyer if I didn't want the building. In a leap of faith, I decided to buy the property. Mr. W.D. agreed to manage the building and finish renovating the units that needed upgrading. He also agreed to purchase the twenty-unit building so that I had enough for the down payment. I believed that ownership of the property would be very difficult the first three years. The principal and interest on the two loans were about $21,000 a month. Add to that $5000 for property tax as well as other operating expenses like insurance, heat, water and sewer, and maintenance, and we were looking at a negative cash flow. But I was willing to take the risk because of the building's location.

After reaching an agreement with Mr. W.D., I had a short period of time in which to raise the down payment. This took two days. Five investors (close friends and relatives) participated. I was straightforward about informing them that the property would probably be a negative cash flow for the first few years. They might have to contribute money to help pay the expenses. Investors were told that every effort would be made to pay off the building in eleven years.

The sale was consummated on May 25, 1995. The first three years went even worse than I expected. The building was riddled with vacancy headaches; sometimes as many as twenty apartments were vacant. The first two winters were especially difficult. High gas bills coupled with high vacancies did not make life much fun. In order to keep the property afloat, I had to borrow money against my stock and feed it to the building. (I did not ask the investors for contributions to cover the negative cash flow.) That's not the kind of leverage you want when you borrow against a stock.

After three years, the financial condition of the building improved. I promoted a resident manager from another one of my properties to be the directing manager. Within two months of taking over, he reduced the eighteen vacancies to zero. In addition, interest rates declined. I was able to refinance the building from about 9.5% (the first mortgage plus the loan from the bank) to 7.75%. (I have subsequently lowered the interest to 4.875%.) Lastly, the property taxes declined by about 20%. Wisconsin voted to fund education from its general revenue fund rather than from property taxes, and consequently, taxes decreased about $12,000 per year. With joy, I watched the checking account balance grow larger every month.

While the financial health of the building improved, the road to a "free and clear" building wasn't without potholes. After September 11, 2001, occupancy dropped from 100% to 79%. Several tenants lost their jobs and could not afford the rent.

Occupancy in the building didn't go over 95% until nine months later. This decline in occupancy was unfortunately widespread; overall occupancy in my properties declined from 100% to 88%.

After the purchase of the seventy-seven-unit building, I did a few other deals:

1. I sold the four-unit building near De Paul University in Chicago, and used the proceeds as the down payment on a thirty-six-unit building located on the east side of Milwaukee.

This was a classic 1031 exchange. I sold the property for $420,000, paid off the existing loans, and with the help of a Deferred Exchange Corporation used the balance of the funds as the down payment on the thirty-six-unit building. My rationale for selling was an effort on my part to get out of directly managing property. Simultaneously with the expansion of my insurance business, I found myself either directly managing or overseeing the performance of managers in Aurora, Chicago, and Milwaukee. My time was becoming too valuable. The amount of time I spent traveling to the Chicago building, coupled with the aggravation, made my decision easier. With a thirty-six-unit building, I could either put it under a management company or at least have a resident manager deal with the tenants. In addition, the long-term income potential and tax deductibility were more favorable with the larger building.

Five years have passed since I made this deal. From my point of view, the acquisition has worked. I've moderately upgraded the building. Consequently, the rents are higher and it is easier to rent.

When I refinanced the property two years ago, the appraisal exceeded my purchase price by $140,000. Since I had owned the building for four years, the value of the property increased by about $3000 per month. More importantly, the building has reduced my personal management time and produced positive cash flow, which I use to prepay the loan from the bank.

2. When I sold the six-unit building in Aurora, I had about $30,000 in cash after paying the expenses and capital gains taxes. I used this to purchase four small condominiums in a famous hotel on the east side of Milwaukee.

The condominiums are really hotel rooms that can be rented by the night, week, month, or even longer. I bought the four condos for $90,000. The sellers carried the $60,000 in debt. A management company runs the hotel operations. Basically, I have to send in my monthly assessment, pay the property taxes and a few other bills, and, of course, deposit the rent checks.

This deal worked out fairly well. The monthly income has far exceeded my expectations, and I have been able to pay off the note in five years. So the condos are free and clear.

Market demand for the condos dramatically improved, and similar units in the building are listing for over $90,000 now. After September 11, 2001, however, the income from the condos did decline steeply. Occupancy dropped from about 80% to between 30-40% . Since the fall of 2002, occupancy has improved, and I hope to be on the positive side of the ledger again soon.

3) An opportunity developed to purchase a sixty-seven-unit building a few doors down the street from the seventy-seven-unit property.

I liked the building because of its excellent location. It was six stories high and had sixty-six studio apartments and one one-bed-

94

room. The building required about $450,000 in down payment. I used three resources to raise the money:

- I sold the six-unit building in the Lakeview area of Chicago. After the sale was consummated, I had about $175,000 in cash left. Using the vehicle of a 1031 tax deferred exchange, I used the money as part of the down payment for the sixty-seven-unit property.

- I refinanced one of the buildings in west Milwaukee and pulled $180,000 out of the property. In retrospect, I originally pulled $30,000 in equity out of the six-unit in Lakeview to purchase the three-unit building in Aurora. After the Aurora fire, I used around $100,000 as the down payment and operating capital on the eighteen-unit in west Milwaukee. Now, through refinancing, I was able to pull out $180,000. All this from buying a six-unit building for $85,700!

- Though it was not necessary, I raised $105,000 from investors to increase the down payment and lessen the amount of the loan. This was protection against a negative cash flow.

I purchased the property in January 1998. A major motivation on my part was to sell the six-unit building so I wouldn't have to directly manage it. As noted earlier, apartment management is time-consuming, and I was getting tired of showing units, handling or coordinating maintenance, and generally overseeing the property. I saw this as an opportunity to grow larger and to gain more free time.

My evaluation of this sixty-seven unit building after four years of ownership is as follows: The building has performed somewhat under expectation. Prior to September 11, 2001, occupancy was as expected, 97-98%. By January, 2002, there were eighteen vacant units – 27%. Occupancy has since improved somewhat.

Unfortunately, I've incurred many capital expenses with the property. Within a week of the purchase, the boiler died, costing over $30,000 to replace. The windows were loose, allowing cold drafts and, in some cases, water into the units. Replacing them was a five-year project that cost well over $100,000. In addition, the parking lot had to be resurfaced, including proper drainage, at a price of around $25,000. Add to these expenses new carpeting, six new washers and dryers, various remodeling projects, and a new roof for $25,000, and one can see that buildings cost money to maintain.

The good news about the property was the appraisal when we refinanced – it was well over $400,000 above the purchase price. Overall, the building was a worthwhile trade, given its location and the fact that I was no longer doing property management.

4. Most recently, I acquired a twelve-unit building on the east side of Milwaukee. The down payment for this property came from refinancing the thirty-six-unit building.

My motivations for this acquisition were different from prior buildings. They were as follows:

- The thirty-six-unit building had financing that was fixed for five years and would thereafter adjust annually, with payment in full (another balloon payment) due ten years after I got the loan. The interest rate for the loan was based on a formula. According to this formula, the loan would soon adjust upward. In shopping the market, I was able to find a loan that was one and a half percentage points lower for the next five years and that didn't require a balloon payment. 1.5% of $700,000 is over $10,000 a year in interest savings. I was actually able to pull $125,000 out of the building and lower the monthly payment. In effect, the down payment was free.

• This opportunity arose around April 15. A few days earlier, I had received a very unpleasant surprise from my accountant, about my income tax liability for the prior year. He mentioned needing more tax shelter that real estate provides. I had never bought a building for tax shelter reasons, but I figured that if the building did a little better than break even, I'd be able to use it as a tax deduction.

• As a reward to one of my valuable employees (and as an incentive for him to stay with me), I gave him a piece of the building. The property was well-located and in excellent condition. My financial analysis showed in the area of a 14% to 16% return on the initial investment, not counting future appreciation. Consequently, I refinanced the thirty-six-unit building, pulled out the down payment, and added the twelve-unit to the portfolio. If I were just starting out, this would have been a big deal to me, but after having purchased several larger buildings over the past ten years, I now considered it a small deal.

It is still too early to determine if this building will be a good investment. After September 11, 2001, it had three or four vacancies. It's been a negative cash flow to date, and I've had to take money out of my own pocket to keep it afloat. For the first time ever, I lowered rents to attract prospective tenants. The rent reduction was successful, and the building is again at full occupancy.

As to future plans, if a worthwhile investment opportunity presents itself, I will probably pursue it. In retrospect, it was fun and exciting to decide to invest in real estate, to learn about it, to search for buildings, and ultimately purchase them. It's been fun making deals and buying larger and larger buildings. It certainly has been exciting seeing my net worth and income grow much faster than anything I could have done from a job or realized from the stock market.

The enhancement to my self-esteem from starting a business with nothing and building it has been wonderful. It's been a fantastic adventure. I still worry and have numerous daily aggravations – costly repairs and insurance problems, for example. Nevertheless, I don't worry about pleasing my boss or losing my job. My sense of personal freedom has increased. I still read books on real estate and self-improvement, as well as biographies. I am far from perfect, but I keep working on growing. When I look back over the last few decades, the positive changes are dramatic. I've lived through many down days and tough times. I frequently thought there was no hope for the future. But I persisted. The bottom line: THERE IS ALWAYS HOPE.

This completes my story. It shows that an ordinary person starting with $10,000 could become a mini-mogul through real estate investing. Similar stories could be recounted by thousands of other individuals. I know many moguls or mini-moguls who did not make it very far up the corporate ladder, or wouldn't have if they tried. They own hundreds or thousands of units and have net worths in the eight-figure range (a few might be in the nine-figure range, but they would never tell you about it).

To be a mini-mogul or beyond, you have to believe it can happen and then take action. Most wealthy investors I know are ordinary people who believed they could make a real estate dream come true. And they did.

Part II of the book will describe some of the things I learned along the journey, starting with the decision to invest in real estate, the search, the acquisition, and the management.

PART II

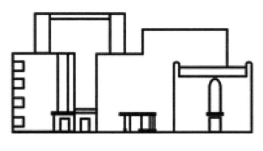

LESSONS FROM
THE STREET

7

THE SEVEN PATHS TO FINANCIAL FREEDOM

To me, the point of investing in real estate is to use it as a vehicle toward attaining financial independence. I define financial independence as having enough financial assets generating enough income after taxes so that you are able to afford the standard of living which you have set for yourself now and for the remainder of your life. These assets produce income independent of your work effort.

As an example, let's assume you are sixty-six years old and retired. Your pension from your job of forty years is $4000 per month, and it will adjust with inflation. Your monthly Social Security check is $1400 and your income from stocks, bonds, and various bank certificates of deposit is $1600 per month. You own your house free and clear. Your children are out on their own and you have Medicare and long-term care insurance. Thus your income before taxes is $7000 per month, or $84,000 per year. Your standard of living where you feel fulfillment in your life is $4500 per month, or $54,000. After paying your taxes, you have well in excess of $54,000. You are financially independent.

As a second example, let's say you own ten apartment buildings free and clear, which are fully rented. You make about $2000 per month per building after all expenses are paid, or $20,000 per month. A management company operates the buildings for you. All you have to do is cash their monthly check. Overall, you are grossing $240,000 per year before taxes take their bite. Your after-tax income is $160,000. You live on $100,000 per year and are insured against future health care and nursing home expenses. You thus find yourself in a position of financial independence.

How do you get to be financially independent? Here are the seven paths to freedom:

1) Inheriting or marrying into financial independence

2) Building or having a business that generates enough income or is worth enough so that you can be financially independent

3) Investing in real estate

4) Being very gifted (or lucky) in a particular area where you can command great sums of money for what you do

5) Working for an employer and saving part of your income, and then perpetually investing it in various investment vehicles such as stocks, bonds, mutual funds, annuities, certificates of deposit, and so forth

6) Hitting a jackpot like a lottery or winning the big prize on the slot machine

7) Some combination of the above six paths

Let's focus on Path #3 – investing in real estate. Real estate investing covers a wide array of alternatives. To simplify matters, I've divided the opportunities into four areas:

• Investing in a Real Estate Investment Trust (REIT)

- Passive investing in a real estate syndication as a member in a limited liability company or as a limited partner in a limited partnership

- Tenant in common ownership interests

- Do-it-yourself investing in "bricks-and-mortar" and land

Real Estate Investment Trusts

When you purchase a REIT, you are buying a publicly traded company that owns, operates, buys, sells, develops, and manages real estate. You are in essence investing in stock in that company. General Motors makes cars. A REIT's business is real estate investing. REITs may specialize in certain categories such as apartment buildings or shopping centers, or they may have a broad range of real estate investments including mortgage lending. Many REITs specialize in specific kinds of property, like shopping centers in certain geographic areas.

If you want to invest in a REIT, there are two approaches: 1) buy individual REIT stocks; or 2) buy a sector mutual fund that focuses on real estate or a REIT Index Fund.

In the latter situation, you are in fact purchasing many REIT stocks when you buy the unit of the mutual fund. You gain instant diversification. Several mutual fund companies offer REIT sector funds or REIT Index Funds. These include Vanguard, Fidelity, and T. Rowe Price.

REITs offer some advantages to the armchair investor. When you buy a REIT, you own real estate, but you don't have the onerous responsibility of managing properties. You simply collect your dividends and watch how the stock or fund performs. The dividends are relatively high, as a REIT in the United States is obligated to pay a high percentage of its net income to shareholders.

This is because REITs are not subject to corporate income tax the way most companies are. The recipient of the dividend pays the tax. In addition, you are often buying instant diversification of real estate assets.

I have never purchased a REIT or REIT fund. I figure that with my portfolio of buildings, a large portion of our net worth and income-producing assets are in real estate already. I wouldn't gain much by investing in REITs.

I do have some limited experience with REITs, though. I am a member of several Limited Liability Companies that own specific properties in the Phoenix, Arizona area. These are garden apartment complexes ranging from sixty-four to one hundred forty-five rental units. Some of the buildings were bought through real estate brokers and some from the Resolution Trust Corporation in the early 1990s. A close relative did the deals, but I was very much involved in the analysis and negotiations.

As buyers, our competition frequently was REITs that specialized in apartments. The REITs were always making high offers and driving the price of real estate up. They had money flowing in and had to keep gobbling up real estate to please their shareholders. We couldn't compete with them, as the high prices they offered simply didn't make economic sense to us.

According to the National Association of Real Estate Investment Trusts (NAREIT), the historical REIT performance shows a total compounded annual return of 24% over the past five years, 15% over the past ten years, and 11% over the past twenty years.

So, if you want investment exposure to real estate but are not in the real estate business, REITs are one way to go.

Investing in Real Estate
through a Real Estate Syndicator

If you want to be an armchair investor and don't want to own real estate through the stock market, you might look for a syndicator (someone who puts together groups of investors and purchases real estate) who is offering the opportunity for you to be a passive investor in real estate. Syndications come in all shapes and sizes. I'm technically a syndicator, since I have investors on some of my investments. Large companies such as Inland Real Estate own and manage many properties which they syndicate or sell interests in to investors. With a syndication, you are typically buying into a particular piece of real estate.

Is buying into a syndication a good deal? There's no one-size-fits-all answer. As an investor, you must analyze each deal presented to you to see if it will work for you. I've known of deals that have done well and others where investors lost everything. In general, I don't invest in syndications. I own enough real estate as it is.

If you are interested in finding a syndicator, there are many resources to help you in your search: real estate brokers, your lawyer, your accountant, your stockbrokers, newspapers such as the *Wall Street Journal*, and even the phone book. You might explore tenant in common or real estate syndication on the Internet (more on this shortly). When you find a syndication opportunity, you will be provided a copy of a *prospectus*. This is a detailed document which provides information about the potential investment, including demographic information, cash flow projections, various risks the investor assumes, the fees, and even the resumes of the syndicators. I've read a few and find them full of legalese and quite boring. If possible, review multiple syndication proposals to compare financial projections, fees, and assumed rates of return. I do enjoy reading about the various ways the syndication charges fees and how the syndicator makes money. If you want to invest through a syndicator, review the prospectus thoroughly.

Tenant in Common Interests

One of the hot areas in real estate investing is a tenant in common ownership interest in a piece of real estate. Let's look at an example.

My friend Charley was getting up in years and was tired of managing several of his small apartment buildings near De Paul University on the north side of Chicago. Over time, they had appreciated dramatically in value and when Charley looked at his return on equity (somewhere in the 1% to 3% range), he questioned whether it was worth even owning the buildings. They made relatively little money.

Charley did some checking around and determined he was better off selling the properties and using the proceeds to buy into a larger property. Along comes the tenant in common syndicator. Charley wanted to sell the buildings, but he didn't want to pay the capital gains tax associated with the sale. He found a syndicator who put together a deal for investors where several people together purchased a large shopping center in Ohio. Key tenants included Wal-Mart and Home Depot. Charley was able to do an I.R.S. 1031 Tax Deferred Exchange (more on this in a future chapter) and defer the substantial capital gains taxes. Charley has what is known as a tenant in common legal interest in the property, as do the other investors.

So far Charley is very happy with this deal. He was able to get a high price for the De Paul buildings and didn't have to fork out any capital gains taxes. The syndicator who put the deal together projected a 7% cash flow return on the money Charley invested. To date, the performance of the property has matched the syndicator's projections. Charley is pleased about getting a sizable check every few months from the syndicator. He's getting a larger cash flow than when he owned the buildings, and he is free from the hassle of management.

How do you find out about tenant in common syndicators? Word of mouth from people you trust would be preferred method #1. For the Internet-savvy, go to one of the search engines like Google, type in "tenant in common," and you'll find a multitude of syndicators who will be happy to take your money.

The "Do-It-Yourself" Approach

The "do it yourself" approach is the path I've taken. In my journey, I've met hundreds of investors who have done likewise and have prospered.

However, this approach is time-consuming, and it isn't for everyone. Hardly a day goes by that I don't have to deal with some real estate matter. I can't say my life is carefree. I have also yet to meet an active real estate investor who views what they do as "armchair" investing. At the same time, I know many real estate investors who have net worths in the millions and robust cash flows. They essentially control their own destinies. They don't have to report to a boss, worry about being victims of corporate downsizing, or play office politics.

Let's briefly look at some of the ways a "do-it-yourselfer" can invest in real estate.

Buying and Holding Raw Land

A vision many dreamers have is purchasing raw land in the path of development, holding it for a period of time, and then selling it for a hefty profit to some developer. I'm sure this is possible, but

I've rarely seen it done in my circle of investor acquaintances. I did see Mr. W.D. purchase a large parcel of well-located land and break it into smaller parcels (called *subdividing*), and he made a nice profit selling these parcels over a period of a few years. I've also seen speculators buy up vacant lots in less desirable neighborhoods, betting that urban gentrification will yield them good returns.

Investing in land has pros and cons. On the pro side, you can make dramatic profits and you don't have to maintain buildings and deal with annoying tenants. On the con side, the land may not increase in value, and you still have to pay the mortgage (if you have one), pay taxes, and insure the land to protect yourself if someone gets hurt. Land can't be used as a tax write-off the way most "bricks and mortar" investments can, because land isn't depreciable. Finally, buildings provide cash flow, whereas raw land doesn't provide any rental income to the owner in most circumstances.

I personally have never invested in unimproved land, but I might someday if the right opportunity presents itself.

Owning or Controlling Single-Family Homes, Condominiums, Townhouses, and Cooperatives

Many people focus on single-family homes or condominiums as an investment vehicle. Some seminars I have attended advocate single-family homes as "THE" real estate investment.

Their logic was simple: well-located single-family homes tend to appreciate in value. If you purchase a $100,000 single-family home with a low down payment ($10,000) and borrow the other $90,000, and if the home appreciates at 5% per year, you are making 50% on your $10,000 down payment, not even counting any cash flow from the property, principal reduction from the loan payment, or tax shelter. Demand for single-family homes is usually strong, and they are less management-intensive than apartment buildings. Having your own home is the American dream.

To me, the key with a single-family home is that if you pursue them, you must have "deep pockets" to carry the property if it is vacant or running in the red. My first real estate investment was a single-family house I bought in the North Hills of Pittsburgh. I didn't actually count it as an investment because I planned to live in it for a long time as my own home. When my job in Pittsburgh didn't work out, it became a rental house.

Let's simply say the house was a financial disaster. I paid $55,200 for it in 1979 and sold it in 1987 for a whopping $46,000 before any sales costs were taken out. If that wasn't bad enough, I lost money every month I rented it out; either it was vacant or the rental income wasn't enough to cover expenses. You can call it a "negative cash flow" property or an "alligator," because it eats you alive. Buying the house in Pittsburgh was not one of my more brilliant moves.

Single-family homes have proven to be excellent investments for numerous real estate investors, however. When I see the graphs showing how the prices of single-family houses have risen year after year in almost every major U.S. city, I am awed.

I have some relatives in Detroit who just love doing single-family house deals. Sometimes they buy a house, fix it up, and rent it out for a small positive cash flow while the house appreciates in value. Often they use a technique known as "lease with an option to buy," where they control what happens to the house but never have to purchase it. They lease it from the owner at one price for themselves and then turn around and lease it to a renter at a higher price. They have an option to buy the house within a certain time period for a certain price. If the real estate market gets hot, they might sell their option or sell the house and pocket the difference between what they sold the house for and their option price. Whenever I see these relatives, they're always excited about the deals they're doing and are quite eager to tell me how much money they're making.

My bottom line is: single-family houses are not the investment for me, but they have worked well for others and are an excellent way to start out in the real estate investment game.

Smaller Apartment Buildings

This category of real estate investment could be viewed as a step up from the single family home. Instead of purchasing one unit, you might buy a two-, three- or six-unit property.

As you may recall from Part I, my first ten years in real estate investing were in the smaller apartment building category.

Many investors I know have done well buying smaller multi-family residential buildings. The value of these buildings tends to go up on a comparable basis with the rest of the neighborhood, versus a larger building whose value is strictly based on the net income/cash flow it produces. A lot of tenants I've dealt with also much prefer living in a smaller building with just a few neighbors, as opposed to a larger building which they perceive as less personal. Smaller buildings feel more homey.

For me, the financial numbers here work better than with single-family properties. A vacancy in a six-unit building for a month or two is easy to absorb. There is also an efficiency of scale. For example, replacing the roof in a four-unit building has never cost me four times the price of a roof for a house. In my view, I am more likely to have a positive cash flow with a multiunit building than with a single-family home, townhouse, condominium, or cooperative.

As with the rest of my properties, I've never calculated the overall return on my smaller buildings. My partner and I bought the six-unit building in 1982 at a price of $85,700, put in about $10,000 over sixteen years, and sold it for $360,000 in 1998. We refinanced it several times to take out money to buy other buildings. We never took any cash flow out and only once put in money – in the beginning, to buy storm windows. Our down payment was $25,000.

The four-unit in the De Paul neighborhood was purchased for about $79,000 in 1983, and sold at a bargain price of $420,000 in 1997. I refinanced that building several times, to pull money out for rehabbing or to buy more buildings. The building was a "nothing down" deal.

My Aurora buildings produced positive cash flow, and all went up in value. I was not unhappy with how they performed. I got out of the small building market because of the time requirements of managing the properties. Some years, my records would show that I made one hundred trips from our home in Wilmette to my buildings to do something or other. Each one-way trip would take from twenty minutes to an hour and a half (you acquire great patience when you have to drive in Chicago traffic when the Cubs are playing). I felt I could buy larger buildings and have other people manage them, and this has worked for me.

Many investors feel most comfortable with smaller properties, however. They don't get whacked with $30,000 bills for new boilers in the middle of winter, and they don't worry about the costs of elevator repair. A smaller building is less intimidating to some people. Getting a loan from a bank is a lot easier on a four-unit or smaller property, too.

My bottom line is: smaller apartment buildings are a great vehicle for getting started in real estate, and one with which you can continue to grow.

Larger Residential Buildings

My definition of a larger residential building is arbitrary: seven units and above. Other investors may differ, but the line has to be drawn somewhere.

At this time, virtually anything I own is seven or more units in size. I won't consider anything smaller unless I can buy it cheaply enough and turn it over right away for a quick profit.

Larger buildings to me are purely economic animals. They produce revenues from rents, parking, laundry, etc., and they have expenses. Appraisers basically value them at a multiple of their net operating income (more on this later).

In my case, I am able to leverage my time by having a management team operating the buildings. If you don't choose to manage your properties yourself, you can hire a management company to operate them. I am more comfortable having my own staff, because I have a much better feel for and more control over what is happening with the properties. On the down side, I have to deal with such "fun" areas as hiring and firing employees, training, payroll taxes, and the myriad of details that come with operating a business and having employees.

Larger buildings have their pros and cons. On the pro side, consider that if you have a building worth $1,000,000 and it goes up 3% to 5% per year, your net worth is going up by $30,000 to $50,000 per year compounded. From my point of view, larger buildings are also easier to manage. Many of my properties are producing acceptable returns. The thirty-nine-unit building I purchased for $625,000 (less the cost of a new roof) in 1991 is worth at least double that today. Having put down about $160,000, we paid the building off in eight years and have positive cash flow in our pockets each month. The same can be said for the eighteen-unit in west Milwaukee and, eventually, for all my properties.

On the downside, since the buildings are large, the expenses associated with ownership can be major, especially when they come up at the wrong time. The properties have to be managed, and one needs more than a mom-and-pop approach to do this. Records must be maintained, and units must be re-leased quickly when vacancies arise. When you need money to buy a larger property, you will be dealing with the commercial loan officer or commercial mortgage broker, as opposed to a personal banker. I haven't seen fifteen- or thirty-year fixed rate commercial loans with zero points, no balloon, and no prepayment in a long time. Lenders have many more stipulations with larger buildings than with your typical loan. Among lenders I also include pension funds and insurance companies.

My bottom line: larger buildings have been a worthwhile investment for me. Most of the investors I deal with in Chicago, Milwaukee, and Phoenix who own hundreds of units own larger buildings. All of them have done well.

Commercial Office Buildings

I view a commercial office building as being similar to a large apartment building. I am not referring here to the small, one-unit office building. With commercial office buildings, the value and return on investment are based on the income and expenses. I have never invested in an office building. From my point of view, I am familiar with rental apartments, whereas owning an office building is beyond my expertise and comfort zone.

Many of my investor friends do own office buildings, however, and are very pleased with them. Leases last for much longer than the typical six- or twelve-month residential lease.

Management is much easier than with residential property, since many of the maintenance items are the responsibility of the tenant. Depending on the location, rents are higher per square foot.

My investor friends tell me it's a pleasure dealing with most of their office tenants, as they are businesspeople who understand that the landlord is a businessperson, too. It's a businesslike relationship where you don't have to deal with the occasional irrational, unreasonable tenant.

The downside to me is the vacancy factor. When one tenant moves out, you don't always just clean up the space, paint, and then rent it out again in a week. Office tenants are selective about the space they use, and renting vacant office space may take months or even years, especially if you have a major tenant who occupies thousands of square feet.

The landlord where my wife works has had about a 25 to 30% vacancy factor this year. When her company's five-year lease ended, her company offered to keep the rent per square foot the same if they could reduce the amount of space they used. After prolonged negotiations, the landlord told them to keep the space they had and reduced their rent anyway, close to 50%. Her company is on a month-to-month lease and could be forced to find new office space if the landlord can fill the space. Unfortunately for the landlord, he hasn't rented one square foot of the vacant office space in the past six months.

In addition to potential vacancies, the owner of an office building may have to put in "leasehold improvements" (which involves finishing and decorating the space to suit the tenant), which may cost the landlord a great deal.

As noted above, I'm not a buyer of office space. I would feel uncomfortable with potential vacancies, and I am inexperienced in commercial lease negotiations. In the apartment rental business, the tenants virtually always sign my simple lease. No one has ever referred the lease to an attorney for review. In the office market, the lease agreement is critical and may entail prolonged negotiation. I don't want to deal with that.

The investors I know who have bought office buildings are also very careful in their financial analysis of the buildings. They have to confirm present rents, thoroughly review leases, estimate the proper rents, figure the future demand, and project expenses. When I buy a building, I do my preliminary financial analysis on a piece of paper in a matter of minutes.

My bottom line: commercial office buildings are an excellent investment for some people. But beware of vacancies.

Retail Space

Retail space typically refers to stores, strip malls, shopping centers, and so forth, where the tenant is a retail merchant of some sort. I view this type of investment as similar to office space, except your tenants are merchants who will hopefully have a lot of people passing through the doors and purchasing goods. The investors I know who own retail space are usually picky about who they choose as tenants. They want whatever the tenant is selling to be compatible with the area, and they want the tenant to succeed. It can take months to evict a nonpaying tenant who has declared bankruptcy, not to mention becoming a creditor of the bankruptcy estate.

Some investors I know do have "armchair" leases here. In these cases, they buy the land, bricks, and mortar that house a tenant such as a Walgreens or CVS drugstore and then earn a fixed return on the investment for a number of years. Several of the tenants in common syndicators offer these as investment opportunities.

Other investors who are approaching retirement and own management-intensive residential property will sometimes sell their rental units and do I.R.S. Section 1031 exchanges into industrial or commercial real estate. Their time is then free. I have a friend in Colorado who owns several industrial and office buildings that have what is known as a "triple net" lease.

This means that the tenant pays the property taxes, insurance, and maintenance. My friend works about two hours a month. He gets his rent checks in the mail, records them, deposits them, and makes his mortgage payments. His life sure is hard. He travels a lot and spends time with his family. In all fairness, my friend is really picky about what he buys, and conducts a very thorough due diligence in his acquisitions.

My bottom line here is the same as for office space.

"Mixed-Use" Real Estate

"Mixed-use" real estate refers to real estate which has more than one use. For example, a thirty-unit apartment building might have three storefronts on the ground floor. In downtown Chicago, high rises are going up where the first five floors are retail, the next several floors are offices, and the upper stories are residential or hotel use. The investors I know who own these like the diversification the various uses offer. They seem content with their investments. Location and the proportion of use (how much is residential versus office) of the building are *very important* in this case.

Industrial Property

Industrial property refers to factories, warehouses, assembly plants, distribution centers, and properties that are geared toward companies that manufacture things. In the Chicago area, certain locales are highly industrialized, such as Elk Grove Village near O'Hare Airport. A number of small and not-so-small companies own or lease such buildings. Many of these buildings are occupied by a single tenant or owner-occupant.

I know a few investors who own and lease industrial property. Most are happy with their investments. This type of ownership isn't nearly as management-intensive as residential real estate. A good friend of mine owns a lot of rental units and also one industrial property. He is, however, not very happy with it. His tenants contaminated the land with industrial pollutants and moved out. Now he is looking at a staggering bill to clean up the property.

Real Estate Developments

I am a member of the Lincoln Park Builders of Chicago. Several of our members are developers who are either building new projects from the ground up or converting existing structures from their current use, such as an apartment building or warehouse, to a new use, like condominiums.

I personally have never converted anything. I have, however, spent time looking for factory and warehouse space in hot areas with the thought of converting it into lofts. Unfortunately, other developers beat me to the punch on those properties I found promising.

If nothing else, it was a useful learning experience. In Chicago, you have to be concerned about zoning for such a project. You can't just go out and buy a warehouse and start tearing it down. The local community has to give its seal of approval. Don't take this as a given. The local alderman has to have his/her say.

The financial analysis is more complex for this type of acquisition than for buying a single-family house or an existing twelve-unit apartment building. You have to consider all kinds of costs. Acquisition costs relate to what you paid for the property. Soft costs include costs you don't see in the finished products, like legal fees or interest-carry or architectural fees. Hard costs involve construction of the bricks and mortar – both the material cost and the labor cost. In addition, you have to estimate how long it will take to make the unit ready to occupy, and how much it will cost to finance the project until the last unit is sold.

Such a project certainly has substantial risk. It's not fun trying to sell a loft unit that cost $300,000 of borrowed money to build and has been sitting vacant for a long time. You are paying interest to hold that property, as well as taxes, insurance, and utilities.

The reward is simple: money. Consider if you developed a thirty-unit loft building at a profit of $30,000 per unit within a three-year period. Thirty units times $30,000 over three years is $900,000 before taxes. That's more than most working folks make. Once the unit is sold, you don't have to manage it – you just invest your profit elsewhere. Imagine if you are doing several projects like this at once. The numbers become staggeringly high.

In my view, developing real estate has great rewards and great risks. I was interested in doing a loft conversion because I had rehab experience, real estate ownership experience, a great contractor who was one of my investors, and a base of income-producing real estate I already owned to fall back on. That reduced my risk. It was also something different from the standard "buy and operate approach." I thought it would be fun as a new challenge.

A major risk involves mistiming the market cycle, especially for large projects that take years to develop. Many big time developers have gotten killed by bad market timing and end up with hundreds of unsold units incurring expenses.

In the end, I kept to my conservative, pedestrian, "buy well-located real estate, manage it, and hold it forever" strategy.

Nevertheless, many of my investor/developer cohorts have done extremely well in real estate development over the past five to ten years.

Other Real Estate

Real estate offers vast opportunities in a number of forms. I wanted to give a general overview rather than try to be definitive. I haven't included investing in mortgages, trust deeds, or delinquent tax certificates for income and possible acquisition of a property. Nor did I mention "flipping," where you buy a house for well under market value and sell it right away to another investor or a live-in owner. Other specialized investment opportunities include golf courses, skating rinks, medical facilities, parking lots, and places of religious worship, to name a few. If you are interested, your local public library has dozens of books to help you learn more about various facets of real estate investing.

The next several chapters focus on a typical real estate transaction, beginning with the decision about what to buy, the search, the decision to pursue a property, due diligence, and closing the deal.

8

Finding Deals: Seek and Ye Shall Find

Let's assume that, having read the overview of investment options, you're convinced you want to pursue the "do it yourself" real estate approach, or continue to do so if you've already begun. Your next decision is "What do I want to buy?"

While this seems simple enough, I personally struggled with this question for a year after purchasing the first six-unit building. The basic choices for the neophyte investor or mini-mogul in the making would be the single-family home, small apartment building, not-so-small apartment building, or a small-to-midsize commercial property (office, retail, etc.). While there is no pre-scribed formula on how to build or maintain a real estate portfolio, my own bias is to start at the smaller end and build up to larger investments.

In my case, my brain had cast in stone that my first acquisition after returning from Pittsburgh would be a structurally sound smaller apartment building with low rents, in need of some cosmetic improvement, in an acceptable neighborhood. Having read several real estate books, I found that this one sentence summed up the target property recommended for acquisition by every book. I eventually found a property that fit this description, and it worked well.

My confusion as to what to buy next related to all the new information I learned after purchasing Building Number 1. I essentially immersed myself in real estate. In the year after the closing, I must have read twenty-five "how to do it" books on real estate. I was also active with a few real estate groups.

My friends at the Lakeview Developers advocated buying apartment buildings. On the other hand, the Wealth Builders' approach was to find a well-located three-bedroom, two-bath single-family house that had the potential to make a profit. After hearing at their meetings how pleased they were buying single-family houses, I wavered between single-family homes and multiunit residential buildings. (Please refer to the chart on page 40.)

A second factor in any decision was my lack of resources. I had very little cash available for a down payment. In order to raise the down payment for the first building, I had saved over half my salary after taxes for a year and a half. I had lived like a pauper. I didn't want to do that anymore.

After wrestling with what to do, I decided to acquire a small apartment building with as little down payment as possible. I liked the idea of getting a few rents rather than just one.

In my early days of real estate investing, I relied on agents. I was working full-time and did not have time to search during the day. When my day jobs disappeared, I resorted to a variety of methods for finding real estate investments.

Now, with two decades of experience and many deals under my belt, I have concluded that the key to finding profitable real estate investments is knowing and having good relationships with as many people as possible. The more people who know you are alive and interested in real estate investing, the more likely you are to hear about a building for sale.

Let's now focus on specific search methods.

Newspaper Ads

Read the real estate ads in your local newspaper. In Chicago, the major newspapers have extensive real estate sections on the weekends. In addition, some the local neighborhood papers have ads that don't get placed in the major newspapers. In a major newspaper, you'll be checking the following sections: houses, town houses, condominiums, and cooperatives for sale or for rent, apartment buildings for sale, commercial property for sale, investment real estate, and miscellaneous real estate. There are essentially two categories of ads: ones for sale by owner (FSBOs); and ones placed by agents. If an agent is placing an ad, the ad should include the name of the real estate office.

The ad usually gives you scanty information, so you have to determine if you want to respond to it. Sometimes the wording will have enticing language, like "motivated seller," "handyman's special," "bargain basement," etc. Other times you'll find financial information which will help you decide if the building has profit potential. These ads might read "twelve beautiful units for $480,000," "six times gross in fashionable neighborhood," or "eight times net." If you have a feel for the market, you may spot a profitable investment.

For example, the ad for the six-unit building in Roscoe Village contained only a few lines. I knew the property was underpriced at $85,000 and immediately phoned to set an appointment. If you are interested in buying a house in a specific neighborhood, you might look for an Open House on a Sunday. This will give you a feel for what the listing price of local housing is. One of my favorite Sunday afternoon pastimes is cruising our neighborhood with my wife, checking out Open Houses. We then estimate what our house would list for if we were to sell. We don't plan on selling, but it's nice to know.

If something in an ad ignites your interest, you'll obviously make a phone call to learn more about the property. Many real estate books I've read advocate calling the ads whose language indicates the seller is motivated. Look for key words like "motivated seller," "must sell," "desperate," "needs TLC," or "handyman's special." I like dealing with owners directly, because you can build a relationship and get information firsthand. If an agent is running the ad, you can either contact that agent directly or through your agent. Once you get information about properties that interest you, you must separate the wheat from the chaff.

One final word: if you are going to peruse the ads as a means of searching for investments, you need to be aggressive. This means getting the Sunday papers as early as possible on *Saturday*, identifying the ads of interest, and immediately calling the phone number in the ad (or going online to check listings as early as possible). I learned this lesson the hard way. An ad for a house I knew of was placed in the *Chicago Tribune* for its Sunday edition. The earliest I could get the *Tribune* in the suburbs was noon. I saw the ad at 12:10 p.m. and called immediately. The seller/owner who had placed the ad told me I was only the second caller, but he had already signed a contract with someone who called at 11:00 a.m. Opportunity waits for no one.

This also means reading the ads every day, especially in the neighborhood newspapers, because a hot deal can come out on in a Wednesday ad, and you'll miss it if you only focus on the Sunday paper.

Real Estate Agents

As an investor, I have dealt with many real estate agents, using them both in the acquisition and the sale of property. I have also bought and sold property without the use of agents. For a time, I even held a real estate salesperson license in Illinois. In this book, when referring to agents, I include both brokers and agents.

Real estate agents can be immensely helpful in your search for an investment. Most agents are out in the market full-time and are endeavoring to do three things: 1) they are trying to find properties to sell (list); 2) they are trying to sell their listings; or 3) they are trying to sell what is formally listed for sale by another agent in the real estate marketplace. In my experience, agents tend to specialize; they might focus on single-family homes and very small multiunits, larger multiunits, or commercial investments. Often commercial agents are also involved in finding and leasing space like an office or store.

If your focus is larger apartment buildings, you need to find agents who specialize in this. They aren't hard to locate. You can find them through newspaper ads they run, through referrals, or simply by phoning real estate offices listed in the Yellow Pages and asking to talk with the agent who specializes in whatever interests you.

An agent can serve you in many ways. Most agents have access to the multiple listing service, which will give you immediate information about potential investments listed with agents who cooperate with the service. More importantly, a good agent will keep abreast of the marketplace and contact you immediately about any opportunity that may interest you.

In my experience, all the agents I have worked with are compensated on a commission basis. They get paid either a percentage or a set fee when a property sells or leases. In essence, they are commissioned salespeople who need to make a sale to earn money. From an investor's perspective, you have to define for an agent what you want, and you have the final decision regarding what to buy and how much to offer.

As an investor, I have mixed feelings about agents. I like to contact sellers directly, because I can ask them questions myself and thus get a much better feel for their position and needs. This also allows me to build a relationship with the seller. While the deal at hand may not work, perhaps a future one will. I am also bothered by the commissioned pay structure of the agents. I want to know that an agent is 100% in my corner. If an agent gets paid based only on a sale, I wonder in the short-term whose interests have priority. Another issue I have with agents is their lack of creativity. Most agents are trained to list a property, to show it in compliance with all the laws that apply, and to use a board-approved contract, with the expectation that the buyer will meet the contract contingencies.

When I mention what I believe are basic alternatives to these methods, I get resistance:

"The seller never will go for it," "The seller isn't a bank," etc. Some of the creative things I suggest include seller-financing, moratoriums on interest payments, low offers, or giving the seller options on how to structure the sale. Agents rarely want to try anything different.

In fairness to agents, they've been very helpful to me in finding and selling properties that fit my time constraints. Virtually all the agents I have dealt with are hardworking, honest, and show total integrity during the transactional process. Working as an agent is not an easy job, and they care about what they do. Their reputation is manifest.

I'm also not exactly an agent's dream. I am picky and don't want to make a mistake. I remember the aggravation I caused agents when I would march through buildings with my checklists and then end up not buying anything. As an experienced buyer, I've improved. If an agent brings a property to my attention that he or she thinks is a good deal, I will make a decision quickly. The agent wants to make a sale and I won't get in the way.

If you find a good agent, you should treat this person like gold, as the agent really is helping you get gold.

Two last comments on agents:

1) The question arises whether you should use multiple agents. What I've done in the past is use an agent for a specific area. I rely upon and trust those agents unless they prove themselves unreliable. I expect them to help me by being on top of the market and contacting me quickly with opportunities.

2) In addition, there are some brokerage houses that focus exclusively on larger properties and don't necessarily cooperate with the multiple listing service. These include national brokerage houses like Marcus and Millichap and C.B. Richard Ellis. With these brokers, you'll want to find an agent within each agency who will serve you as needed.

Thus, if you are looking for a property, you might have a local agent plus use agents from a large brokerage company.

Canvassing Specific Areas

Canvassing areas involves picking specific locales where you want to acquire a property, then searching those areas. In Chicago, I have walked every block and viewed every building in Ravenswood, Logan Square, Bucktown, east and west Ukrainian Village, Roscoe Village, and Old Irving Park. I did this before most of these areas became "hot." I'd get there in the morning with a pad of paper and look for multiunit buildings in need of repair, identify them by address, make notes, and then trudge down to Cook County headquarters to get the name and address of the taxpayer of record. At the time I started out, resources like the Internet were not available. I would then contact the taxpayer of record by mail about my interest in the building and wait for the phone call back that hardly ever came. If I could find the taxpayer's phone number, I would call. Eventually, I did get some responses – sometimes a year or two after my letter was sent.

This is what real estate agents do when looking for a listing, and it works. You need patience and persistence, though.

I've even heard of some investors who employ high school or college students to comb specific areas, and compensate them based on their production if they identify by address run-down or boarded-up properties. Taking this one step further, you could print flyers for your target area and have students distribute them. One of my first jobs as a high school student was distributing promotional flyers for a Kentucky Fried Chicken franchise.

As an owner, I am on the other end of the phone now. I am constantly bombarded by agents who tell me what great buildings I own and how much they can get for my properties.

Individual buyers also continually contact me directly, either by mail or phone. While I plan to die with the buildings (unless a better opportunity comes along), I do remember the people who call me every six months, and I'd probably give them a chance to buy the property before I listed it with an agent. I save their letters and keep their phone numbers.

Some of the ploys these people use are quite interesting. One buyer offered to fix me up on a date with a very beautiful actress if I would sell the property. Since I am a happily married and faithful husband, this person really failed to find my "hot button." Another agent said his mysterious client had sold his property and had to find and close on a property within a certain period of time (his client had forty-five days to identify a property and one hundred eighty days to complete the purchase after the sale date), or he would have to pay capital gain taxes. The agent called several times, and I told him I would take $3,000,000 for a property worth about $1,000,000. The agent then attributed many undesirable characteristics to me. I simply explained that the building had net operating income of $85,000, most of which was tax-sheltered. If I received $3,000,000, paid various taxes at the highest tax level on the capital gain, and invested the remaining balance in thirty-year U.S. Treasury Bonds at 5%, my investors and I would end up at the same amount of income. I never heard from that agent again.

Eventually, when you canvass specific areas, you get to know the owners on a first name basis. An owner may not sell a particular building but may have another one to sell, or have a friend who has something to sell. It helps to build up your people contact base. If you do find something when canvassing an area, the key is to act quickly, assuming that the building meets your requirements.

Mass Mailings to Building Owners/Taxpayers of Record

In my free and easy days, I would drive out to the Tax Assessor's office in Aurora, Illinois, and go through the records to identify the name and address of the taxpayer of record for every multiunit building in Aurora. I would then send out a mass mailing to the owners. A few called me back, but I wasn't able to find any bargains. This is easier to do today than in 1989, since all records were manual back then.

The mass mailing approach is similar to the canvassing approach, except you are sending an impersonal letter to everyone. I never had success with this approach, but my real estate agent friends tell me they have procured listings with it. Again, persistence is the key.

Running Your Own Ad

One of the things I learned from real estate books and seminars was to let sellers find you. Most local newspapers have a section in the classifieds entitled "Real Estate Wanted."

These advertisements typically state that the buyer will purchase or lease your property in any location, in any condition, for all cash, with a quick closing. They may say they will pay your asking price (but with their terms) for a quick closing.

Over a period of time, these ads work. The people who place them are looking for very motivated sellers who want to unload property quickly. The advertiser is looking for a bargain. Sellers will call you. You may buy one or two properties a year, but hopefully the money you make on the deal will pay for all the advertising costs, plus you will end up with money in your pocket. Year after year, you see the same ads run every day by the same people.

One of my fellow members in the Lincoln Park Builders Club has run an ad like this for years, and he's done very well for himself finding properties this way.

You can even take this a step further. I've seen boldly printed advertisements stating, "I'll buy your property with all cash, in any condition" on public benches, on automobiles and vans, and on billboards.

I've run ads myself seeking multiunit buildings, where I'd pay the seller's price, but wanted my terms (no interest, or very low interest). The ads were effective; I got calls. Some were from agents who wanted to sell me property and some were from sellers. However, most of the properties were outside my target areas and were in poor condition. Even with 0% interest, I didn't want the aggravation of operating these properties. I stopped running ads after a few months, because I did not find anything suitable and could not afford the advertising cost at the time.

Tracking Legal Notices

Sometimes someone else's pain is your gain. More specifically, property owners may experience unfortunate events that can create real estate opportunities. These include death, divorce, disability, or bankruptcy, to name a few. Often a public notice is posted in the newspaper. Real estate investors monitor these notices closely, in hopes of finding an opportunity.

In Chicago, the daily legal newspaper publishes death notices and notices of bankruptcy proceedings or real estate foreclosure developments. Companies exist in most major metropolitan areas that provide a summary of pertinent notices every day. The Internet also makes this information accessible. Based on the notices' information, the investor then contacts the appropriate person, such as the homeowner or the executor of an estate, and tries to make a deal.

I spent a few months tracking down opportunities of the recently deceased/probate properties. My efforts were to no avail. I never directly contacted the family of the deceased; I dealt with their estate attorney or the public administrator instead. I was also in touch with several funeral directors. Typically I'd send a letter and follow it up with a phone call. I met with great resistance. It was not uncommon for me to be called an insensitive brute or a vulture.

I did not get anywhere here.

Many investors do well finding properties via the legal notice route. Several books and seminars are available on buying foreclosures and other properties with owners who are in a distressed situation. A trip to your public library or local bookstore is a good beginning if this is the direction you want to go.

Other Investors

You are in competition with other investors to find bargain real estate. Some may be willing to flip you their property at an under market price where both of you still come out ahead.

For example, if an investor finds a house for 30% under market value and flips it to you for 15% under market, you both profit. While you may feel some sour grapes about not finding the property first yourself, a purchase 15% under market may still fit your investment parameters. Mr. W.D. has done this with me several times.

Real Estate Investor Groups

I've been a member of three real estate investor groups: the Wealth Builders, the Lakeview Developers, and the Lincoln Park Builders. Many deals have been struck that started with casual conversations at their meetings. I have standing orders that if I ever want to sell any of my properties, Person X and Person Y want to know about it first. I also know these investors are out to get a bargain.

If you are a buyer, you put the word out or call other members. If you are a seller, you let the other members know. We have certain unwritten rules, such as not talking about a deal until it is closed.

The key here is knowing and relating well to people. I am aware of most of the larger buildings in Milwaukee, and I have no reservations about calling the owners when I'm in the market to buy or sell a building. We all talk to each other.

Attorneys, Accountants, and Other Professionals

Attorneys, accountants, and other professionals serve clients who are active real estate investors. Other professionals include property managers and real estate appraisers who are active in the real estate market. To help a client, they may be willing to give your name, address, and phone number to that client. In a few cases, I've written simple letters to real estate and estate planning attorneys about what I want, inquiring if they know of any clients that might be selling at that time. I then follow up with a phone call. This approach has yielded little for me except good will. Periodically I'll hear from one of their clients, but they usually just want to pick my brain rather than sell me anything.

While this approach has yielded little for me personally, I strongly believe in the importance of using as many means as possible to find an investment. Your chances of success are much greater.

Lending Institutions

Many books on the subject of buying real estate foreclosures recommend buying foreclosed property from a lending institution, such as a bank or a savings and loan. The term "REO" or "Real Estate Owned" by the lending institution refers to this category of property.

In the real estate foreclosure process, a lending institution may get stuck taking back a property if no one outbids the lender at the foreclosure auction. Lending institutions aren't eager to have foreclosed properties on their books, as they are in the business of lending money and making a profit. They are not real estate investors or managers. The lending institution could be viewed as a motivated seller that will sell you property at either a good price or with good terms, or both.

I have occasionally contacted lenders for REOs, but with little success. I do, however, have relationships with several banks and savings and loans. I'm a preferred customer, since I owe them lots of money. Chief commercial lending officers and bank presidents have brought to my attention opportunities to buy from their real estate inventory. My guess is they have offered me these opportunities because they know they'll have a good-performing loan with me rather than a nonperforming loan that would look bad on their balance sheet. I've taken a pass on these opportunities because I don't want to own houses which need work, even though there might be profit to be made.

At foreclosure auctions I've attended, I've found that most of the properties get pulled out of the auction for some reason. I've also noted that the majority of the other properties are purchased by the lender for the loan balance plus the bank's costs. Very rarely have I seen a bidding war.

Many "how to profit from real estate foreclosures" books advocate contacting a key person at the bank after the auction, such as the president or chief officer in charge of REOs.

Investors I've talked to who have made the effort to contact the key bank officer were frequently frustrated by these persons' individual nonresponsiveness.

I believe it really does help to have an ongoing relationship based on mutual trust with a banker in order to find real estate investment opportunities held by a bank.

An additional lead source that is sometimes overlooked is a mortgage broker. Mortgage brokers may periodically get calls from owners in distress about refinancing their properties to get cash to meet some kind of urgent need. These desperate owners may not qualify for a mortgage because of bad credit, unemployment, etc. For a fee, the mortgage broker may provide you with the name, phone, and address of the lead.

Auctions

Sometimes you can find real estate bargains at public auctions. The legal notice route described earlier will lead you to some auctions.

In addition, newspapers periodically announce public auctions promoted by brokers and so forth. Several government agencies also conduct auctions. These include the Internal Revenue Service, the U.S. Marshall Service, the U.S. Customs Department, the U.S. Department of Housing, the U.S. Department of Veteran Affairs, the FDIC, and the Small Business Administration. You can find out about these auctions by calling the departments or checking their Web sites.

Family, Friends, and Others

All the world loves the real estate investor. I have often experienced shy and quiet individuals who open up when queried about real estate. They want to show you what they know and generally want to be of help.

When I am looking for real estate, I let the world know. I even have business cards that say "I buy real estate." My suggestion: tell everyone you know that you are in a search mode. This includes family, friends, business associates, and coworkers (so long as it doesn't jeopardize your employment). Include on this list your banker, hairstylist, grocery store clerks, store managers, car mechanics, and any others whose path you cross. Some investors have scouts or "bird dogs" who tip them off for compensation about real estate opportunities.

In the event you are given a lead, remember to keep the referral source informed as to whether the deal worked out or not. If I give a person a referral, I get great inner satisfaction when I find out I've helped someone.

The Internet

A few months ago, I decided to sell my three-unit building. I put a notice up on an Internet site known as Craig's List (www. craigslist.org) that the property was for sale. Within twenty-four hours I had six phone calls. Within seventy-two hours the property was under contract. (It later closed with no hitches.) Obviously a lot of investors are checking Craig's List for deals.

Many opportunities for sale are to be found on the Internet. Virtually every brokerage office has their listings on the Internet. Government agencies such as HUD have their properties available for purchase through the Internet. Auction houses show their opportunities on the Internet. The real estate section for most urban newspapers is available on the Internet. You can communicate over the Internet through e-mail.

So how does an investor make use of the Internet? Here are some possibilities:

- Do a search for topics related to real estate investments for sale. Check out:

   1) real estate for sale

   2) houses for sale

   3) investments for sale

- Check brokerage Web sites

- Check government agency Web sites

- Check the real estate section of the newspaper for the area in which you want to invest

- Contact people at the real estate investment group Web sites

- Check what's available on Craig's List

- Be creative in your search

Concluding Remarks

To me, the hardest part of real estate investing is finding the right deal. It's very important to "buy right" so that you will profit.

There are many methods for finding worthwhile investments in real estate. Finding a property is like fishing – you put many lines into the water in hopes of pulling in the big one. Thus you might employ several methods at one time, such as contacting agents, running ads, contacting owners directly, and contacting professionals affiliated with real estate in some way.

Your efforts create a momentum that will generate leads. Persistence is paramount.

9

WHAT MAKES A GOOD DEAL?

Hopefully your search efforts have paid off with many opportunities for you to consider.

Now comes the hard part – separating the wheat from the chaff. Your knowledge of both the marketplace and of real estate operations is critical.

I view real estate investing as a numbers game; I use what I call the numerator/denominator theory of investing, a formula I've used for over twenty years. The numerator is the positive benefits you earn from the investment. The denominator is the money you initially put into the investment as the down payment, closing costs, or for rehab costs.

The numerator – the positive benefits – has four components: 1) appreciation (app); 2) positive cash flow (pcf); 3) principal reduction when you make your mortgage payment (prin); and 4) reduced income tax (tax) due to an operating loss as defined by the federal government on your tax return.

The denominator also has components: 1) the amount of money it takes to purchase the property (including your down payment); 2) lending fees, title insurance, and appraisal, and 3) any capital improvements or other expenses you plan to put into the property after acquiring it.

A few examples will clarify this:

EXAMPLE 1

Let's assume you buy a twelve-unit building with one-bedroom apartments for $480,000. The down payment is 20% or $96,000. When you factor in appraisal, loan costs, attorney's fees, and initial working capital that you deposit into the building's checking account, your total take comes to $100,000. The property is in excellent condition and doesn't need any capital improvements. You now have your denominator: $100,000.

To get the numerator, you need to add four numbers. After projecting annualized revenues and expenses, you determine that all income after vacancy and lost rents due to nonpayment is $85,000 per year. This is the amount of money you deposit into the building checking account.

All expenses (including mortgage payments) are $80,000 per year. You have what I call a positive cash flow of $5000 per year ($85,000 – $80,000).

Let's now say your mortgage payment is $36,000 per year for principal and interest. Of this, $30,000 is interest and $6000 is principal or debt reduction. The $6000 represents the second component of the numerator.

Let's now assume that the building appreciates in value by 2%. This equals $9600, assuming that your purchase was fair market value ($480,000 X .02 = $9600).

Lastly, when you project the state and federal income tax liabilities, it appears that you will have a $4000 tax loss on the property because of a $15,000 deduction the government[1] allows for

---

[1] The tax loss is calculated as follows: the I.R.S. allows you to depreciate the bricks and mortar of the residential property in an equal annual amount over twenty-seven and a half years. Let's say that portion of the investment is valued at $412,500 ($412,500 divided by 27.5 years is $15,000 per year). On your tax return, you would list the gross income of the building at $85,000. You then deduct all the expenses, including interest equaling $74,000. The principal

an expense for depreciation (more about depreciation later). Let's assume you are at the 30% marginal tax bracket (both for federal and for the state in which the property is located). 30% of the $4000 tax loss is $1200.

Thus, we have an investment opportunity that looks like this: Numerator 1 ($5000 positive cash flow) plus 2 ($6000 principal reduction) plus 3 ($9600 appreciation) plus 4 ($1200 tax savings). Denominator: $100,000 down payment, closing costs, and initial working capital.

Now we do the arithmetic:

$5000 (pcf)

+ $6000 (prin)

+ $9600 (app)

+ $1200 (tax)
_____
= $21,800

$100,000 = $100,000

The projected first year return on investment is 21.8%.

EXAMPLE 2

Let's say you purchase a run-down, ten-unit building for $300,000. At $425 per month, the rents for the one-bedroom units are low. Because you know the rental market in the area, you are aware that with some improvements the units should rent for $550 per month.

_____

payment that is part of your mortgage payment is not a deductible expense. This leaves you with $11,000 on the profit side of the ledger. You can then deduct $15,000 for one year of depreciation – you bought the property on January 1st. $11,000 profit less $15,000 depreciation gives you a $4000 loss for the year.

You make a down payment of $75,000, including all closing costs and working capital. You finance $225,000 at 7% over a thirty-year amortization period ($1496.95 per month rounded up to $1500.00 per month).

If you assume that you will keep the building "as is" and the rents and expenses will stay constant, a return on investment in Year One would be as follows:

The denominator – your investment – is $75,000. The numerator is:

- Positive cash flow of $3000 ($50,000 adjusted annual gross income, factoring in income from a coin-operated washer and dryer, 5% vacancy, and lost rents due to nonpayment less $47,000 for expenses, plus mortgage payments)

- $2200 principal reduction

- $6000 appreciation, using a 2% appreciation factor

- $1230 tax loss, assuming you are at the 30% marginal tax rate based on your income

Here's the arithmetic for the math whizzes:

- Numerator: $3000 (pcf) + $2200 (prin) + $6000 (app) + $1230 (tax) = $12,430

- Denominator: $75,000

- Return on investment: $12,430 divided by $75,000 is 16.4%.

Recognizing, however, that you have an upgrade possibility, let's look at what happens in Year Two, if you instead choose to rehab all the units in Year One.

Let's assume that it costs $5000 per unit to do a moderate upgrade (landscaping the outside of the building, new lighting and carpet in hallways, new carpet in each unit, new tile in kitchens and bathrooms, updated lighting fixtures, new stoves, refrigerators, counters and sinks in kitchens, new vanities and medicine cabinets in baths, repainting of each unit). Based on the existing leases, you don't renew leases when they expire. You upgrade the units and rent them out at a higher rent when they are finished. You borrow $50,000 at 7% for one year to do the rehab. The additional interest cost is $3500.

The first year income on the building drops to $45,000 because of the downtime it takes to upgrade a unit when the tenant vacates it. Once the rehab is completed, the units rent for $550 per month.

Given this information, let's refigure the performance of the property in Year One and Year Two.

Year One performance would be as follows:

Numerator:

- $45,000 income received, less $47,000 expenses, including first mortgage interest. On top of this is $3500 interest on second mortgage. Thus, the operating loss is $5500.

- $2200 principal reduction

- $6000 appreciation

- $5100 tax savings based on a 30% marginal tax bracket. The tax savings increased because the building had $3500 additional interest and the depreciation expense increased by $5000 ($50,000 of capital improvement divided by ten years equals $5000 depreciation expense per year).

Denominator:

- $75,000 (I didn't add $50,000 for the upgrade because

143

this was borrowed money, rather than money the investor took out of his/her pocket).

Thus, the first year return on investment is as follows:

- Numerator: $5500 (ncf)[2] + $2200 (prin) + $6000 (app) + $5100 (tax) = $7800

- $7800 divided by the $75,000 denominator equals 10.4%.

Now let's look at the second year. Let's assume that with the improvements, you are able to refinance the building after Year One, for $275,000 at 7% interest with a thirty-year loan. This covers paying off the original loan (now $222,800), the $50,000 upgrade cost, and $2200 in refinancing costs. The mortgage payments in the first year of this loan add up to $21,955. Of this, about $19,055 is interest and $2900 is principal. The denominator remains at $75,000, since the $50,000 to pay for the improvements was borrowed. If you used your own funds to cover the $50,000 in upgrade expenses, in my analysis I would add it to the $75,000 in the denominator.

The numerator: because the rents have increased by $125 per unit per month, the new adjusted annual income is $64,000. This amount less $30,450 (I increased operating expenses by 5%, or $1450, in Year Two) less the new mortgage payments of $21,955 leaves a positive cash flow of $11,595.

The principal reduction in Year One of the new loan is approximately $2900. There are no tax savings. In fact, you have a taxable gain of $222, even after adding in the depreciation.

The tax on this is $67 at the 30% marginal tax rate. (The tax gain is $11,595 cash flow plus $2900 principal reduction less $14,273 for depreciation, equaling $222.)

---

[2]ncf stands for negative cash flow. This means you paid out more than the rents you collected. The $5500 has to come from somewhere – most likely your pocket.

In light of the fact that you've increased the income substantially, relative to the expenses, the building will have increased in value in the eyes of other investors. You have increased the net operating income in Year Two to $33,550. (Net operating income equals all the revenues actually collected for the year, less the expenses for that year. It excludes mortgage payments.)

Because you've updated the building, it has increased in value. The new value set by an appraiser is $372,778. The property would be valued by a formula: net operating income ($33,550) divided by the cap rate (9%). (More on this later.)

Thus, in Year Two you see the fruits of your rehab efforts, and the building has increased in value by $66,778 over what it would have been if you had left it "as is."

To summarize the return on investment in Year Two, the numerator and denominator would be as follows:

- Numerator: $11,595 (pcf) + $2900 (prin) + $66,778 (app) − $67 (tax) = $81,206

- Denominator: $75,000

- The return on investment in Year Two equals 108.3%.

Was it worth the effort to rehab the property? Let's look at this from two other perspectives.

Perspective 1

Let's say you used your own $50,000, which had been sitting in your money market account, to finance the improvements. Your monthly income on the building would increase by $125 per unit. $125 per unit times ten units is $1250 per month additional income. This is reduced by 5% for vacancy factor and credit loss to $1187.50. When you multiply $1187.50 by twelve months, your annual extra income because of your $50,000 of improvements is

$14,250. Your annual return on your $50,000 investment is 28.5%. With the increased rents, it would take about three and a half years to get your $50,000 back.

Perspective 2

In this case, you borrow $50,000 for the upgrade. In the example, you borrowed the $50,000 against your house at 7%, and eventually borrowed the money on a long-term basis when you refinanced the property after one year at 7% interest with a thirty-year amortization. The additional cost to add the $50,000 to your original loan is $322.66 ($50,000 at 7% over a thirty-year payment period). Since your monthly income has increased by $1187.50, you are earning an extra $896.86 per month in income after factoring in the additional mortgage payment. It clearly was worthwhile to upgrade the building.

Now let's look at some more examples.

EXAMPLE 3

You purchase a single-family house for $200,000 at fair market value. You make a down payment of $20,000 and finance the property with a low-interest loan. At closing, you only have to bring $20,000. You get a $180,000 loan at 7%, payable over thirty years. The monthly payment is $1197.56 ($14,370.72 for the first year). After one year, approximately $1800 of this is used to pay off principal, and the balance of $12,570.72 is interest. You rent the property for $1600 per month. The expenses, besides interest, are $4500 for the first year. The house goes up in value by 5%, or $10,000.

To sum up the first year of this investment:

- Numerator: Positive cash flow is $19,200 ($1600 times twelve; you have 100% occupancy) less $4500 expenses and $14,370 mortgage payments.

- This comes to a whopping net income of $330. Principal reduction is $1800. Tax savings at 30% tax bracket is $1215. Appreciation is 5% of $200,000, or $10,000. Denominator: $20,000

- $330 (pcf) + $1800 (prin) + $1215 (tax) + $10,000 (app) divided by $20,000 = 66.7%.

Most of this is from appreciation.

EXAMPLE 4

Instead of purchasing a property, you lease a single-family home for a period of three years with the right to sublease the house. The owner gives you an option to purchase the house for $150,000 anytime during the three-year period. You make a security deposit of $1000, and you pay $2000 for the option to purchase the property for $150,000. The monthly rent is $950 the first year, $1000 the second year and $1050 the third year. You are able to sublease it out over the three-year period for $100 more per month. The location where the house is gets "hot," and you are able to sell the property at the end of the three-year period for $172,000 – a profit of $22,000 over your option price. You get your $1000 security deposit back after three years.

Let's consider this from a three-year perspective:
The numerator is as follows:

- Positive cash flow $3600

- Principal reduction $0 (you didn't have a loan on the property.)

- Tax savings are zero, since you don't own the property. The $3600 is, however, taxable. Using a 30% marginal tax rate, over three years you'd pay a tax of $1080.

- Increase in value is $22,000 over the option price less the $2000 for the option. Assume for the sake of simplicity that there were no transactional costs to sell the house. Thus your profit is $20,000.

The denominator is $2000 for the option. I'd view the $1000 security deposit as a security deposit rather than an investment. Thus, after three years, the overall performance would be as follows:

- Numerator: $3600 (pcf) + $0 (prin) − $1080 (tax) + $22,000 (app) = $22,520

- Denominator: $2000

- $24,520 divided by $2000 = 1226% rate of return over three years, or well above 100% per year compounded increase.

Virtually the entire benefit on this investment is the increase in the value of the property. The high rate of return is helped by the low option price. Theoretically, if you were able to get the option for $0 (or for $1), you could claim an infinite return.

Now let's look at some shortcomings to my approach. If you are a "nothing down" buyer fortunate enough to have a positive cash flow with an increase in property value, or you are flipping a property under contract, this analysis won't work. Since you don't have a down payment, the denominator will be zero. You will have an "infinite" return on investment.

Don't get too excited yet though. In this case, you need to look at the value of your time, the risk you are assuming (such as having a serious negative cash flow without having the money to support that negative cash flow), and how much you are gaining by flipping after taxes. If you spend one hundred hours doing a deal where you make $5000 after taxes, you're making $50 per hour.

Another shortcoming of my approach is that it doesn't take into account the time value of money. My accounting and business school professors taught that this concept was critical in any financial analysis. It relates to the timing of when you spend money and when you receive money.

When conducting a net present value analysis, you are trying to determine if the stream of payments (like monthly rents or the eventual sale) you receive at a certain rate of return you choose – say, 10% – exceeds the current value of your down payment. Most financial calculators can figure this out for you. I prefer my approach, because it is simple and has worked for me to date.

Virtually all the investors I know use my approach in some way. When they are "numbering out" a potential investment, they are usually estimating what the current or potential income is, the timing and expense of any rehab, the operating expenses based on their method of running a building, the financing, and whether the building will make money.

A few successful investors I know don't even do any analysis. In a lot of cases, they know the building and its owner, they learn the asking price, and they make an offer on the spot. They know what the property is worth. Since I'm numbers-oriented, I love to do financial analyses of potential investments; I wouldn't feel comfortable not doing one. This has never, however, stopped me from making a quick offer on a building. I figure I can do an analysis after the contract is signed. I always have language in a contract to allow me to get out of a deal if necessary.

With this as background, let's again look at the question, "Is this a good deal?"

Here are my definitions of seven ways to make a good deal:

1) Investing in a property in a desirable location where, based on your financial analysis, you get an acceptable return on your investment – e.g., 15%.

2) Purchasing a property under market value, where you can sell it at an immediate profit.

3) Leasing a property with an option to buy or re-lease, where you can make a profit when you option or lease the property.

4) Developing a property for profit.

5) Purchasing a building where the net operating income can be substantially increased by either better management and/or physical upgrades.

6) Putting a property under contract, and then making a profit by assigning the contract to another purchaser (similar to #2 above).

7) Purchasing a property at fair market value, where you don't expect such a high rate of return in the beginning, but the location is very desirable and you expect to get substantial appreciation in the future, as well as improved cash flow.

Let's take a closer look at these.

Property with Acceptable Return

The return on investment that I personally look for is 15%. In the numerator/denominator analysis I described above, the return on investment has to be at least 15%, and the building must be in a desirable location. When I calculate the 15%, I exclude appreciation and tax savings from the analysis. My thinking here is that I'm buying the property for cash flow or future cash flow, and any appreciation is gravy. I don't plan to sell the property unless a better opportunity arises. As to the tax advantages, I think it's great to have a loss, but I'd rather have the building operate well and pay income taxes. I know I will always be able to take depreciation expense to help lower my taxes.

I use 15% as my standard. My thinking is that I can get about 5% by investing in very safe thirty-year U.S. Treasury Bonds and get a 10% average return by investing in the Standard and Poor 500 index fund. The only work I have to do with an index fund is look at the newspaper periodically. I therefore require an additional 5% for all the work, risk, and aggravation that go into purchasing and managing real estate.

Flipping

It has not been my modus operandi to buy a property and immediately resell it. According to the appraisals, which I believe to be low, my last two acquisitions were $20,000 and $75,000 under the appraised value. I figure it's hard enough to find a worthwhile investment, and so I'd rather keep what I buy.

Flipping has worked well for many investors, though. To do this, you need to know the value of what you are buying and then purchase it for enough under market that you make a justifiable profit when you resell.

As noted previously, I further recommend that you consider the value of your time. If you flip a property and make a $10,000 profit after paying taxes, and it took you 125 hours to find the property, buy it, and then sell it, you are making $80 per hour – an okay return (unless you do this 2080 hours per year). If, on the other hand, you can make $75,000 for 100 hours of work, that's $750 an hour. If you can make $750 an hour in a 2080 hour year, you will earn $1.5 million. It won't take long to attain financial independence at that rate.

151

Lease with an Option to Buy

Here's a simple example. You sign a two-year contract for a single-family house at a monthly rent of $1500. When you sign the lease, you also obtain an option to purchase the house for $250,000 within the twenty-four month period. You pay the owner $5000 to have this option. If, after two years, you don't exercise the option, the owner keeps the $5000, and your lease is over.

On the other hand, if the real estate market heats up and you sell the house without an agent for $280,000 during the option period, you have just made a profit of $30,000 less sale expenses. Leasing with an option to buy is a low-cost, low-risk way to gain control of a property with a substantial future profit.

I've never done a lease with an option. My Detroit relatives have done several and are very pleased with the results. They've often received a positive cash flow and a nice payoff when it comes time to exercise the option.

Rehabilitating Property

The tried-and-true approach in real estate is to find a well-located, run-down property in need of inexpensive upgrades that you can improve cheaply, so that it yields higher rents and higher value. I've done this several times, and many of my investor friends have also used this approach to build their income and net worth. There are several keys to making this work:

- You have to find an acceptable property in need of some repair.

- You need to determine what improvements will work for the location, how much they cost, and how soon you can get them done.

- You need to decide what the rents should be and the impact on the value of the building once you do the rehab.

- You must have access to the resources necessary to pay for the upgrade as well as to perform the work.

- When you purchase the property, you need to build room into the deal for yourself, so that you will make a profit.

This is a conservative approach that works. Improving a property can be done in three ways:

1) You can increase income

2) You can reduce expenses

3) You can do cosmetic improvements that make the property more desirable.

Income can be increased by improving occupancy, by simply raising rents if they were too low, by adding new revenue sources that did not previously exist (e.g., laundry or vending machines), or by making improvements in the building which allow you to raise rents. Expenses can be reduced by renegotiating existing contracts such as scavenger services, by making cost-effective energy improvements such as weather stripping, insulation, converting to tenant-paid heat and air conditioning, preventive maintenance, better purchasing practices, and lowered maintenance costs.

Other improvements that will increase the value of a property include landscaping, painting the building, fixing broken windows, or upgrading the interior by redecorating. Each improvement increases your net operating income. This translates into an increase in the value of the investment and puts more money in your pocket.

To determine if purchasing and rehabbing a property is a good deal, you need to do the previously described financial analysis on the building.

Development/Conversion

Development refers to building something from the ground up. It could involve buying a parcel of land and building a housing development or office building on the land. Or it might involve buying an older house in a desirable area, tearing it down, and building a bigger, more valuable house on the land.

Conversion involves changing the use of a property. For example, you might purchase a large single-family house in an area with commercial potential and physically change it into a building with several small offices. Or you may have a twelve-unit apartment building and substantially upgrade each unit and the common areas, and then convert it into a twelve-unit condominium building. In these cases, the building becomes more valuable in its converted state.

To use a real estate term, you are converting the building to its "highest and best use." To be a developer/converter, you need to be able to visualize the potential of a property.

In the Chicago area's northern suburbs known as the North Shore, many developers look for small houses on large lots in very desirable areas. They buy the houses, tear them down, and then build larger homes consistent with the neighborhood. When these developers add up all their expenses, the proceeds from the final sale and the time involved, they make a very hefty profit.

When you see a dilapidated factory in an area that is just beginning to develop, a greater vision is required for you to convert it into loft condominiums.

I'm not the kind of investor who has this kind of vision, and I'm not willing to take the big risks necessary for this kind of development. The investors I know who are major developers are very careful with their numbers. They typically know exactly what they will build, how much it will cost, how to finance the project, what it will sell for, and how long before the project sells out. A better way to view this type of investment is not asking, "Is this a good deal?" but rather "Will this project work?" While the acquisition cost may be small, the development cost may be large.

Investors need to be aware of their political and community environment, and they need to know that the supply/demand factors are on their side. Many of my developer friends have been stymied by community groups who don't want change in their neighborhoods. They have had to attend numerous community meetings and do everything they can to appease community groups and politicians.

Lastly, several developers I know have become very wealthy.

Speculation

While you cannot subject speculation to the numerator/denominator analysis, it is so common today that I am including it in the section on good investment deals.

What is speculation? When you visit downtown Chicago these days, particularly the near south, near west, and near north sides, your view is obstructed by building cranes and the sight of high-rise residences being built. At it's core, Chicago is a mecca of development.

When a new project is announced, the residential units go on sale. The developer prices units so they will sell and not sit empty when construction is complete. The speculator, knowing the desirability of the location, looks at the layout of the various units, considers the view, and picks what he/she thinks will be the most desirable units for future buyers. The speculator signs a contract, plops down some earnest money, and waits for the project to be built. The speculator is never planning to move in, but rather is gambling that the units will go up in value by the time the project is done, typically two years.

Before the units are finished, the speculator assigns the contract to a buyer and pockets the difference between the price he/she paid and the selling price. In the event the speculator can't sell a unit, he or she either rents it out or walks away from the earnest money and loses the gamble. The developer has recourse in the event the speculator walks away, and may sue for damages or to perform as the contract dictates.

My developer friends estimate that a large percentage of the marketplace in Chicago is made up of speculators. Speculators are also active in new housing developments and typically will put a preconstruction unit under contract in the hope of selling it at a profit before completion.

To speculate successfully, you obviously need to have the earnest money available, the skill to select the most desirable product, and a knowledge of the relative value of the units you purchase. In the past five to ten years, this has been a profitable way for investors to make money.

Buy at Market – Bet the Future

Sometimes you have to look at more than just the numbers on an investment. If your intuition tells you an area is going to get "hot," but not for two to five years, you may want to accumulate buildings in the area, manage them, and wait for the area to command higher rents and values. When I bought the four-unit building in the west De Paul area in 1983, I figured I'd have to put up with management headaches for some period of time, but eventually the neighborhood would become the "in" place to live.

I was right sooner than I had expected. The rents and property values (along with the property taxes) leapt up dramatically. When I tell other investors what I paid for the property, they think I'm a genius to have bought it for so little. And I honestly felt at the time that I overpaid.

The numerator/denominator analysis may not always work if an area hasn't "turned" yet and you believe it will. When I bought the four-unit for essentially $79,000, I don't believe anyone would have imagined it would appraise for $237,000 after just a few years. I've had similar dramatic upswings in value in several buildings, including the original six-unit, the thirty-nine-unit, the sixty-seven and seventy-seven-units, some condominiums I bought near downtown Milwaukee, and even the three-unit building that was rented to low income tenants.

In the case of these acquisitions, I conducted my conservative analysis, but the dramatic appreciation became a bonus. The point here is that if you really believe in a location and plan to hold for the long-term, you may be willing to sacrifice your return on investment percentages for the first few years before you see the area take off in value.

Let's summarize the good deals discussed above:

- A purchase that satisfies your long-term return on investment

- An under-market purchase where you can make an immediate profit by reselling

- A project where, through cost-effective management and/or rehab, you can substantially increase the cash flow and value of a property

- Low-risk methods, such as a lease with an option to buy, where you can make a lot of money with a small investment

- Development/conversion projects

- Buying at market value in an area on the upswing

- Buying on speculation and flipping the contract

You need certain skills and abilities to identify good deals:

- The ability to know the value of a property as it is, what the value would be after improvement, and what it can be sold for if you want a quick profit

- If you are a rehabber, knowledge of what improvements are appropriate for the location. Furthermore, you need the resources to get improvements done correctly and on time.

- Knowledge of market rents for the space available, especially after making improvements

- The ability to project operational expenses

- The ability to project the cost and time required to make various improvements

- The ability to judge which housing units will be most desirable if you speculate

- The ability to determine what locations will be "hot" in the future

- Knowledge of the financial marketplace from which you will borrow money

Since these are critical skills and abilities, the next chapters will focus on determining current market value and the specifics of financial analysis.

10

WHAT'S A PROPERTY WORTH?

One of the key skills to develop as a real estate investor is accurately determining the value of a property. It's basically a
matter of simple arithmetic. If you're shopping the market, you can
quickly gauge what something is worth.

Having paid for numerous property appraisals and having built
relationships with several appraisers, as well as tax assessors, I can
give you an idea of the methods an appraiser will use. There are
three basic approaches to appraisals: 1) the market valuation approach; 2) the cost approach; and 3) the income, or cap rate, approach.

The Market Approach

The market approach is especially useful when valuing single-
family houses, condominiums, cooperatives, town houses, and small
apartment buildings. You are essentially comparing the property
you are looking at with other similar properties, and figuring its
value relative to those other properties.

For example, let's say you are interested in purchasing a three-
bedroom, two-bath, all-brick 2100 square foot ranch house in excellent condition in location A. The house is on a 6250 square foot
lot. It has nice landscaping and a two-car attached garage. The

asking price is $225,000. As a buyer, you then compare it to what you've seen in the general area. If there is a three-bedroom, two and a half-bath (a half-bath being a powder room – it has a toilet and sink but no tub/shower) that is 2200 square feet, with an attached garage, on a 6250 square foot lot listing for $250,000, you have to ask yourself why it is listing for $25,000 more. You then compare features of the houses. Some differences are obvious. In this case, the second house has a half a bathroom more, and one hundred more square feet. In addition, it has a finished basement, compared to the unfinished basement at the first house.

If you've ever bought a house or condominium, you've most likely comparison shopped to figure out the value of the house relative to the market at the time. When an appraiser determines a valuation on a house or condominium, he or she uses a uniform appraisal form.

The heart of the appraisal involves a comparison between the property being appraised and the three most similar houses or properties the appraiser can find. The appraiser will consider the house's condition, square footage, number of rooms, bedrooms, bathrooms, and any special features of the house. When the comparable house has something different, like a fourth bedroom, a fireplace, or an upgraded, more modern kitchen, the appraiser will make some sort of downward adjustment to the value of the house being appraised. If your house has something extra that the comparable house doesn't have, the appraiser deducts this from the value of the comparable house.

The appraiser then looks at what the comparison house sold for, deducts dollars for any extras it had over your house, adds its shortcomings versus what your house offers, and comes out with a comparable value if that were your house. This is done for three nearby properties that have hopefully sold within the past six months which had conventional financing.

The appraiser then makes an estimate as to the market value of your property. He or she might take an average of the three, or use the lowest value. A very simple analysis for an appraiser follows:

Subject Property	Comparable #1	Comparable #2	Comparable #3
111 Central Anywhere, IL	121 Nearby Anywhere, IL	131 Close Anywhere, IL	141 Neighbor Anywhere, IL
Sales Price	$215,000	$235,000	$250,000
Gross Living Area 2100	2000 (+$5000)	2200 (-$5000)	2300 (-$10,000)
# of Bathrooms 2	2	2	2.5 (-$5000)
Fireplaces 0	0	0	1 (-$5000)
Value of Subject Property	$220,000	$230,000	$230,000
Indicated Value of Subject Property $226,666 (average of the three comparables)			

For simplicity's sake, everything else about these properties is assumed to be the same. In the case of comparable #1, you added $5000 to the sale price because it was somewhat smaller than your property. Comparable #2 had its sale price of $235,000 adjusted downward because it was somewhat larger than your property. Comparable #3 was larger, had a half bath more, and had a fireplace. It was adjusted downward by $20,000 to equalize it with your property. The comparable sales all closed within the past six months.

Thus, if your investment strategy is to have a portfolio of single-family houses or small residential properties, you need to keep abreast of your marketplace.

The listing price is different from the selling price. A real estate agent can give you a good idea as to how the listing prices and final selling prices vary. You can also pay for services that provide details on "sold" properties in your area of interest. "Sold" properties are a matter of public record if you want to investigate the records for a particular house.

Lastly, if your plan is to rent the property, you will need to be aware of the rent level in the neighborhood. The most effective way to learn this is to shop the market just as a renter would. It's a lot of work, but after you do it once, you have a general feel for the rent levels.

I'm the only landlord I know who has done this. Most of my fellow landlords talk to other landlords and set their rents accordingly. Or they boost their rent by a percentage (for example, 3% or 5%) or a set amount per unit such as $20 per month. My observation is that over a period of time, most landlords end up setting their rents too low. Their view is that the building is performing well, and they are happy with the income they receive. They do not want vacancies.

A second method to determine proper rent levels is to pay someone who knows the market. This could be a real estate agent, a rental agency, or an appraiser. I favor rental agencies, because they are very aware of market trends. I prefer to pay them a fee rather than get a free estimate. The payment ends my obligation to them.

The Cost Approach

The cost approach for appraisals looks at what totally replacing a property would cost in current dollars, and then deducts some amount for what is known as *depreciation*. To this number, the appraiser adds a figure for site improvements, such as landscaping or a driveway, and finally adds a figure for the value of the land.

WHAT'S A PROPERTY WORTH?

An example will make this clear. In the prior example where the property was appraised for $226,666, the livable square footage was 2100. If it cost $120 per square foot to replace this, then the replacement cost would be 2100 times $120, or $252,000. The appraiser would then deduct certain amounts for the physical wear and tear the property has endured since it was built, any functional obsolescence, and external wear and tear. Depreciation is the term that describes the gradual wear and tear that a property receives over a period of years. Furnaces wear out, roofs eventually need to be replaced, and so forth.

Functional obsolescence refers to parts of the property that had a function at the time the property was built, but do not now. An example of this would be small bedrooms without closet space, or anything that doesn't reflect current living standards or lifestyles.

Returning to our example, the appraiser determines that the forty-year-old house has had physical depreciation of 18%. 18% of $252,000 is $45,360. The appraiser deducts this amount. This leaves the property using the cost approach at $206,640. To this number the appraiser adds $10,000 for the landscaping and external improvements such as the concrete driveway. The appraiser also adds $50,000 for the value of the land. This adds up to $266,640. This would be considered the value of the property, using the cost approach.

When you compare the cost approach to the market comparison approach, the cost approach is substantially higher. This points to one of the truths about real estate: properties often have a market value of less (sometimes much less) than the replacement cost, or the replacement cost less any adjustments for depreciation. As an investor in apartment buildings, I don't use the cost approach in estimating the value of a building.

A few examples from my experience might be of interest:

• When I had the fire at the three-unit in Aurora, the insurance company estimated that the replacement cost would be $229,000. I had it on the market at $85,000, and no one snapped it up.

• A one hundred twenty-four-unit building acquired in Mesa, Arizona was purchased in a Resolution Trust Authority auction for $2,225,000. (My wife and I are part owners of the building.) Research on the history of the building showed that the prior owner, the builder, originally had a $4,500,000 mortgage on the property. We figure that was what it cost the developer to build the property.

To balance this, it's also possible for the market value to far exceed the cost value. When I visit friends in California, I am startled by the high market valuations versus my estimate of what properties would cost to replace.

I basically ignore cost approach appraisal figures and either use the market comparison approach or, much more likely given the size of the property, the income approach.

The Income Approach

When using the income approach to valuing a property, you determine the net operating income and divide by the *capitalization rate* to estimate the property's value. Stated differently, you first determine the net operating income of a building and multiply it by a certain number to determine the value. Let us call this number the *net income multiplier.*

Let's say you are appraising an eighteen-unit apartment building in a desirable location. The rents are $600 per unit, and the laundry facilities generate $8 per unit per month in income. Overall, each unit generates $608 per month or $7296 annually. Since the building has eighteen units, the maximum income (or Gross Potential Income – GPI) expected in a year is $131,328 ($7296 x 18). From this amount the appraiser would deduct some percentage for vacancies and credit loss (credit loss refers to tenants who don't pay their rent and have to be evicted). The percent the appraiser uses depends on market-specific conditions. If the appraiser uses 2%, then market conditions are tight and it's a landlord's market. If it's a slow market, the appraiser might use 10% – a renter's market. In our example, let's use 5%. We then deduct 5%, or $6566, and end up with actual annual income (Effective Gross Income – EGI) of $124,762.

The appraiser would next estimate the annual operating expense. Ideally, the appraiser will look at a rent roll as well as accurate information about all the expenditures of the property over the past few years. Annual tax returns are helpful data sources here. Otherwise, the appraiser will estimate these figures based on other sources of data, such as appraisals done recently for comparable buildings. The appraiser also factors in replacement reserves for items like carpeting, dishwashers, stoves, and refrigerators. Interest expense and principal reduction are not considered in the appraiser's estimate of annual expense.

In our example, the appraiser has determined that annual forecasted operating expenses are $56,143 (45% of income). When we subtract the anticipated expenses ($56,143) from the EGI, the difference is $68,619. The difference between the GPI adjusted for vacancy and credit loss ($124,762) less the operating expenses ($56,143) is the net operating income ($68,619). The term net operating income is often referred to as "net" or "NOI."

The next step in the appraisal is to plug in the capitalization rate. Let's make the capitalization rate 9%. The formula to determine the property's value is:

$$\frac{\text{Net Operating Income}}{\text{Capitalization Rate}} = \text{Value of Property}$$

$$\frac{\$68,619}{.09} = \$762,433$$

If you like to multiply numbers, then you might multiply the Net Operating Income by the Capitalization Rate multiplier. In this case, the multiplier would be 1.00 divided by .09, which equals 11.111. To simplify this, you'd multiply the NOI by 11.

The question arises as to where a capitalization rate of 9% comes from. The capitalization is the rate of return an investor would expect if he or she paid all cash for a property.

In the example above, the investor would pay $762,433 in cash for the property and expect a cash return of 9%, or $68,619, annually.

If the investor paid $100,000 in cash for a property and expected a return of $8000, the investor would be expecting a return of 8%. The cap rate would be 8%.

The cap rate for income-generating properties in very desirable locations would be lower than for less desirable locations. Investors are willing to accept a lower rate of return in a desirable area. I've seen cap rates as low as 3% for condo-conversion properties in Chicago's most desirable locations and higher than 20% for its least desirable areas.

Over the past ten years, I've seen cap rates decline as real estate has become a more desirable investment vehicle.

Cap rates are not set in granite. Appraisers determine the cap rates based on recent sales of similar properties in a given location. If the area gets "hot," investors are willing to pay a higher price, and the cap rate goes down. If, on the other hand, the local economy dictates, the supply/demand pendulum will favor buyers, and the cap rate will tend to rise. Lower interest rates tend to lower the cap rate.

If you want to find out a cap rate for a specific area, your real estate agent should be able to obtain the information. If not, call in an appraiser. Each appraiser determines what he or she believes to be the correct cap rate. This can result in appraisers establishing different values for the same property. Appraiser A might use a 9% cap rate, while Appraiser B uses 9.5%.

A recent example shows this can happen. We were refinancing our sixty-four-unit in Phoenix. The lender required an appraisal. The appraiser estimated the value at $2.1 million. This value struck us as far too low based on recent nearby comparable sales, and we complained to the lender. The lender agreed to allow a second appraisal. Appraisal #2 was $2.6 million, almost 25% higher. In reviewing the appraisal worksheet, the first appraiser used comparables five miles south of our property, in a much less desirable location. He used a higher cap rate, which devalued our building. In my opinion, his appraisal was worthless. Interestingly, we put the property up for sale a year later. Our broker recommended a listing price of $3.3 million, and we sold it for $3.075 million.

Many of the appraisals on my investments have been required by banks for lending purposes. I've often felt that the appraisals were low. When I called the appraisers to discuss their assumptions and their final figures, they weren't in disagreement with me. Appraisals for lenders tend to be conservative, especially if you are refinancing a property. Lenders don't want to take unnecessary risks when lending. They want to know a property has enough equity in it if the lender has to foreclose.

Investment real estate is a numbers game. When investing in a commercial property such as a large apartment building, or a retail or office space, the income approach to valuation is the key.

When I am analyzing a potential investment, I project the expected revenues and expenses to see if the property will give me my minimum 15% first year return. I don't care what price the building is so long as I like the location and will get my required return, but I don't want to overpay. After checking to see if a property meets my required return, I will plug in a cap rate based on my own experience, and see how I would figure the value. In addition,

I'll usually figure out the asking price per unit (e.g., a seventy-unit building of one-bedroom apartments with a $2,800,000 asking price is priced at $40,000 per unit), and compare that with what I value my other properties at or what I know of recent transactions in the marketplace.

Most of my fellow investors aren't as analytical as I am. Much of the time, when they learn that a specific building is on the market, especially a larger one, they are familiar with the building already and often know who the owner is. They have an immediate feel for whether this is a good opportunity or not. The investors I know typically use their own methods of valuation.

Mr. W.D. uses price per unit. Other investors use some multiple of gross income, like six or seven times gross. Still others base it on something along the lines of ten times net. I'm comfortable using my numerator/denominator approach, then figuring the value based on a multiple of net operating income. For my analysis to work out, the overall monthly rent is in the range of 1 to 1.5% of the purchase price.

Unfortunately, when an opportunity comes on the market, if it is underpriced or a profitable rehab opportunity, it won't sit on the market very long. As a buyer, you need to be decisive and make your offer quickly, often upon your initial inspection. You can usually void the contract if you put in contract contingencies to protect yourself. When I sold the six-unit in the Lake View area of Chicago, the demand for commercial rental real estate was so strong that fifty people looked at the building in the first week, and I got six offers. I negotiated the offers upwards until I got the highest all-cash price, with no contract contingencies. I don't believe I underpriced that building; the buyer/seller pendulum favored the seller at the time.

For me, one of the keys in the acquisitions process is accurately projecting the income and expenses. The next chapter will cover this.

11

WORKING THE NUMBERS: SHOULD I DO THE DEAL?

Almost always when you ask a real estate agent about a property listed for sale, the agent will provide a brief summary of the property. Usually you'll see a photograph, a short description of the building, and a section called income and expenses. For the income, you'll typically find one overall number, such as the annual rental income. Reported expenses usually include taxes, insurance, gas and electric, water/sewer, and scavenger fees. Most seasoned investors place little confidence in these numbers, because rents are at their highest value with 100% occupancy, and the expenses are incomplete and often understated. I always tell the agent that the seller is showing next year's rents and last year's expenses. Let's look at how to avoid inaccurately estimating these figures.

The Income Projection

The income projection is a matter of simple arithmetic. If you have accurate rental information (which you can find in the lease), you can then add all the rents, apply a monthly vacancy and credit loss factor, and finally estimate a monthly and annual income.

Several problems can make this difficult. First, the rents on the lease may not reflect accurate market rents; they may be too low. In this case, you'll want to raise the rents the first chance you get.

169

Secondly, the lease expirations may take place throughout the year. You may pencil in a rent of $550 for a given unit, but will boost it to $580 when the lease expires in seven months.

Or you could even run into the same problem that I had with a recent purchase. The owner had the tenants sign a lease at one rent and then orally agree to take a lower rent for the duration of the lease. Imagine my surprise when I went to collect lease-based rents. All the tenants complained that their rent was lower than the lease figure. I had a lot of fun getting that one resolved. I eventually got the lease-based rents from the seller, but I had to pay some hefty legal bills to get my rightful money.

I had a similar experience at another building. The owner stated that all the leases were month-to-month oral agreements, but he gave some of his favorites long-term written leases at low rents after the contract was signed. While in both cases my contract to purchase had protections against these situations, dealing with them was still aggravating and time-consuming. I had to involve attorneys, and this certainly did not help build constructive relationships with my tenants.

In general, when figuring the income, I rely on the lease figures, factor in the lease expiration date, and adjust the rent from there. Usually I have an idea about fair market rents, and compare those with the stated rent. I often find that the seller's rent schedule is on the low side.

When presenting your contract, you'll want to put in a contingency stating that your offer is subject to the review and approval of the existing leases (more on this in the chapter on negotiations). While these aren't available to you when you make your offer, I'd suggest you set a deadline by which you will obtain them. I won't buy a property if I can't review the leases.

Let's look at a simple example of figuring out the income.

You are interested in a building with twenty-four one-bedroom units with a stated rent of $600 per month. All the leases are May 1 to April 30. You know from your experience that the $600 rental figure is on the low side. From what you've seen, you believe the units could get $650 per month.

Therefore, you have a fair amount of confidence that the $600 per month figure is accurate. You then figure in a vacancy and credit loss factor and deduct this from the annual rent. In the case of this building, assume that you'll close on the property July 1 and will have rents of $600 per unit for the next ten months. You will then raise your rent figure to $650. Here's how the arithmetic works:

24 units x $600 for 10 months = $144,000

24 units x $650 for 2 months = $31,200

This totals $175,200.

From this number, you deduct the vacancy and credit loss factor (we use 5%).

$175,200 x .95 = $166,440

Thus, your projected income on the rentals is $166,440.

In terms of applying a vacancy and credit loss factor, there is no one, solid, infallible number to use. Instead, you need to exercise judgment. In Milwaukee, I typically use 2%. After September 11, 2001, my vacancy rate went to 14% by January or February. In Aurora, it ran about 10%. On the north side of Chicago, I ran close to 0%. In sunny Phoenix, our typical vacancy rate is in the 15-20% range, but this has gone as high as 40%. A helpful appraiser can give you an idea if you don't know what to use for a vacancy factor. You might also check with the local Chamber of Commerce or the local Planning Commission.

This, then, gives you the monthly rental income. To this number you need to add other numbers for the various services you might offer tenants. Some of these could include laundry facilities, vending machines, parking, and other types of services available in larger buildings and commercial real estate.

Coming back to our example, let's say that the building has two washing machines and two dryers. These are owned by the building rather than leased. Hopefully, the seller has provided some information about the laundry income. I know from my experience that I usually collect in the range of $8 to $10 per month for an occupied unit ($1 for a wash and .75 for a dry, based on local conditions). Assuming $9 per unit per month with a 5% vacancy factor, we have $9 per unit times twenty-four units times twelve months less 5%, or $2,462 for the year.

Let's say you have a soda vending machine in the laundry room. I net about $1.25 per unit per month. The arithmetic works as follows: $1.25 per month times twenty-four units times twelve months less 5%, or $342 per year. The $342 may seem like a small number, but if you are valuing the property using the income approach with a capitalization rate of 10%, this increases the value of the building by $3,420.

Assuming that there are no other revenue sources, you would estimate revenue sources as follows:

Net rental income	= $166,440
Laundry income	= $2,462
Vending income	= $342
Total expected income	= $169,244

The Expense Projection

When figuring the expense projection, I endeavor to think of all the potential expenses an investment can have. Often I estimate these. When I am really serious, I have to do some research. Because I've owned various sized apartment buildings for a number of years, I can usually estimate pretty quickly when evaluating a building. After I put the building under contract, I refine my numbers.

The first comment I would make here is that the six expense categories I typically see on a listing sheet are an inadequate list. At minimum, you should consider using the categories on the I.R.S. Form 8825 – Rental Real Estate Income and Expenses of a Partnership or a Corporation. In reviewing my tax returns, I usually have eight or ten additional expense categories that my accountant adds to the I.R.S. Form.

Let's look at the key components:

TAXES

Taxes include property taxes, sales taxes, and payroll taxes, such as social security and withholding tax and unemployment taxes. Getting the current property tax is easy; you call the county tax collector and try to get as much information as you can. WARNING: oftentimes investors mistakenly assume the taxes will stay level or increase modestly in future years. In Milwaukee, I usually get a reassessment the next year, using my purchase price as the market value. The assessor there, as well in Aurora, basically knows every building and continuously checks the real estate transfers and recordings for new purchase prices, and even refinanced loan amounts.

Consequently, I project the property taxes on my purchase price. Often, if the seller has owned a building for a long time, the property taxes could be low and will be adjusted by the assessor at the first chance. The other taxes I would include under salaries. It's important to include the 7.65% that comprises the employer's part of social security, and state and federal unemployment. The Workers' Compensation premium falls under insurance costs.

173

INSURANCE COSTS

Beware of simply plugging in the number the seller gives you for the property insurance cost. I might use the seller's figure in calculations, but I always ask my insurance agent for an independent quote for the coverage I want. I've found a couple of problems with using the seller's figure: 1) he or she may be under insured; and 2) he or she may have several buildings that are part of a package deal – these might be properly insured, but the premium will be lower than anything in the marketplace.

Presently, the property insurance market is awful from a buyer's perspective. This year my premiums increased by 30% for the same coverage as last year, and I didn't even submit one claim. Mr. W.D. and my partner in Arizona had some claims on their properties and had their coverage cancelled. They each ended up buying less coverage for a more than 300% increase in their premiums.

The bottom line: to get an accurate number for property insurance, it's best to get quotes from an independent agent. You should also get a copy of the seller's policy and have it reviewed by your agent. If the coverage is adequate and the premium is a good value, the best option might be for you to continue with the current insurance, as long as the existing insurer allows the transfer.

ADVERTISING

This is typically a relatively small expense. I rely on the seller's figure. If it seems low, I add to it based on my experience. If you want to be exact, you can contact the publications you'd advertise in, get their rates, and estimate how much advertising space you need for a year.

INTEREST

This is generally the interest to the loans you have on the building. When you are looking for properties, you should be aware of the rates and terms of lenders for your type of property. For example, a lender might offer the following deal for a non-owner-occupied single-family house: $1,900 closing costs, 10% down, 6.5% fixed interest, with a thirty-year time duration for the loan. Once you know how much you will need to borrow, it is simple to determine the interest expense in each year of an amortizing loan. A lender can provide this or you can to www.bankrate.com/brm/ mortgage-calculator.asp to get it.

AUTO AND TRAVEL

Since most of my properties are within an hour and fifteen minutes of my home, I don't consider this. When I purchased property in Arizona, I figured I'd make two visits per year.

UTILITIES

Utilities include gas, oil, electric, water, sewer, and telecommunications. Many sources of information are available here. I start with the seller's figures. I'm usually also able to get a figure from the gas and electric provider and the government agency that's in charge of water and sewer. I start by calling their toll-free customer service numbers, and then track down the right department. I don't worry about expenses like telephone costs. These are relatively minor. BOMA, the Building Owners and Management Association, usually has a database that provides utility figures for certain types of buildings in a given locale. BOMA can be reached at (202) 408-2662.

Unfortunately, the footprints of the past may not be predictive of the future. A few years ago, the price of natural gas more than tripled, right in the heart of winter. Even with a discount, I was paying close to $1 per therm for natural gas, and my monthly gas bills were coming in at the $15,000 to $20,000 range. The previous winter my costs were in the $.30 per therm range. This sharp increase hurt my profits for that year. I had no choice but to pay whatever the public utility charged. Not one of my landlord friends saw this situation coming either.

When determining utility costs, you may want to consider whether you plan on making any energy saving improvements, such as energy efficient heating and air conditioning, water conservation methods, insulation, and so forth.

Lastly, some locales offer alternative energy providers in addition to the traditional sources. For example, in the Chicago area you can purchase natural gas directly from a pipeline supplier.

This can be an opportunity to save a lot of money. What amazes me is that each supplier has its own special deal. It's up to you to analyze each vendor's program to determine which one best meets your needs.

CLEANING AND MAINTENANCE

Cleaning and maintenance refers to the periodic cleaning of the property as well as cleaning when turnover occurs. Maintenance refers to ongoing building needs such as lawncare, snow removal, monthly elevator servicing, heating and air conditioning servicing, etc.

For apartment buildings, I typically employ a resident manager in charge of cleaning, and so I include this amount in the manager's salary. For larger projects, you can contact various services such as janitorial contractors, elevator maintenance companies, or snow removal contractors, and then plug in their costs.[3]

COMMISSIONS

Commissions refers to the compensation you pay to contractors who provide you with certain services. For example, if you have

---

[3] Some investors I know use $500 to $600 per year per unit. This figure includes repairs.

commercial or apartment space to lease, you might use a real estate broker to lease the space, and you would pay them a commission to lease the space.

In the past, I've usually paid between 50% to 100% of one month's rent to rental agents. For a commercial property, I suggest you contact a commercial leasing agent to get an idea of their charges.

LEGAL AND OTHER PROFESSIONAL FEES

Legal fees relate to what you pay attorneys based on the services they perform. Other professional fees might include fees you pay your accountant, engineer, architect, or other professional who helps you solve various operating problems.

When you are purchasing a residential or commercial structure that is in satisfactory condition and you do not anticipate making significant changes, this cost would be low. I typically figure that I might have one or two evictions per year at a cost of $350 each (for which the evicted tenant is liable).

If you are planning to build from the ground up, or perform a significant rehabilitation, you will need to factor in these costs. Your professional advisor should be able to give you an idea of what the charges would run for a project.

REPAIRS

Repairs are a difficult cost to estimate. Your initial assessment of the building should give you an idea if the property is in good operating condition or whether there is a lot of "deferred maintenance." Deferred maintenance can be very expensive, especially when you look at the cost of tuck-pointing the building's brickwork, fixing leaky pipes that are not easily accessible, or replacing an old, inefficient boiler. Obviously a "clean" building will require fewer repairs than the "deferred maintenance" type.

177

A second factor is how you plan to have the repair work completed. If it is a small apartment building and you have the time and the skills, you will do the repairs. In this case you would put in a low repair expense. If, on the other hand, you are all thumbs like me and have no interest in snaking out a clogged toilet, then you'll factor in a higher expense. If you are going to have a salaried maintenance staff, then your repair expense will be low because you are paying salaries to employees who will do the repairs.

When I'm doing my estimates, I use 3-5% of total revenues for the repair expense. In looking at my annual tax return, this figure seems to work. If the building is run-down and in need of repair, you can either put in the specific repair costs or use a higher percentage.

WAGES AND SALARIES

If you are acquiring a property and plan to have either a salaried or hourly staff or plan to use independent contractors, you would include their projected annual compensation as a cost.

In addition to their salary or hourly rate, you'll need to add in other costs related to employment.

This includes the employer's responsibility for social security tax (7.65%), federal and state unemployment tax, workers' compensation insurance, and any benefits you provide employees, such as health insurance or a 401K plan.

DEPRECIATION

I don't include this as an expense. Instead, this is covered under "Capital Improvement and Replacement Reserves." Many important expenses fall under the I.R.S. category of "Other."

MANAGEMENT

When you own a property, it has to be managed. Either you

manage it directly, you hire employees to manage it, or you hire a management company to operate the investment. When you are figuring out the expense for management, you'll want to come up with a number, even if you plan to manage it yourself. For most larger investments, an appraiser will include a figure for management. While I don't use a management company, I have employees who perform the day-to-day management. I also pay myself a management fee. For me, the total in management costs turns out to be about 6% of gross revenues.

In my experience with residential buildings, management fees run from 4-10% of gross income. Probably 5-6% is a safe number to use. If you purchase a smaller property like a four-unit rental that you plan to manage yourself, you might still want to include a management fee when you are doing your financial analysis. You don't have to take the fee, but can use it as a negotiating tool with the seller. In the event you become disabled and are unable to manage the property, you will need to hire a management company to operate the building, so it's a good idea to factor in this management fee.

CAPITAL IMPROVEMENT AND REPLACEMENT EXPENSES

One of the unfortunate aspects of investment properties is that various parts wear out and need to be replaced, sometimes at the worst possible times. The replacement often costs a lot of money. How I love to write checks for replacement roofs, new boilers, major-size hot water heaters, tuck-pointing, or new windows!

Assuming that the building is in good operating condition when you purchase it, you need to think about a reserve for replacements when they come due. I use 3% of the gross revenues as my replacement reserve. If the building is in poor condition, I usually figure that certain replacements are needed immediately, like a new roof, new windows, new carpet, and landscaping. I figure out the actual costs of these improvements, and since they are needed immediately, I put the amount in the denominator and figure it will be a rehabilitation expense.

After these improvements are finished, I use my standard 3% as the replacement reserve.

SUPPLIES

Over and above capital improvement and specific repairs, you'll need other materials to operate a property. These include small items such as paint and painting supplies, smoke detectors, batteries, glass, and so forth. I use a 1% of gross revenues figure here.

SCAVENGER AND RECYCLING FEES

Depending on the type of building and the locale, you may be required to hire a scavenger and/or recycling service. In Milwaukee if you have an apartment building with less than four units, the city provides this service at no charge. If the property is larger, you'll have to hire both a scavenger service and a recycling service. To find out the cost of these, just call a local provider.

EXTERMINATING

If you didn't include this in as a maintenance cost, you need to factor it into your estimate. Exterminating is usually not a planned event, but cockroaches, mice, termites, and other pests are not well received by tenants. Furthermore, I have yet to meet a cockroach who paid me rent.

For larger buildings, I do preventive maintenance and have an exterminator go into every apartment periodically. A phone call to a local vendor can give you an expense estimate here.

MISCELLANEOUS

You may incur small, irritating expenses when you own a real estate investment. These include licenses and fees paid to government agencies, credit report checks, criminal background checks (if you choose to do these on prospective tenants), Dunn and Bradstreet reports, bank charges, tenant referral fees, pool maintenance, cable TV, leased furniture, and so forth.

I usually put in a small figure for miscellaneous costs, depending on expected tenant turnover. I do charge tenants who apply for apartments a modest fee for their credit report and criminal background check. I break even on these. This periodically dissuades a potential tenant from applying for an apartment. My suspicion in these cases is that the tenant has something to hide and probably wouldn't meet my rental standards anyway.

While figuring the rental income is fairly simple – a matter of adding several rents together with other revenue sources – the expense side is more difficult. There are many more expenses, and some, like electricity and gas, fluctuate unexpectedly. Nevertheless, I always try to get an estimate.

Some investors use a very simplified approach to estimating expenses. They figure expenses are 40-50% of revenues for a building where the tenants pay utilities (except water and sewer) and 50-60% of revenues when the landlord pays all utilities.

My overall track record on estimation has been mixed. Sometimes I'm too optimistic and underestimate expenses, and sometimes I'm too pessimistic. If nothing else, for each property I get a feel for what I expect to happen, and I gain a sense of having control over the property.

After estimating the revenues and expenses, we come back to our question, "Is this a good deal?" My main criteria for answering this question are an acceptable location and a 15% cash return on my down payment and other costs. If the investment looks like it will perform in that range, I'll pursue it. If it looks like it will be a negative cash flow, I don't bother. The 15% is not a set-in-granite rule. If a location is very attractive to me, but the investment will make a little less than 15%, I can live with that. I think about the future, because I don't ever plan to sell, and I visualize owning each building twenty-five to fifty years.

Other investors use different approaches. When a building is run-down, but located in a good area, they offer a reasonable price. Some just want to acquire property and simply say something like, "If I can get this for $60,000 per unit, great. I'll offer $55,000."

The wealthiest investors I know own a lot of property and aren't shy about offering a somewhat low price.

In the end, you have to find your own answer to what is a "good deal" for you.

A Word on Negotiations

After you've done your inspection of the property, reviewed the listing sheet or the information the owner has provided, and figured out whether the property has the potential to be a good investment, it's time to make a decision. Do you want the property? If so, you need to make an offer and begin negotiating the price and the terms of the deal with the seller. If not, move on to the next opportunity.

This leads me to some comments on contracts and negotiations. When I first became a serious real estate investor, I read several books, and every book seemed to offer its own view of the ideal contract. Many of the books had sample contracts. I studied every contract and took notes. When the time came to start making offers on properties, I went to my attorney and asked him to develop a contract that was a compilation of all the contracts I had seen. It was quite a masterpiece, and it cost a tidy sum to produce. I felt confident that I had the perfect contract.

Unfortunately, I was working with various real estate agents who were used to using the standard Chicago North Side Real Estate Board-approved contract with its approved riders. I could only imagine what they thought when I eagerly said I was ready to make an offer and pulled out my fancy-shmancy contract. They all resisted using it, but I insisted. Not surprisingly, the sellers would turn down my offers and not even respond. The real estate agents suggested I drop my contract and use their approved contract. I suspected that the agents weren't totally committed to pushing my contract on the sellers. Against my better judgment, I eventually compromised: I'd use their agreement to purchase real estate and put the additional items from my contract as part of an addendum or rider to their agreement. This seemed to work.

When the six-unit building because available in the Lake View neighborhood, I figured I'd better not play around with my contract and decided to use the approved North Side Board agreement. I did, however, add several additional requirements (known as *contingencies*) that I pulled from my own contract.

I used this approach more and more as I acquired property. I also switched from using the approved North Side Real Estate Board contract to the one Chicago Title and Trust printed. In my view, it was more neutral to the buyer and seller than the board agreement. Of course, I still added my contingencies.

One situation I don't like to be in is when I am the assignee on an existing contract. Over the years, Mr. W.D. has flipped some contracts to me, meaning that I've had to assume the contracts he was assigning to me. They didn't contain the language I like to see in a contract, but in most cases the buildings worked out well.

Having bought and sold several buildings, I have mixed thoughts regarding contracts. The positive thought is that they are important to have and are helpful in setting the behavior of the buyer and the seller. On the negative side, I have been party to blatant contract violations, and given the costs and time to litigate for either damages incurred or to make the seller perform his/her responsibilities, I'm not 100% confident that an agreement will be fully respected.

When I was selling my rental house in Pittsburgh, the property was under contract but the buyer didn't show up at closing and never purchased the house. I was very angry, since I'd had my tenant evicted so the buyer could move into the house. I was so mad, I sued for damages and won in court.

When I put a six-unit building under contract for $85,000 – meeting the full asking price of $85,000 – the seller's attorney advised the seller that she was giving the property away and cancelled the contract. The seller listed the property for $120,000 a few days later and it soon went under contract.

My attorney advised me that I had grounds to sue for damages. He further advised me that years might pass before I obtained a verdict and recovered any money, while the legal fees would eat into much of the potential profits. Rather than give in to my anger, I moved on to the next deal.

Having been party to other contract violations, my current philosophy is to avoid dealing with people if my gut feeling tells me they are untrustworthy, to use a contract with various contingencies, and not to assume anything.

I currently use a standard contract where I fill in the blanks. Before even submitting a contract, I may generate a letter to the seller and his or her agent stating that I intend to submit an offer for $X with the significant terms noted. These terms might include the down payment or how the financing might be arranged. I'm hoping the seller will respond so I have an idea of the seller's level of motivation.

On my contract, I add several contingencies or requirements for the seller. The contingencies will vary with the property in question; however, my standard contingencies are as follows:

1) I reserve the right to have an inspector of my choice fully examine every room of every unit, the exterior, the roof, and any areas that house storage or mechanicals, such as the boiler or electrical service.

I request that this be done within fourteen business days of the signing of the contract. Because of weekends, that gives me almost three weeks. (The seller's position is not to have an inspection at all, and if there has to be one, to have it done as soon as possible.) Frequently the inspection will reveal some defect that will enable me to get a concession from the seller, like a new roof or a price reduction.

I have mixed feelings about actually using an inspector, which in my case is usually a structural engineer. Having owned several buildings, I've overseen the replacement of roofs, boilers, windows, and hot water heaters. I've hired electricians to upgrade electrical services and paid plumbers to do every sort of plumbing and sewer job. In short, I've seen and paid for a lot. Although I am mechanically challenged, I can go through a potential building and can generally assess the heating, plumbing, roof, electrical, and other structural and mechanical aspects of the property. In recent purchases, I've done my own inspection and haven't discovered very many unpleasant surprises after acquisition.

Structural engineers are not cheap. Nevertheless, if I see something I am uncomfortable with, such as walls that bow in or out, evidence of water damage or asbestos, or floors or walls that are not level, I'll hire a structural engineer to do an inspection. It's a lot cheaper to pay the engineer and pass on the property if necessary than to have to pay for major structural repairs. Some lenders, in fact, require an engineer's report.

By inserting the inspection contingency, you're giving yourself the leeway to use an inspector as well as having the opportunity to see everything in the property.

2) The next contingency relates to reviewing and approving the operating report for the past three years. This is ideally found in the seller's federal tax return. It clearly helps you fine-tune your numbers if you are using the numerator/denominator approach to investing.

The review will often help you raise some interesting questions to the seller.

Examples of such questions are:

"Why were the gross rents lower in 2001 than in 2000?"

"Why is the repair cost so low?"

"How can a thirty-six-unit building spend only $220 on advertising in a year?"

"Why are the management fees approximately 10%?"

"Why was the plumbing expense so high in 2000? Did you replace anything?"

I favor the tax returns, because it is to the seller's tax advantage to show as low a profit as possible. Operating expenses aren't likely to be overlooked, especially over a three-year period. Appraisers will often want this information when conducting their appraisals for a lender.

Most of the time, the seller will agree to provide the information. I do find resistance on occasion, when:

• The seller doesn't have historical information.

• The seller is flipping the building.

• The seller hasn't owned the building for three years.

• The seller has rehabilitated the building in the last year or two.

• The seller has grossly underreported rental income.

• For whatever reason, the seller doesn't want to provide the information.

In the first three cases, I can understand the situation and work out a compromise on this contingency with the seller. In the latter situation, I am very leery. Why would the seller not want to provide the information? It creates a feeling of mistrust, and it forces me to make a decision: does the building seem to be such a great investment that I am willing to forego this contingency? That's a decision to be made based on each particular situation.

As I noted above, the language of the contingency states "subject to review and approval." What I am seeking here is satisfactory answers to my questions from the seller of the building. If the seller is evasive, I question whether this is a worthwhile investment. Sometimes the explanations are interesting; the seller might be padding the expenses for tax purposes, or undercounting the laundry revenues.

My bottom line here is that I feel uncomfortable if I don't have anything to review, especially on a larger building.

3) The third category is that the agreement is subject to the review and approval of my attorney within a set time period, usually ten working days.

While I usually use a standard contract where I fill in the blanks and add my contingencies, my attorneys always seem to make some worthwhile comments. In the event you are involved in a 1031 tax deferred exchange, it is critical that your attorney and a competent accountant review the contract, so you will be in compliance with the I.R.S. rules for 1031 exchanges.

I confess that I've cheated here. I don't always follow my own rules and have bought properties without the services of an attorney, and these transactions have worked out satisfactorily. If you are purchasing a rental house and have already purchased forty other rental houses, you probably don't need an attorney. For me, most of the time my comfort level is increased when I know I have an attorney behind me.

4) A fourth contingency that I include relates to my being able to review and approve existing leases within a set period of time.

If a tenant is on a month-to-month lease, I request the original lease that later became a month-to-month lease. If the tenant was always on a month-to-month lease, I want this confirmed in writing by the seller.

In reviewing the lease, I'm seeking to confirm the figures the seller had stated as well as the lease expiration date. I'm also looking for any special concessions the seller may have made to the tenants, such as a free month's rent or leasehold improvements. My review of the leases may bring up various questions I want to ask the seller.

5) Another contingency I find necessary to include is that I have other investors who will be funding the project, and so I'll need a certain time period to raise the necessary funds.

I usually allow myself two weeks. Sellers are obviously concerned that I don't have the money. My track record, however, has been excellent. I usually have my investors on board within two or three days of signing the contract. My investors have proved reliable and have always delivered the promised funds on time and signed all the necessary documents. In order to be fair to the seller, I work diligently to raise any necessary funding.

How I Fill in the Blanks

When I am generating an offer, I use a neutral contract where I fill in the blanks. I am very careful to be as specific as possible with what I put in the blanks. Here are some examples of how I fill in the blanks:

- I put my name as the purchaser, followed by a comma and the words "and/or assigns."

189

- I put in the purchase price.

- I put in the down payment amount. I typically will put in the lowest down payment a lender will allow (e.g., 20% of the offer price), even if I plan to make a larger down payment. My reason is that in the event the appraisal turns out to be lower than the agreed purchase price, this allows me the opportunity to go back to the seller and say, "Oops, I agreed to too high a price and the bank won't give me the loan at our agreed price. Can you help me here?"

- I spell out the exact terms of the financing. This includes the specific interest rate, the length of the loan (e.g., an amortization period of thirty years), the amount of the loan, and the points a lender might charge. If the loan is adjustable, I include the initial interest rate, the adjustment period, any floors or ceilings on the interest rate, and whether a balloon payment is due within a certain time period. I also state the maximum prepayment penalty. Lastly, I set a time frame in which the loan will be approved.

  I'm usually very aware of what lenders are offering when I make an offer. If necessary, I can make a quick call to the lenders, so my information is fairly accurate on the offer. If I can't find the loan I'm looking for within the set time frame, I have the flexibility to withdraw from the contract. Over the years, I've endeavored to maintain good relationships with lenders, and so I can get a loan approved quickly when necessary. This is a good bargaining point with sellers. A seller's confidence in me and in the likelihood of the deal going through increases when the seller knows I can get a loan approved quickly.

- The contracts I use require "earnest money" deposits. Such a deposit shows in hard dollars that you are sincere in your efforts to purchase a property. While I can't deny that I am eager to purchase a property, I always endeavor to put as little as possible into my earnest money deposit. Local custom often dictates how much earnest money you provide. Where I live, house sellers assume that you will make a 10% of purchase price earnest money deposit, generally after the inspection contingency is cleared. This is nevertheless negotiable. My earnest money deposits tend to be in the $1000 to $10,000 range. If I renege on the deal, I am at risk of losing my earnest money, but to date, I've never had to concede a dime of earnest money.

- Another blank relates to what personal property and fixtures stay with the property after closing, and here I try to be as specific as possible. Therefore, I put in the specific number of stoves, refrigerators, air conditioners, maintenance equipment, washing machines, dryers, and so forth. This makes it clear who gets what after closing. A word of warning: make sure the seller doesn't replace existing appliances with older models after the contract is signed.

- Still another item to clarify relates to prorations. You want the contract to indicate that there will be prorations based on the day of the closing. Thus gas, water, sewer, electric, property taxes, rents, and other income, as well as monthly maintenance contracts would be prorated so that the seller pays for his or her fair share and you, the buyer, pay your fair amount. On the property taxes, some counties are a year behind on their collections, and you won't know the actual property tax amount until the next year. Some counties collect taxes for the current year. I prefer to have the seller set aside a specified amount of money that is an estimate of the tax liability, to be held by an independent third party. When the property tax bill comes the next year, you then figure out the actual tax proration. If the seller put in too much money, you give the seller the overage. If not enough money was deposited, you have the legal right to have the seller provide extra money.

The reason I suggest this approach is that it protects you against dramatic tax increases. As I've noted before, the tax assessor is usually aware of real estate sales and will make an immediate adjustment in the tax assessments. Having property taxes prorated on the actual tax bill can save you thousands of dollars when you receive the tax bill the first year after the closing.

- The final item of note is the closing date (the date the title transfers to you from the seller). This should certainly be set after your financing has been approved. My preference is to set it late in the month during the winter months. I am located in a cold weather climate, and about 70% of the gas cost is incurred during the first three months of the year. In addition, I'd rather close after March 1 if possible, because the rental markets improve then and I can more easily fill vacancies. In a warm weather month, I try to close after the sixth of the month. This forces the seller to collect the rents, and I get a credit at closing for all the rents collected. This also gives me time to connect with existing tenants before the next rent collection cycle occurs. Of course, this is negotiable.

Negotiation is an important part of real estate investing. Numerous resources are available if you want to learn more about negotiation strategies. Your local bookstore is a good starting point. There are also negotiation seminars you can attend. I suggest you search the Internet under "Negotiation Seminars," or check adult education courses in your area.[4]

While I won't be discussing theories of negotiation, I will share my basic principles and describe my negotiation process.

In my experience, negotiation is a battle of wills. In the negotiation dance between buyer and seller, the party who wants the deal more strongly is at a disadvantage and will give up more in order to get the deal done.

Principle #1: As much as possible, operate from a position of strength.

Thus, if you are in a buying position, your viewpoint should be, "I like what I see, but I will not be forced into buying it. If the numbers work out, I'll buy. If not, I'll walk away from the deal and look for the next opportunity. This deal won't make or break me. I can live without it. No deal is life or death. There are always more opportunities. I'm patient and not under any pressure."

Always be ready to walk away from a deal, even if you spent time and money trying to make it happen. I'd rather walk away from a deal that has revealed something I don't like than have to live with it a long time. Stated differently, better to have a little pain now than a lot of pain later. I've never seen a deal that will dramatically improve how I will live my life. As a person licensed to sell life insurance, I've learned that the life expectancy of real estate operators is about 15% longer than the average (unfortunately my source, a life actuary, won't let me cite the confidential source

---

[4] In the Chicago area, I see courses offered by either the Learning Annex or the Discovery Center.

of this information). I figure I'll be around for a while, and new opportunities will arise.

If you are in a weak position, do whatever you can to expand your options and strengthen your position. Therefore, if you have just sold a property and want to use the sale's proceeds as part of an I.R.S. 1031 exchange, the deadline weakens your position. You have a forty-five-day period to identify potential properties for purchase, and you have to complete the purchase within one hundred eighty days of the day you sold your property. If you want to avoid paying any income tax, you are in a "must buy" position. To strengthen your position, aggressively seek out real estate investment opportunities. You want to maximize what is available. The goal is to find several potential opportunities and to have multiple negotiations available, so you have options when you run across an inflexible seller.

Principle #2: Keep your emotions out of the negotiation.

Try to be as objective as possible. Real estate is a business, and to me, it's all a matter of numbers. I don't want to waste energy feeling angry and insulted by the other party in the negotiation. I definitely don't want my judgment clouded by emotion. I simply wish to purchase a property that meets my requirements and will give me a long-term return on my investment. I don't care if the seller calls me an idiot or a greedy, worthless vulture. My goal is to make a deal, not to satisfy any emotional need.

Principle #3: Keep your ego out of the negotiation.

Don't have either an inflated opinion of your overall importance or a deflated opinion of yourself. Be respectful of others. I see no reason to antagonize the other person with disrespectful comments and actions; there is little to gain by that. I don't feel a need to pay too much in order to buy a big building so I can impress my friends and neighbors. I need an investment that will give me the long-term return on investment I require. When negotiating, I leave my ego at the door.

Principle #4: Be honest and consistent.

The negotiating process is one of building trust. If I don't trust the other party, I'll pull away from the negotiation. When negotiating, I am honest with both the agent and the seller. If I'm interested in a property, I say that I want the property, but I let the seller know that it has to meet my parameters. Since I speak only the truth, I don't get caught lying, which reduces one's credibility and trustworthiness to the seller. I believe that my approach of being honest allows the seller the freedom to be honest too.

Another factor to consider is your reputation. When you are dealing in larger properties in a certain location, there are a limited number of owners. I usually know many of them on a first-name basis. We all talk about each other. If you are dishonest and misrepresent something, the word gets around, and people are leery of you in future negotiations. I want a reputation for honesty among my peer group of investors as well as with my bankers, investors, employees, tenants, and contractors. This pays huge dividends over time.

The last piece of this principle relates to keeping your word. Simply stated, if you are going to do something within a certain time period, do it. This builds trust, and the other person knows you can be counted on.

Principle #5: Know your market.

Negotiating from strength doesn't mean much unless you know the market. Become familiar with:

- What similar properties have recently sold for

- The rents for similar properties

- The financing that's available

- What else is on the market and how it compares to the subject property

- Market trends, such as increasing demand

- What the cap rates are for the area at the present time

When you are aware of market conditions, you won't unknowingly overpay for a property. You are able to compare the property for which you are negotiating with the rest of the marketplace. This gives you strength in the negotiation.

I put this principle into practice when I bought the sixty-seven-unit from Mr. W.D. Since I owned and managed the building next door, I knew the rents, the value per unit, the market trends, and the financial marketplace. I wasn't going to overpay (the appraisal was $75,000 above what I paid).

Principle #6: Learn as much as you can about the seller's style and needs.

When you are purchasing real estate, you want to find out, "Why is the seller selling?" and, most importantly, "What is the absolute best deal I can make with this seller?" You're trying to find out the reason the property is being sold; you want to know whether the seller is motivated, or waiting to get a specific price.

I'd love to plant a little transmitter in a seller's brain to give me these answers, wouldn't you? Unfortunately, you'll need to figure out the answers by asking questions and looking for clues.

Learn as much as you can about the seller. What are his or her current circumstances? How long has the person owned the building? What did he or she pay for it? What is the remaining debt? Does the seller have an outside occupation and if so, what is it? Does that occupation get in the way of managing the property?

How does the seller manage the building? Is it profitable? Does he/she own other buildings? Are these for sale? Has the property been on the market long? Have there been other offers? How did the seller respond to those offers?

You'll be able to find out the answers to some questions, and with others, you'll end up guessing. When I bought my first building, I knew the seller was retiring. His plan was to sell his house and building by spring. With the five-unit in Aurora, I knew the seller had incurred significant hospital bills due to medical care needed by his child, and he didn't carry health insurance. The hospital bill collectors were pursuing him, and unfortunately my down payment ended up going to the hospital. I actually contacted the hospital to see if they'd discount the bill for him. They wouldn't. The seller had to cash out his equity to pay them.

On some of the deals with Mr. W.D., he wanted the cash as operating capital, or he had to sell buildings to raise down payments for larger properties. In many other cases, I could only speculate as to why the sellers put the buildings on the market. I'll never know if I got every last cent off the price of a building when the final deal was worked out. I suspect that on most deals I was close to bottom, if not at bottom.

Knowing the seller's position allows you to make a deal that benefits you and works for the seller. The best ways to find out about the seller are by asking questions, through observation, and by researching the seller's background.

Principle #7: Set a maximum limit on price and terms before negotiation begins, and stick to this.

When you make a first offer, you don't want to offer your maximum price; you'll want to allow yourself fall-back positions. You do, however, want to set a maximum, which you keep secret. You absolutely shouldn't share this information with a seller. Many sellers I know figure a negotiation will end up "splitting the differ-ence." For example, if the seller is asking $100,000 for a house and you make an initial offer of $90,000, the seller will figure that the two of you will split the $10,000 difference. You'll go up $5,000 and the seller will drop the price $5,000. This doesn't have to be the case. If you set $92,500 as your maximum, then stick to that.

Thus, if the seller drops to $97,500, you might counter at $91,000. Maybe you'll agree at $92,500 or maybe you won't. Please don't pay beyond your maximum. Every dollar beyond the maxi-mum will most likely have to be financed, and you will be paying this difference on your loan for years to come.

Principle #8: Meet the seller face to face; build a relation-ship.

I like direct contact with the seller, even though not everyone agrees with this approach. Since I'm very unemotional about real estate and have had years to make dumb mistakes, I believe I have developed good people skills. I can see where the seller is at, and through my own perceptions I can get a feel for him or her. I don't like to rely on a middle person, like a real estate agent. I especially like, over the period of negotiation, building a relationship with the seller. I still stay in touch with several of my sellers, years after the deals were done. I feel we're in the real estate game together and should try to help each other.

Others disagree with me and think there should be a middle person between buyer and seller. A broker does offer some advan-tages:

- Buyers and sellers can freely vent their emotions about the other party to the broker. You as a buyer might scream at the broker that you think the seller is a dis-honest, greedy old coot who can't be trusted and is to-tally inflexible. If you said this directly to the seller, it would not bring your negotiations closer to completion. The broker will listen to you, but will not repeat what you said to the seller.

• Brokers are experienced negotiators who know the market. The broker may be able to bring a seller to a mutually agreeable point because he or she can share market information with the seller. The broker may be more credible to the seller than you, the buyer.

• Because of their personality, some people do not make good negotiators. My wife, for example, will not negotiate for anything. If a car dealer is asking a manufacturer's suggested retail price for a new car, she'd just as soon pay it rather than get into a negotiation. I've tried to empower her to be a negotiator, but to no avail. Some people simply abhor negotiating. Those with abrasive personalities are better off using a middle person, also.

You might ask what my personal style is in negotiating a real estate deal. After examining a property, I project revenues and expenses and try to estimate net operating income. I then figure out a down payment and factor in loan costs such as interest rate, duration of loan, monthly payment, and origination costs. At certain price levels, I figure out my return on investment, based on the numerator/denominator approach. I exclude appreciation and tax savings from the numerator. For example, a price of $1,000,000 may give me a cash-on-cash return of 12%, where a price of $950,000 may yield 14%.

Most often, I generate an official offer. I try to present this to the seller face-to-face. I ask questions of the seller and try to build a relationship. Then I wait for the seller's response. As a backup, I have my financial analysis available. My target, as you will recall, is a 15% return.

If necessary, I show the seller my numbers and let him or her adjust them as necessary. If I agree with the seller's opinion, I change my analysis; however, I'm usually right.

If the seller wants to make a deal with me, he or she will lower the price or terms. I know I am competing with other buyers. The negotiation is a matter of wills. How strongly do I want to buy, versus how strongly the seller wants to sell? I'm never extremely motivated. If I can buy the property to get my required return, that's great. If not, it wasn't "meant to be."

I abide by the principles noted above: I operate from strength; I am honest; I keep my word; I learn as much about the seller's needs as possible; I don't feel as though someone is holding a gun to my head to make a deal; I leave my ego and all emotion out of negotiations, etc. I don't feel I have to "beat" the seller in order to "win." I don't think of negotiation as a win/lose proposition. I am trying to purchase something according to my preestablished needs.

At the same time, I don't want to overpay. My investments in real estate have worked out well over time.

I had an interesting insight about this while looking at the MLS books from ten or twenty years ago. When I first started looking for real estate investments in 1981, I could have paid full price for anything listed and been a happy investor today. Appreciation does wonders, so long as you have the deep pockets to carry a property.

Once you've negotiated the deal and the contract is consummated, the time has come to conduct your due diligence.

13

SHOW ME THE MONEY

One of the key contingencies in real estate investing is getting the financing in place within a certain time period. This chapter will be devoted to arranging financing.

In my view, an investor has two significant sources of financing: 1) nonconventional lenders such as the seller, your relatives, or private lenders who may even want to be your equity partner; and 2) conventional lenders such as banks, savings and loans, credit unions, pension funds, insurance companies, and REITs. Let's start with the nonconventional ones.

Non-Conventional Financing

When I became a serious real estate investor in 1981, the prime lending rate had exceeded 20% and conventional lenders were making loans at very high rates. On a commercial property, lenders were demanding interest rates of at least 15%, three origination points (3%) on the loan, and three- to five-year balloon payments.

Sellers who really wanted to sell their property often had to offer "seller financing." Many real estate seminars and books of the time called this "creative financing" and covered the subject

201

in great detail. The first five buildings in which I invested all had some element of seller financing. Buildings #1 and #3 were completely financed by the seller. I assumed existing financing in Buildings #4 and #5, and in #4, the seller agreed to hold a second mortgage (both the first and second mortgage on #4 were at 0% interest). With Building #2, I got a conventional loan for 90% of the purchase price and the seller held a 15% second mortgage. (I borrowed at 105% – more than the building was valued at.)

Other buildings I bought in Milwaukee had seller financing as well. Seller financing is my favorite kind of financing. Unfortunately for me, it's not as available now as in the early 1980s.

Why do I prefer seller financing?

• Only one seller ever wanted to see a credit report (note: my credit report is very clean). Every bank wanted to see one.

• Only two sellers ever asked to see a statement of my net worth. Every bank did.

• I have never had to pay a loan origination fee as well as a lot of other loan charges when I have gotten seller financing.

• Sellers don't stick you with nuisance fees that do nothing but cost you money.

• Sellers don't have lending standards like loan-to-value maximums or debt coverage ratios.

• The seller's loan is approved as soon as the contract is consented to.

• I've always gotten a lower interest rate than anything I could find in the conventional marketplace.

- I don't have to deal with bureaucratic structures like the loan committee.

- There is far less paperwork.

- Sellers may accept services instead of a down payment. Thus, if you are a roofer, plumber, or electrician, you may be able to provide services and receive a credit toward the down payment.

- Unusual financial terms that I propose, such as a six-month moratorium on payments at the start of the loan, 0% interest, or deferred loan payments when the building isn't doing well, would never be accepted by a conventional lender. They have been accepted with my seller-financed properties.

Here's my wish list when I get seller financing. I may not get everything I want, but if I ask, I'll get something:

- A below market interest rate. A call to conventional lenders will give you an idea of the fixed or adjustable rates on the market at the time.

- Interest in arrears rather than in advance. You pay the interest due at the end of the month rather than the beginning.

- If possible, a loan that fully amortizes, preferably for a thirty-year period. This means that you have a set monthly payment, and if you make every monthly payment, the loan is paid off in thirty years. If the seller wants payment of the loan balance in full by a certain date (a balloon payment), then I want that payment as far in the future as possible. As a precaution, I'd want to add a clause that says if I am unable, despite my best efforts, to find a new loan to pay off the seller's loan, then the seller will extend the payoff date by a few years, but I will agree to pay a sweetener such as a fee or higher interest rate.

• No prepayment penalty. I can pay as much extra as I want.

• A moratorium on payments. Typically, I say that I expect to have a lot of start-up costs when acquiring a new property, and I'd appreciate if the seller could wait a few months before I begin the loan payments. As an option, I ask for 0% interest the first six months of the loan, so I can get the debt balance down. Some sellers agree to this. I also ask that there be one month a year when I don't have to make a payment – typically January or February, when heat bills are high or real estate taxes are due. This usually doesn't work, but is a good bargaining chip to give up for something else. The key is to ask for it.

• As the owner, I pay the real estate taxes and insurance premium directly rather than be escrowed with the seller. I will provide annual proof of payment and will provide a copy of the insurance policy to the seller.

• The property shall be the sole security for the loan. Thus, in the very unlikely event that the seller/note holder has to foreclose (I have never missed a mortgage payment), the seller can take back the property but can't personally come after me if he or she has to resell the property and doesn't get enough money out of the foreclosure sale to pay off the debt. I feel this is justified because I typically make a substantial down payment.

- The loan should be assumable to a new buyer in the event I sell. I request that the seller not unreasonably withhold his or her approval when this occurs. If a buyer does assume the loan, I have no further liability for the loan. In truth, I tend to hold my buildings a long time and have never sold a building where a new buyer assumed an existing loan.

- I ask for a discount of some percentage or amount if I pay off the loan within the first six or twelve months. This gives me an incentive to refinance. Some sellers have gone along with this.

- I ask for a fifteen-day grace period when the monthly loan payment is due.

- In general, I prefer a fixed interest rate rather than an adjustable one. If interest rates at conventional lenders go lower than my contract rate, I ask the seller to reduce the interest rate. I argue that the seller is better off at an interest rate of something like 7% with a safe risk like me than with an annuity or money market fund. If the seller refuses, I refinance.

- I ask to see the note or notes for the underlying loan the seller has. These may be assumable at favorable interest rates. I would then get a second mortgage from the seller. The note holder may let me pay off the note at a discount.

- I want the title of the property to pass directly to me; I do not want a land contract where the seller holds the property title and can more quickly foreclose on the property.

In my experience, many of these terms are acceptable to the seller. Whenever I have gotten seller financing, I pushed myself to get something special like 0% interest, below market interest, or a moratorium on loan payments. I've always gotten something from the seller. On the flip side, I never got any of these special terms from a conventional lender.

Seller financing can often make the numerator/denominator method of purchasing work. All that has to be done is lower the interest rate or increase the length of the loan term (amortization period).

The question arises, "How do I find a property with seller financing"? Back in the early 1980s, it wasn't very hard, since virtually every property was seller financed. Now this isn't as common, but often when a seller will offer financing, he or she will advertise this. If the property is listed with a real estate broker, the broker is usually aware of this. Some sellers will offer a "10% second." This means that they want you, the buyer, to get a conventional loan (a first mortgage) for 80% of the property value, and the seller will carry another 10% of the loan.

In this case, your down payment would only be 10%. If you decide to buy a property with a 10% seller financed loan, I strongly recommend you check with the lender of the first mortgage to make sure they allow this. Many lenders want to see 20% or more cash down payment on a commercial property and won't allow such a transaction. You are then forced to have a "secret second."

If the seller isn't advertising any financing, you'll want to explore it as a possibility with him or her. You'll need to get important information from the seller. Pose questions such as:

- What do you owe on the property?

- What are the terms of the mortgages if any exist?

- Are the mortgages assumable?

- What do you plan to do with the sale proceeds?

- What are your needs?

- Would you consider financing some or all of the deal?

- Would you consider an installment sale where you get some of the sale price now and more at various times in the future?

When you learn the seller's position, you may be able to structure a financial package that is better for the seller than if he or she received all cash. The key is asking questions and coming up with workable solutions based on the answers.

Another type of seller financing is leasing a property with the option to purchase within a designated time period. Under this arrangement, you don't purchase the property; you lease it from the owner. The owner continues to make the loan payment (assuming there's a loan on the property). Hopefully you can re-lease the property, perhaps even for a profit. If your lease payment includes a portion that is deducted from the option purchase price, within a few years you may have substantial potential equity in the property because of appreciation, increased operating income, and any reductions your lease payments made off the option price. If you want to execute on your option, you will have to go to a conventional lender to get a loan to pay off the option. One important factor here is that you want the loan based on the current appraised price of the property, rather than the option price. If the value of the property has increased, you'll be able to get a larger loan that will cover the option price.

Another nonconventional lending source is friends and relatives. Personally, I have never borrowed from friends or relatives. I'd feel very uncomfortable going to a family wedding or party knowing I owed someone money. I'd feel even more uncomfortable if I defaulted on the loan. I value my family and friends and don't ever want to do anything to diminish those relationships.

I do not loan money to friends or relatives, either. It's often been said that the best way to lose your friends is to lend them money. I have done so in the past and have gotten burned. Unfortunately, I have an indelible memory of these loans and have often felt like a dope for having made them. The nonpayment put a serious damper on those relationships. My current philosophy is to respond to such requests as follows:

"I don't lend money to friends or relatives. If there is a genuine need, I give money as a gift. If it comes back, great. If it doesn't, it was a gift in the first place and was never expected to be returned."[5] (For those of you who like this idea, be aware that if your gift exceeds $11,000 in a given year, the balance is subject to a federal gift tax.)

Using this approach, my anger and disappointment are abated. I also feel less guilty, because I find it much easier to say "no" to giving a gift than to making a loan.

If you do choose to borrow from friends and relatives for real estate deals, I strongly recommend that everything be specified very clearly in writing. You can purchase a model note from a stationery store or use one from a bank. All the details should be spelled out, including interest rate, monthly payment, the timing of the monthly payment, what, if anything, is the security for the loan, the date the loan is to be paid in full, and what happens in the event of default. This will reduce any confusion later.

A last nonconventional source might be a private lender who makes real estate loans. If you choose this route, be careful and again, make sure everything is in writing and reviewed by your attorney. Some of these lenders might want to be an "equity partner."

---

[5] I am not looking for any new friends whose friendship is based on my gifts of money.

In short, they'll lend you money, but will want a piece of the action such as a percentage of ownership or the future appreciation. You as the investor will have to determine if it is worth your while to have the lender participate in your project. My preference is not to have a lender be an equity partner.

Conventional Financing

While seller financing is preferred, most of the time you'll need to search for conventional sources of funding real estate transactions: banks, savings and loans, mortgage brokers, pension funds, insurance companies, and so forth. You can shop mortgage loans on the Internet. Search under "real estate loans," "home loans," "mortgage loans," and "commercial real estate loans." The lender you seek depends on the amount and type of loan you want. If you are buying a condo, single family home, or small multiunit rental (up to four units), you would seek out a bank, credit union, savings and loan, or a mortgage broker. Many government agencies offer special loans for those who qualify (first-time buyers, low-income borrowers, borrowers in target areas). In the Chicago area, our local newspapers are filled with quotes every weekend from mortgage brokers as to current rates for single family homes.

If you need a loan for a multiunit of five or more units or a commercial loan, these quotes won't be found in the real estate section of the local newspaper. Multiunit properties with five or more units are considered commercial and require a commercial loan.

You will need to make phone calls to many lenders to get your rates. For loans under $1,000,000, your best sources are banks, savings and loans, and commercial mortgage brokers. For loans in excess of $1,000,000, I'd also include insurance companies, pension funds, and REITs on my list.

Your local Yellow Pages will provide an extensive list of lenders and mortgage brokers. Journals and publications such as *The Wall Street Journal, The Real Estate Forum,* or *Real Estate Finance Journal* will often provide you with the name and phone number of many commercial lenders. The Internet can also provide leads. If you have a larger property to finance or refinance, the lenders in this arena have the amazing ability to find you.

The major key when you are getting a loan from a conventional lender is to shop around. You should call as many lenders as possible to see who is offering the best deal at the time you need financing. Most likely you will need to spend a day or two talking to lenders to get the details of their loan program, and the results will be worth it. If you could save one-fourth of a percentage point on a $100,000 thirty-year loan (7% versus 7.25%), the difference in the monthly loan payment would be $17.50 per month ($665.31 vs. $682.81). Over the course of 360 payments, this would add up to $6300.00 – not bad for a day's work.

One interesting thing about the money you borrow is that $100,000 borrowed from a major national lender like Wells Fargo is just as good as $100,000 borrowed from your local community bank. The key is the terms of the loan.

Here's what to ask when you make your calls on a single-unit family residence. These are preliminary questions; there are a few more to ask later, before you commit to the loan:

- What is your current interest rate?

- Is it fixed? For how long? Fifteen years? Thirty years?

- Can it be lowered with a larger down payment or with more origination points being paid?

- If so, how does that work?

- Will the rates change if I don't plan to live in the home?

- If so, how?

- Is this an adjustable rate loan? If yes, how often is the adjustment made?

- What determines the adjustment?

- Is there a maximum amount that the interest rate can be raised or lowered annually over the life of the loan?

- Is there a rate floor or ceiling?

- What is the least amount of down payment that is allowed?

- What are the various costs related to getting a loan from you?

- Is the loan based on a percentage of appraised price or contract purchase price?

- How long does it take to have a loan approved?

- What is the Annual Percentage Rate (APR)? The APR is an interest rate calculation that includes all the costs of the loan including the closing costs.

- If I plan to upgrade the property, can a loan be made based on the projected value of the property because of planned improvements?

- Can the costs for these planned improvements be included in the loan?

Once you receive information from several lenders, you compare this information and pick best choices. I typically focus on the interest rate, the frequency of the adjustment to the rate, if the lender has a balloon or prepayment penalty, and how the adjustment works. I look for the lender who offers the most favorable combination.

If one lender stands out among those you contacted, you'll want to ask a few more questions:

- Is there a prepayment penalty and if so, how is it determined?

- What do you require of the borrower in terms of income to mortgage ratio, what percentage of debt is allowable, job longevity?

- Can the loan be made assumable?

- Can the property be the sole security for the loan, or do I have to sign personally for the loan?

- Do you require taxes and/or insurance to be escrowed (held by the lender)?

- What documentation do you need from the borrower (e.g., tax returns, personal financial statement)?

- If under a 20% down payment, is private mortgage insurance (PMI) required?

- Is there a balloon payment due on the loan?

You hope that most of the answers will satisfy you. To be honest, I have yet to find a perfect loan from a conventional lender. My loans at present are all commercial loans. They vary in terms of the interest rate, length of the loan, and prepayment penalties. Some have fixed rates and many have adjustables. One has a ten-year balloon, while the rest don't require balloons. I don't like balloon payment loans generally, because after a period of time you are forced to sell or seek out a new loan. If I sell the buildings, I have prepayment penalties of ninety days of loan interest due. I personally guarantee all the loans.

If you are seeking funding for a two- to four-unit residential building, the questions to ask are similar to those mentioned above. A key question here relates to whether you intend to live in the building or not. Lenders prefer owner-occupied property to non-owner-occupied. This is reflected in the rates they offer as well as the minimum down payment required.

When your loan package is evaluated by the "loan committee," the extra income that the rental units produce will be considered when making the loan. The lender adds this to your income and makes it easier for you to qualify for the loan.

In my experience, anything from a condominium, a co-op, or a house up to a four-unit residential is considered by the personal lending department. The loan terms are well-established and the documents are generated by computers. Most lenders I've dealt with sell these loans to organizations like the Federal National Mortgage Loan Association (FANNIE MAE). These loans have to conform to the standards set by which organization is buying the loan.

When you get to five or more residential units, or any of the other commercial real estate properties like office buildings, shopping centers, or industrial property, you've entered the realm of the commercial mortgage lending department. Lenders will assume that you, the borrower, know what you are doing. I have found that there is more leeway here. When I call about a commercial loan, I haven't found a fixed rate loan in quite some time – all the loans are adjustable. Most commercial lenders have prepayment penalties and more costs to the borrower. Simply stated, when you're into commercial borrowing, you're in the big leagues.

If you're looking for a commercial loan, call a variety of lenders to learn what kinds of loans they offer. When you call to get a quote, you can expect to talk to a human being who isn't reading from the daily quote sheet. The loan officer you talk to will want to know some of the specifics of the property: what the property is, if it is under contract, how much you want to borrow, what the contract purchase price is, and so forth. I often find that the lender doesn't give me an immediate response, but will call back within a day or so. You need to ask most of the questions already noted. (Obviously, if you are buying a strip mall, you are not going to inquire about special rates for owner-occupied properties.)

Some of the differences I've found in commercial loans versus smaller residential loans are as follows:

- Lenders want to know who will manage the property and how it will be managed.

- They may request environmental audits on the property to make sure there won't be any environmental liabilities, such as radon or asbestos.

- They almost always require prepayment penalties.

- They may want an engineer's report on the property and may insist that certain structural repairs be completed within a specified time.

- They may specify origination points on the loan.

- They will want to have their attorneys review the paperwork for the loan, and may charge you as the borrower for the attorney's fee. As the borrower, you have no control over what the attorneys charge.

- Their interest rates are not necessarily set at the time of quote. I've had very unpleasant upward rate adjustments a day or two before the closing because the rates floated over an index until closing. I've had to go along with the increased rates, but the lender's action certainly didn't build my loyalty to that lender. I have felt quite angry in this situation, but was stuck in the short term. To prevent this, you might inquire about whether the lender can "lock" rates for you and at what cost.

• Commercial lenders usually want some of their fees when they provide the loan commitment, so that if you walk away from the loan you lose your deposit, which can amount to several thousand dollars.

• They may or may not require a personal guarantee (a nonrecourse loan). This is a negotiable item.

• Their lending standards may impose certain unique requirements, such as adequate parking.

• They will want to see the appraisal and operating figures for the building. Lenders use a ratio named the "debt coverage ratio" (total revenue less operating expenses divided by annual principal and interest payment) to insure that the property will have adequate cash flow to pay the loan. Debt coverage ratios are typically 115% to 125%.

• They usually want to see that the borrower has enough of a down payment or equity in the project and personal financial strength, so that their risk of not recovering their money is very low. In my experience, the commercial lender wants the loan-to- value ratio (LTV) to be 70% to 80% of the property's value. Stated differently, they want the borrower to have at least a 20% to 30% equity position. It helps to have a strong financial statement on top of that.

215

- They want to have certified rent rolls, operating statements, and financial statements annually.

- Commercial loans are a businessperson to businessperson transaction. This means they are subject to negotiation. That is why it helps to know what each lender is offering so you can negotiate one lender against the other. The negotiation essentially comes down to how badly you want the loan versus how strongly the lender want to make the loan.

In my experience, a lender will be much more interested and flexible on a big loan such as $10,000,000, than on a small loan of $200,000. The amount of work on the lender's part isn't that much more for the bigger loan. In any case, always try to get a lower rate or better loan terms. It also helps to develop a personal relationship with a lender or two.

When a lender is evaluating a commercial loan prospect, he or she is evaluating both the actual investment risk and the character of the borrower. Every time I've gotten a commercial loan, the lender has run a credit report on me. In addition, I've had to meet face-to-face with someone of importance, such as the president of the bank, the senior vice-president, or the chief real estate investment lending officer. The meetings are always quite interesting; the lenders want to know my investment philosophy and what my specific plans are for the operation of the property, such as what improvements are planned and if I will raise rents or cut expenses. In short, they want to know whether they will get their loan back.

I, on the other hand, try to pick the brains of the lenders. I ask questions like:

- What do you see as the future of the location?

- What is your lending philosophy?

- To whom are they making loans at present and for what?

- How have recent developments worked out?

The key for you is making a good presentation. I often put together a package with detailed information on the property, the management plan, and the investors.

I suspect that commercial lenders usually have mixed feelings about me as someone they want to lend money to. On the plus side, I am a very safe risk. I've never missed a loan payment, I usually always borrow an amount of money that leaves a large equity cushion if the bank has to foreclose, and I don't mind personally guaranteeing loans. On the minus side, the lender may not make as much interest as hoped for off my loan. I'm told lenders don't like the fact that I make extra principal payments every month so the loans get paid off more quickly than if I were just making the required minimum payment (by doing this, I reduce the overall interest expense). They also are aware that I will shop around to refinance the loan as soon as interest rates drop. If they make a twenty-five year loan, they know I won't be with them for the whole twenty-five years.

The lenders' position is that they want to make a safe, profitable loan. Lenders are motivated to make loans because that's how they stay in business, and they need to make good loans.

After contacting all the lenders, select the one who offers the best package regarding the interest rate and other terms of the loan. One strategy is to select two or three promising lenders and negotiate one against the other until you get the best possible deal.

For example, you might call Lender B and tell them that Lender A is twenty basis points lower with the same terms and ask if they can do anything to compete.

217

Special Loan Situations

In addition to borrowing money for the acquisition of a property, you will probably have other borrowing needs.

The first type of special loan is a rehabilitation loan. In this case, you acquire a run-down property and must borrow the funds to upgrade it. You need to know where the rehab money will come from before you begin the project. You don't want to be in the position of purchasing such a property without having the money to repair it.

The lenders in a rehab situation will want to see a complete timetable as to what will be done, how much it will cost, and when it will be completed. In short, they want to know that you have a sound plan to complete your rehab. The key again is to call specific lenders who make these kinds of loans. If you call Bank A and are told they don't make commercial rehab loans, ask the lending officer to recommend a lender who will. Find as many lenders as you can.

Be aware that additional issues must be addressed on a rehab loan. The lenders often place the money in escrow, and then they will either inspect or pay someone such as a title insurance company to inspect the property before they release any money to you to pay your contractors. They or their representatives will want to make sure that the work was done properly, and will require that the contractors sign off that they have been paid in full (they will require a waiver of lien from the contractors and any subcontractors).

Although I have done several rehabs, I have never gotten a rehab loan. Instead, I have refinanced existing properties to pull out the cash I needed before beginning the work, used funds from the cash flow of an existing property, or used my own funds to finance a rehab. I do this to avoid the red tape of lender inspections and payments out of the rehab escrow. My contractors very much appreciate being paid on a timely basis. They have often prioritized my work orders over other customers because I pay on time.

A second type of special lending situation is a construction loan. I've never built from the ground up, but several of my real estate friends have. They've typically developed a relationship with a lender who finances the construction. Once the construction is complete, they find a lender who will make a permanent loan, since the construction lender may not be able to offer a permanent loan. If you are a first-time developer, you'll want to build relationships with lenders who offer construction financing, because lenders tell me that they are very cautious when making loans to first-time developers.

Other types of loan needs aren't quite as favorable. Here you need money quickly for something that has to be done immediately. Examples include needing a new boiler in the middle of winter, having to make a real estate tax payment on time, or, worse yet, needing money to cover a negative cash flow. Solutions to these problems are not simple. I've solved negative cash flow problems by borrowing against our personal residence or against my stock portfolio. Another solution that has worked for me is approaching my suppliers and other vendors early to see if payment arrangements could be made. I've always found my vendors very accommodating in working out financial arrangements with me. They know they will be paid.

One type of loan you may want to have prearranged is an unsecured line of credit or a signature loan. If you do business with a certain bank, you might ask the lender to consider offering you an unsecured line of credit. With an unsecured line of credit, you have an automatic loan available when you need money. The loan is approved up to a certain amount, such as $50,000. When you need the funds, you simply write a check and are charged interest beginning when the check clears. While the interest rate is negotiable, you want the lowest rate you can get, like less than the prime interest rate. Remember, you get the loan by asking for it.

Do I Refinance?

As this is being written, interest rates are near forty-year lows. When I started investing in real estate in 1982, no one foresaw that in twenty years you could get a thirty-year fixed rate loan on your home for under 6%. I am very grateful for the low interest rates that prevail today.

As an investor, you will find opportune times when it makes financial sense to refinance your property. When I consider refinancing, I look at the opportunity from two perspectives: 1) the amount of time required to pay back the refinance costs in terms of loan interest savings; and 2) the return on investment based on my loan costs.

Let's look at an example:

I owe $270,000 on an eighteen-unit building at 8% interest, with a fifteen-year amortization. The prepayment penalty is $3800, and the current lender doesn't want to offer lower interest rates, although these prevail in the current marketplace. Some lenders are quoting 5% interest fixed for five years and then adjusting annually based on an index. These loans are based on a fifteen-year amortization. The costs to acquire a new loan are $3,500 including origination points, title insurance, appraisal, and all the other fees the lender would charge. Thus if I refinance with a new lender, it will cost me $3,800 in a prepayment penalty plus $3,500 in costs associated with the new lender. This adds up to $7,300. I then look at the interest I would be paying under the existing loan compared to the new loan to see what the interest savings are over the period of the loan. This is found by looking at each loan's amortization schedule.

Lenders will provide you with this if you request it. You compare the interest on the current loan to the interest on the new loan. In this case, the interest on the new loan was about $700 per month less than the current loan. I look to see at what point the interest savings equals $7,300.

Let's say it's in eleven months. I would then view this as having an eleven-month pay-back period. If I plan to hold the building longer than eleven months, the refinance makes sense.

The second perspective concerns the return on investment. Let's say that the refinance cost is $7,300, and rather than having this added to the new loan, you pull $7,300 out of your savings account and pay the prepayment penalty and all the loan costs. The question is what do you get for your $7,300 investment? You then need to consider your interest savings over the life of the loan. Be sure when you do this analysis that your new loan is paid off at the same time as the current loan.

For example, if your current loan was originally set to pay off in fifteen years and you have already made the first sixty payments, you have ten years left on the loan. I would then look at the new loan with a ten-year payment period before it is paid in full. With $7,300 as my denominator, I have the interest savings over ten years as my numerator. Most financial calculators can provide you an amortization schedule to figure the principal and interest. You can also ask the lending officer to provide this. I divide the numerator by ten (for each year) and then see what percentage return I get. If the number is over 20%, the refinance looks promising (if I save over $1,460 per year in interest).

Mathematical purists reading this might ask why I don't figure the net present value of the stream of monthly interest savings over a ten-year period or consider the internal rate of return. My response is that this way works for me. If you have a financial calculator that can figure out the net present value or the internal rate of return, you could also check this. You want the net present value to exceed $7,300 in our example, or the internal rate of return to meet your requirements.

Before refinancing, I factor in two other considerations. First, do I plan to sell the property in the next year or two? If so, it probably doesn't make sense to refinance. Secondly, I consider my relationship with the current lender, and ask whether I am burning a bridge that I may need in the future. Perhaps one day I'll need a lender to approve and close on a big loan to pay for a new boiler in the middle of January. In general, the lender isn't going to be happy to lose a safe, profitable loan. Nor will the lender be thrilled to be paid off and not be able to reinvest the funds at as high an interest rate as he or she had been getting. If the benefits of refinancing are marginal, I may decide to keep the original loan. Often the lender will be willing to do a "loan modification" to keep the loan. If the refinancing benefits are substantial I'll proceed, but I'll let the original lender know why I am moving the loan, in case he or she wants to make a last effort to keep me.

If you consider refinancing, shop the loan. A recent event I experienced is illuminating. I own an eighteen-unit building with a loan balance of about $270,000, and with an interest rate of 8% over a fifteen-year amortization. Naturally, I called my existing lender to see what they could do for me, and was unfortunately told "very little." I then called several other lenders where I had loans as well as a banker who had approached me about borrowing money from his bank at a recent real estate seminar. All in all, I went to five lenders. The best rate I found was 5% fixed for three years, or 5.8% fixed for five years, with adjustment based on an index after that. The loan origination fee was 2.5% of the loan amount, plus the usual loan transaction costs.

Since I was in the midst of writing this chapter, I figured that perhaps I should take my own advice. I pulled out the Yellow Pages, took the day off, and called every potential lender I could find – approximately twenty. To my surprise, I found a lender who was offering 4.75% fixed for five years, with annual adjustments after that time. I didn't care about the adjustments, because the building would be almost paid off in five years. The bottom line: it pays to check around and to negotiate on a commercial loan.

Index Adjustments and Prepayment Penalties

Two more facets of commercial loans merit attention: 1) index adjustments; and 2) prepayment penalties.

As noted already, many lenders will offer a fixed rate loan for a period of time and then base the interest rate on a published index of some kind. You, as a borrower, have two choices: 1) accept this basis of adjustment; or 2) work with the lender to get a more favorable adjustment basis. Some lenders are totally set on the index that they will use, while others offer some flexibility.

The kind of index bases I've seen are as follows:

- The prime interest rate

- The London Interbank Offering Rate (LIBOR)

- An index based on the cost of the funds of one of the federal reserve districts

- The interest rate on various treasury bills, notes, or bonds

The lender will usually add some margin or spread over and above the index rate. For example, one lender recently quoted me an adjustment of three hundred basis points, or three percentage points, over the one-year LIBOR rate. Not surprisingly, my investor friends and I have had some very boring discussions as to the merits and demerits of any particular index. Everyone had his or her favorite, and no consensus was reached. If any index was the winner, it was the federal eleventh district cost of funds.

When you borrow money, you may not have a choice of which index a lender uses. As this is written, LIBOR seems to be the favored index on commercial loans. If you have a choice of indexes, ask the lender to forward to you information on the historical performance of the indexes. Choose the one that's lowest and/or has more stability in its fluctuations. If you don't have a choice, try to negotiate as low an adjustment as you can.

In my recent refinance efforts, one of the lenders offered me the prime interest rate plus .25% (twenty-five basis points.) The rate would fluctuate monthly. I asked for a chart showing the performance of the prime over a twenty-year period. I was dismayed to see that the prime rate rose rapidly or dropped quickly, depending on the lending climate. I knew I'd be pacing the floor with worry as the prime rate climbed three percentage points in a year, and I could do nothing about it except pay more interest. Some of my friends were really hurt by the 20% plus prime rate in the early 1980s. The bottom line: if you have a choice, carefully check your index adjustment.

A second area of concern relates to how a lender sets the prepayment penalty. Most investors I know shop interest rates and adjustment factors and rarely ask about the prepayment penalty, but instead take this as a given. Prepayment penalties are an impediment if you want to refinance the loan or sell the property.

My current commercial real estate loans either have no prepayment penalty or a penalty of sixty to ninety days interest. In the event I refinance the property, my lenders have always waived the prepayment penalty if I used them to refinance the loan. Of course, the new loan then had a new prepayment penalty written into the note.

In one of my Arizona investments, a special prepayment penalty clause is written into the note that always causes alarm bells to go off whenever I hear these words from a potential lender: YIELD MAINTENANCE PREPAYMENT PENALTY.

Under the Yield Maintenance Prepayment Penalty, the lender expects to get a certain yield on the loan for the loan amortization period (e.g., ten years, fifteen years, etc.). If interest rates go down and you want to refinance the loan, the lender will want to get the expected return for the ten-year or fifteen-year period. An example will make this clear:

On the property noted above, the original loan was $809,000 at 9.75% interest amortized over twenty years (the loan was originated in 1993). Interest rates have been well below 9.75% for several years. Unfortunately, the loan has a yield maintenance prepayment penalty. After eight and a half years, the loan balance is $600,000. If we were to sell the property or refinance it, the prepayment penalty would be $60,750, more than 10% of the current balance. Ouch! Fortunately, the prepayment penalty was imposed for only the first ten years of the loan, so we were able to refinance after the tenth anniversary.

Another thing I don't like about Yield Maintenance Prepayment Penalties is that you can't prepay even an extra dime when you make your monthly mortgage payment. This is entirely unsatisfactory to me, as I always put something extra in each of my mortgage payments to help pay down the loan.

If you are considering a loan with a Yield Maintenance Prepayment Penalty, you might ask the lender to structure the loan in two pieces – a first mortgage with a fixed interest rate and a Yield Maintenance Prepayment Penalty, and a second mortgage with an adjustable rate and a small prepayment penalty. This is a way for you to reduce your prepayment liability.

My general rule: avoid Yield Maintenance Prepayment Penalties unless they're your only option.

Flavor of the Day Loans: Interest-Only and Negative Amortization Loans

I got a call a few months ago from a loan broker who told me about some "fantastic" new loan programs his company had put in place. He knew I'd just love their deals, and he could show me how I would be able to reduce my monthly payments dramatically and substantially increase my cash flow. Could he come to my house and show me his bells and whistles? I said, "Sure, come on by."

Loan #1 was what he called an interest-only loan. With this loan, I would only pay interest on the loan amount, not on the principal. For example, if I borrowed $120,000 at 10%, the annual interest would be $12,000, or $1,000 per month. This would lower my payment and increase my monthly positive cash flow. After a few years (three or five years – my choice), the loan would adjust and I'd then be paying principal and interest. At this time, the monthly payment would go up. With this approach, the building would qualify for a larger loan and I'd keep my monthly payments down. The loan broker could hardly contain himself.

The next loan type was even better. I currently have a loan on the thirty-six-unit building where the principal and interest payment is about $5,500 per month. The interest was 6% fixed. The broker told me I could get a loan from his company with an interest rate of about 4.25%, adjustable monthly based on an index. The monthly payment was around $2,300 per month. That number seemed so low, I took out my pocket calculator and figured that the monthly payment was even less than the 4.25% interest rate would require.

"Why is the monthly payment so low?" I inquired. The broker told me that the loan was really a negative amortizing loan. The monthly payment at a minimum should really be about $2,800 per month, and the lender would tack approximately $500 per month on to my principal balance at a future date. He argued that my interest rate would be lower, my monthly payments would drop precipitously, and my cash flow would increase. How could I go wrong?

The broker left a package of sales materials, and I politely escorted him to the door.

As I thought about it, I didn't like either kind of loan. My own bias is that I like amortizing loans where principal is paid every month and I can envision paying off part of my loan balance every month. I like the thought of a paid-off building producing cash flow. Neither of these loans did that.

Here's my take on interest-only loans:

For some borrowers, the interest-only loan is great. If you want to qualify for as high a loan amount as possible with the lowest monthly payment, this is a possibility. If you are planning on owning the property for a short period of time and selling it at a higher price, an interest-only loan will maximize your profit. If you can put the extra monthly cash flow into investments that perform better than your loan's interest rate, then go for it.

The downside of interest only-loans worries me. What if we're in a real estate bubble and the property value declines? You could have negative equity in the property – the loan amount due might be higher than your property value. If you plan to hold the building a long time or if you live in it, the future interest rate adjustment can hurt you, especially considering the historically low fixed rate loans now available. When you have a traditional amortizing loan, you know you are making progress every month paying off the loan. You are building equity. When you are paying interest only, you are never making progress paying off the loan balance. You are giving up one of the four financial benefits of real estate. The rates I noticed for interest-only loans seem in general slightly higher than comparable loans where the loan pays both principal and interest.

The advantages of the negatively amortizing loan the broker presented to me are the same as the interest-only loan: higher loan amounts approved, lower monthly payments, and improved monthly cash flow.

The downside is even worse than with the interest-only loan. The loan balance grows every month, and this can lead to negative equity even more quickly. As the man in the commercial says, "You can pay me now, or you can pay me later." My preference is to pay now rather than have regrets later.

Final Words on Financing

Overall, the financing you have on a property is a key ingredient in the success or failure of the investment. It's to your advantage to have a complete package available to the lender, so that it's easy for the lender to say yes to your loan request. Shop the market wisely to get the best deal you can from your lender. A quarter of a percentage point on a million dollar loan adds up to a lot of interest over a five- or ten-year period.

With the financing in place and the various other contingencies met, you are now ready to finalize, or close, the purchase agreement. Let's move ahead to this in Chapter 14.

14

THE FINAL DESTINATION: CLOSING

Once you have your commitment letter regarding the financing, and you have cleared all the contingencies, you are well on the path to closing the deal. Either you or your attorney will want to see a title report on the property to make sure some unforeseen nuisance, like a mechanic's lien or a dispute related to the property, won't haunt you when you become the owner. If a blemish is found during the title search, get it resolved before the closing, or at least find out what the problem is. In all likelihood, your lender will insist that you have clear title prior to loan closing. If you buy a property with a title problem and you don't correct it, plan on dealing with it again when you sell that property.

I do not attend closings. I am superstitious. I attended the closing for the house in Pittsburgh and that turned out to be an awful investment. So when I bought the six-unit in Chicago, I refused to attend the closing. I'm on a roll. Every property I bought after the house in Pittsburgh has worked out well. That's seventeen profitable purchases in a row. Not attending closings sure makes a difference for me. I am up front with my attorneys and lenders about not attending closings. They know that all the documents have to be ready a few days ahead of time for me to review.

229

Having reviewed many closing documents, I find them incredibly boring and chockful of legalese. I do pay close attention to the closing statement, though. It enumerates the purchase price, how much money goes to the seller, and all the costs that I will incur as a purchaser.

The closing statement also contains the prorations for real estate taxes, utilities, rent, and security deposits transferred by the seller. I rework all the numbers to my satisfaction. I have caught many questionable items in my reviews that have required immediate answers. I've been disappointed to find that about half of the closing statements need to be revised. The errors relate to incorrect prorations or fees that I am being charged that I don't believe are my responsibility. I also review the note to make sure the interest rate and other terms of the loan are what I expected.

When closing in this way, I sign whatever documents I can (sometimes a notary is necessary), and give my attorney a power-of-attorney letter to sign on my behalf. I've rarely had problems closing because of this. I've made sure that everything is in place, and the closing is just a matter of everyone signing the documents and the various monies being transferred to the right place.

Once when I sold a building, a messenger service delivered the payoff monies with a certified check to my lender on a Friday afternoon. The lender's employee signed the receipt and managed to misplace the check. It was never found. About a month later, I started getting loan delinquency notices, and late charges and other fees started piling up. The lender was less than receptive when I phoned and explained the situation.

After a few months of wrangling, I was able to obtain a copy of the delivery receipt with the employee's signature, and documentation from the title company that closed the transaction. The title company issued a new check. The lender cried "uncle" and waived all the charges. Unfortunately, the lender also tarnished my credit report by stating that I was three months delinquent on a real estate loan (an R-3). I wasn't aware of this until I applied for a loan to acquire a new property, and the new lender asked me to explain the loan delinquency.

Regrettably, the errant lender had been sold to a bank. The bank that acquired the lender could not find any documentation on the transaction and so refused to correct my credit report.

Nevertheless, my loan was approved, and I couldn't claim damages against the lender. What it amounted to was just a lot of aggravation and wasted time. Other than that, all of my closings have gone smoothly. As noted above, they are primarily a simple matter of the closer passing documents around for signatures.

In the event you are doing a double closing – purchasing a property and flipping it at a profit to a buyer – my advice is to use an attorney and a closing officer who are familiar with what has to be done at double closings. I have been in the end-buyer position at a double closing, and my attorneys have reported that the seller was upset that somebody made a quick profit on his or her underpriced property. The seller would rather have made that profit. A few words of advice: check your state laws on disclosure in the case where you are flipping a property, as written disclosure may be required in your state.

Once the closing is over, you are the brand-new owner of the property. You get the keys, the leases, the deed, and letters of introduction from the seller. You will now proceed with your original plan for the property, which could be:

- Sell it right away

- Rehab it and rent it

- Rehab it and sell it

- Develop it

• Keep it as it is and manage it

If you are going to resell it at a higher price or better terms, you know what you are going to do. If you are going to rehab it or develop it, you know what your next step is: you start the rehab/development process. If you are going to keep it, you will have the glorious experience of managing it.

Let's move on to the next chapter.

15

"MANAGEMENT IS THE DREGS"

When I had the six-unit building in Chicago inspected in December 1981, the inspector was very thorough. After taking notes for three hours, his final comments were, "It's a good building; you'll do O.K. I personally hate management. Management is the dregs."

I wondered, "What am I getting myself into buying an apartment building?" My two years of training at the University of Chicago in business administration didn't include one minute of instruction in setting rents, showing apartments, or evicting non-paying tenants.

What qualified me to manage an apartment building? What was I going to do?

I was scared. In response to this fear, I went to my local bookstore and bought several books on managing apartment buildings. During the two months before the closing, I read all of them. I developed forms and leases, had rental ads ready to go in the event of vacancies, and even spent my weekends looking at available rentals in the neighborhood, so I could price my units correctly. Still the final words of the inspector haunted me. Had I gotten in way over my head?

The closing was March 8, 1982. My first official act as a real estate manager occurred that evening, when I had to shovel four inches of snow off the building's sidewalk. I also slipped a note under each tenant's door introducing myself and providing my phone number in the event of maintenance needs.

Later in the week, I began calling tenants to set up meetings in order to get better acquainted. I was into the heart of management. The meetings with tenants went better than expected. For the most part, they were nice, reasonable human beings. Still, meeting with them wasn't easy for me. For one thing, asking if everything was O.K. in their apartments generated a lot of work orders. I also had to inform the tenants that I planned to upgrade the building, and their rents would be upgraded as well. My plans were to install an intercom with a buzzer so tenants could know who was in the lobby and buzz people in. Under the prior owner, visitors simply walked right into the building and knocked on a tenant's door.

Other plans included landscaping the front, putting up new storm windows, installing washers and dryers, and upgrading the electrical capacity of the building.

Surprisingly, the tenants were excited about everything. To my shock, they all stayed on and agreed to the rent increase. One gentleman made the error of telling me his checkbook was open after I described the changes. His rent magically went up an extra $10 a month. I made the promised improvements and I increased the rents. My real estate management career had begun.

I still think about that statement, "Management is the dregs." Twenty-plus years into the business of residential apartment management, I believe I understand the basis of this comment.

Residential management takes time – lots of it. Showing rental units means devoting weekend and evening hours to meeting with prospective renters and selling them on living in your building. Many prospects never bother to show up. Then come the repairs that need to be done. Standard maintenance, like cutting bushes and grass, or cleaning, is necessary. Rents must be collected and deposited. Bills have to be paid. It takes time, and the job never ends. Worse yet, a small number of tenants are very adversarial in nature. Their life's purpose seems to be making the landlord miserable. I believe this is what the inspector meant. What he didn't say is how important management is, and that it is indeed a survivable occupation.

My experience has been in managing residential real estate, and my comments in this chapter focus on that. Many in my peer group have moved into investing in office buildings, retail, warehouse, and industrial real estate ownership. I often hear relief in their voices when they express how easy management of a warehouse or industrial property with just one tenant is.

When you acquire a property you plan to hold, you then have to decide how you will manage it. Your initial choices are simple: you can do it yourself or you can pay a management company to do it for you. Each approach has advantages and disadvantages.

If you hire a management company, you gain the services of someone experienced in the business who knows how to operate a property. You also gain free time and you hope you'll have less aggravation. On the negative side, your expenses will probably increase with a management company. In my experience, the management companies charged me anywhere from 4% to 10% of gross revenue for the privilege of managing my building. I also was charged an hourly maintenance rate that exceeded what their paid staff made for any maintenance requests. If I wanted a major capital project done, such as rehabbing an apartment unit, they'd hire out the contractors and supervise the work, and I would pay them a general contractor's fee.

In addition, you are obviously giving up the control of the property when you hire a management company. While the company may confer with you on important decisions, the appointed manager will be responsible for day-to-day management issues, such as renting units, collecting rents, evicting delinquent tenants, paying bills, and so forth. Depending on your relationship with the management company, you may have very little knowledge of what is going on day-to-day in your asset.

I have used both approaches. Over the years, I have employed the use of seven management companies to run buildings. I have also either managed the properties directly or hired my own staff to operate buildings. My preference is to manage my properties myself or hire my own staff to operate the properties. My attitude is that I care more about the properties than anyone else. I have a good feel for how many vacancies I have and what I need to do to rent the units. I know what is happening in the buildings. I sign all the checks.

Of the seven management companies I used, some were better than others. In general, all the companies did the best they could, but none of them cared about my properties as much as I did.

Unless you don't have the time or interest, my recommendation is that you manage your own properties.

However, management is not for everyone. If you are a professional in a busy position, direct management may not be for you. If you don't like showing rental properties or dealing with irate tenants (this happens no matter how hard you try), hire a management company. If you really want peaceful evenings and weekends, don't manage – hire out. If the thought of fixing clogged toilets or cleaning dirty stoves and refrigerators is abhorrent to you, avoid direct management. (Note: you can hire contractors to do these services.) Realistically, though, management is survivable and is not that difficult.

If you decide to use a management company, I recommend that you talk to several before selecting one. Ask for referrals from people in the business. When you meet them, they will want to walk through your property with you and give you recommendations on how they can bring your property to its highest and best use. Check the references they give you, or better yet, contact the owners of other properties the company manages. Pick the firm you feel will best serve your interests. When you sign a management contract, be sure to insert a provision that allows you to terminate the agreement within thirty days.

If you use a management company, you need to monitor how well it manages your property. Keep track of the occupancy and of the company's response to maintenance requests.

Check whether the rents they set are in keeping with the area. Review their monthly status reports. You are paying that company to manage your property, so follow up to make sure you are getting good value for your money.

If you're on the "I'll manage myself" side of the ledger, I'd strongly recommend that you read some of the many useful books available in your library or bookstore. In this chapter, I'll give you the key lessons I've learned from managing hundreds of units and thousands of tenants. Even if you own several properties, I believe it's a good idea to read books on how to manage – they might contain ideas worth money to you. To be honest, though, most of my landlord friends have never read a "how to manage" book. They simply bought their first property and started managing from there. Appendix 1 has a listing of books I've found helpful and thought-provoking.

If you do it yourself, you have two choices: 1) you can literally do everything yourself; or 2) you can hire staff and build an organization to do it for you. You then become a manager of managers.

If you own a few buildings with, let's say, twenty apartment units, you don't have enough to have a staff person. You might, however, offer a tenant a rental discount to help with janitorial needs or minor maintenance requests. The tenant may even be able to show apartments for you.

As your size increases, you can hire staff. Edward N. Kelley, in *Practical Apartment Management,* talks about having one full-time employee for every sixty units. I figure that if a management company charges 5% or 6% of gross revenues, that's what I could afford. For buildings of twenty or more units, I have a resident manager. The resident manager gets a free apartment and may receive compensation over and above that. Obviously, for a sixty-seven or seventy-seven unit building, a rent-free apartment isn't enough, so I provide additional compensation. My resident managers show apartments, take applications, perform janitorial functions, respond to maintenance requests, and help resolve tenant problems.

In addition, I have a supervisory manager who oversees the day-to-day activities of all the buildings, and I have an employee totally dedicated to performing maintenance. I oversee everything and make all the major decisions (setting rent levels, when and how to rehab a building, where to hold the holiday party, etc.). My overall costs come in at about 6%.

The key to my system is finding and keeping good resident managers. A good one makes your life easy. A lousy one can drive you crazy with worry and anger. Moneybags gave me my first piece of advice regarding resident managers: "Make sure they're honest and don't drink." Over the years, I've had good ones and bad ones. If you have a good one, do everything you can to keep him or her. If it's not working out, terminate the relationship as quickly as possible. Sources for finding resident managers are the existing tenant population, referrals from hardware stores, retirement centers, and anywhere else that comes to mind. My best source over the years has been my existing tenant population.

Here are some important lessons I've learned from twenty-plus years of hands-on management:

Your building is only as good as its tenants.

If you rent to anyone who applies (and doesn't even have a security deposit), you're not screening your tenants and will probably have problems. It's important to screen all applications based on your rental standards, so that you are satisfied with the quality of tenant. All prospects and applicants should be held to the same standards. I'd rather have a vacancy than a problem tenant. Set your standards high.

Rent is due the first of the month; a five-day grace period is allowed.

Tenants who are unable to pay on time must work cooperatively to develop a payment plan. If we haven't heard from a tenant by the sixth of the month, we issue a five-day notice to pay the delinquent rent or move. If the tenant hasn't paid or done anything after the five days are up, we immediately file with the county to get an eviction court date. The tenants know we mean business. Over 95% of the rents due are collected by the fifth of the month. We have few, if any, five-day notices to deliver. We actually go to eviction court about once every two years. When there is a problem, like a job loss or job transfer, we work out a payment plan with the tenant.

The important thing is that you need to be aggressive in rent collection. Otherwise, it may take months to get a nonpaying tenant evicted from an apartment, especially if the person declares bankruptcy. I can't tell you the number of times I've heard from some landlord that a tenant who owes thousands of dollars is finally being evicted because the landlord put off doing anything to evict the tenant.

Management can be stressful.

Some tenants have major senses of entitlement where they make constant demands to have repairs done right away, even ones that are a much lower priority than other maintenance needs. They scream and yell and are persistent in their never-ending efforts to have their own personal Taj Mahal. Tenants like these aren't fun.

There have been three times in my management career when I've had to tell my wife that I loved her, and I might not come back alive from a difficult eviction or landlord-tenant issue. Some tenants are very confrontational, especially when they are drunk. Avoid dealing with drunk tenants.

In my early days as a manager, I was very sensitive to every tenant demand, no matter how unreasonable. But now I feel more like a duck in water – I just let the water roll off my back and move on to the next project. It no longer bothers me when tenants make fun of my name, calling me Mr. Cockroach or Mr. Pot Roast. I do try as much as possible to be responsive to my tenants and any building maintenance needs.

Every landlord I know has his or her own horror story about the tenant from hell. However, I have noticed very few of them getting out of the business due to an aggravating tenant. Most are busy acquiring more properties.

Your tenant is not your friend. You have a business relationship, not a personal one.

As a landlord with a paid staff to deal with tenants, I realize that it's easy for me to follow my own advice here. My problems arise when one of my resident managers befriends a tenant. They may go barhopping or start doing other social things together. Guidelines have to be set for your staff. It is very frustrating when employees have a personal relationship with a tenant. That tenant gets better service and may not get the same rent increase as everyone else. All tenants should be treated equally.

This leads me to a major management "no-no": Don't have sexual relations with your tenants or your employees. If nature must take its course, either have that tenant move or get out of managing the property. These are the days of sexual harassment lawsuits. Keep strictly to business, and require that your employees do the same. I have each employee sign a form stating that he or she has read my policies on employee/tenant relations and agrees to comply with them.

Respect and honor your vendors.

I'm told my vendors very much appreciate me because I pay them quickly with good checks. They know I keep my word, and I know that if I have a high priority project, they will drop whatever they're doing and get my project done at a reasonable price. They are also flexible if my cash flow is a little tight and I must write a postdated check. I go out of my way to pay promptly any moonlighter who paints an apartment with two hours' notice or fixes a serious plumbing problem immediately after I call. These are golden resources that I want to keep.

You don't need a highly mechanical aptitude to manage a building. Home repair do-it-yourself books proved useful to me. I would often read them before a contractor showed up to bid a job. Usually the contractor thought I knew what he was talking about when I started asking questions.

If it comes down to a choice between managing property or preserving your marriage, my vote goes to preserving your marriage.

Real estate management is a demanding and time-consuming job. If you have one or two smaller properties within a few minutes of your home, that's one thing. But when you have ten or more properties, and you find yourself running out every night and on weekends to show rentals or fix something, it can be wearing. On numerous occasions, I've sat in empty apartments waiting for prospective tenants to show up, to no avail. When I get home, my wife innocently asks how everything went, and Mr. Grump just glares.

I know of property owners who have developed marital difficulties because of the time-consuming, stressful nature of real estate management. Your marriage or domestic partner arrangement and your family relationships are the most important things you have and should be valued.

In the past, I've tried to encourage beginning moguls to get into real estate. One of my former tenants became motivated and, with some encouragement from me, bought a couple of buildings. After a few years, he was fed up with tenants writing bad checks and damaging the units. He recognized that he didn't have the temperament for management, and sold the buildings. I respected him for trying and for valuing his marriage over the potential profits from real estate.

Let me reiterate: real estate management is not for everyone.

Have a transition plan in the event that you die or become disabled.

A friend of mine owned several apartment buildings. He was slim, and exercised religiously. One day after his morning run, he sat down in his favorite easy chair and proceeded to have a massive, fatal heart attack. His unfortunate widow not only had to deal with the painful loss of her husband, but found herself immediately thrust into the role of manager for the buildings. My friend did not have a transition plan, and his widow didn't know where to begin. She didn't even know where he kept the keys.

This situation is avoidable. Death and disability are facts of life. Actually, you are much more likely to be disabled during your productive years than you are to die. A transition plan is immensely helpful to those around you who will have to take over the management of your properties. This plan involves identifying how you want the properties operated, who is responsible for what, and who the key vendors are. It also involves appointing someone you trust to be a back-up signee on your checks.

Putting together a transition plan takes time and thought. That's the bad news. The good news is that if the need arises, the plan will be very helpful and your loved ones will be very grateful.

Several years ago I spent a number of days developing a transition plan. It was around twenty pages, and directed my wife on exactly who to call and under what circumstances. I even provided assessments of the strengths and shortcomings of each vendor. After I had stressed how important it was that my wife review it, she glanced it over quickly and cheerfully informed me that if I died she wouldn't want the buildings and would sell them at a bargain basement price. I was very upset. Her comment was made to get a rise out of me.... She was certainly successful.

We are not immortal or invulnerable. So, please, have a transition plan.

Value your tenants.

Tenants have tremendous power. They choose to occupy your space. They have the power to make your life difficult or pleasant. And most importantly, their rent checks pay the bills and the mortgage, and possibly put a little money in your pocket at the end of the month. I've always tried to be fair and responsive to my tenants. I appreciate that they occupy my space.

When you operate a building, you hope to get it under control so management becomes routine, rather than a difficult challenge. When the building is under control, the next question is: under what circumstances do you keep it or sell it?

16

WHY SELL?

Once you own a property, you have two basic decisions as to what to do with it: hold onto it, or sell it.

I've owned several properties that I have made the decision to sell based on various reasons. Some of my reasons have had to do with good circumstances; some with less fortunate circumstances.

In my view, there are good circumstances under which to sell a building, neutral circumstances, and unfortunate circumstances.

Good Circumstances

1) You find an investment opportunity that yields a higher return on investment.

For example, let's say you own an eight-unit building free and clear that produces $40,000 of net operating income per year. Its market value is $400,000. Not a bad situation. The opportunity comes along to purchase a forty-unit building for $2,000,000 in a more favorable location. Your numerator/denominator analysis indicates that with a $400,000 down payment, your annual return (positive cash and principal reduction) would be $60,000. This is a 15% return versus a 10% return on the property you currently own. It makes sense to sell and to execute a 1031 tax deferred exchange on the property. The two buildings I sold in Chicago and the twenty-unit I sold in Milwaukee both reflect this situation.

You might ask whether refinancing 80% of the building at 8% interest and then using the refinance proceeds as your down payment would make more sense. This is a valid question. The source of the down payment for many of my purchases in fact came from refinancing existing buildings. If you have enough equity to raise the down payment, you may not need to sell a property. If you feel that you have a winner and want to keep it, refinancing may be the simple solution. Nevertheless, if you want a larger portfolio, it will grow more quickly if you sell a building and acquire a larger property. You are using all your equity and trading up to a larger property.

The second point relates to annually evaluating the return on equity on your investment. In essence, you need to increase the denominator every year, based on the market value of the building. An example will make this clear. The first property I bought was a six-unit building, purchased for $85,700. My partner and I made a $25,000 down payment. Over the years the property value went up, as did the cash flow.

Let's say that it generated $5000 of positive cash flow and principal reduction in Year #1. Simple arithmetic shows it had a 20% return on investment ($5000 divided by $25,000 down payment). When we move the clock ahead fifteen years, the property is paid off and is now valued at $360,000, producing $25,000 of income. You have two perspectives from which to view the investment return of this building. You might say that you now have a 100% return on your original investment of $25,000. Or you could say that you have a investment return of about 7% ($25,000 income divided by current equity of $360,000). In the latter case, a better return on your money might be found elsewhere.

In my view, you should use the "what is my current equity?"

value as your denominator when evaluating the performance of a building. You have to look at its performance right now, assuming its current value, not on a historic purchase price or potential future value. Since larger properties are valued based on their capitalization rate (cap rate), eventually when your properties are paid off, they will yield the cap rate, which may be 5%, 7%, 10%, and so forth.

2) You decide you no longer want to own a certain type of property, but instead want a different type of real estate investment.

One of the reasons I sold the four-unit and the six-unit in Chicago was that direct management was taking up too much of my time, and I figured that with larger buildings I could hire staff to operate the properties, while I managed the staff.

The numbers worked out, and those sales proved to be correct decisions. Other owners I know who are in their sixties have sold their residential portfolios and executed I.R.S. 1031 tax deferred exchanges into industrial properties, or into purchasing the physical structure that houses a Walgreen's drug store. These sellers have stayed in the real estate game, but have gotten a personal benefit – more free time – by selling. They lease out the properties, and the tenants operate them. In this situation, you are gaining something based on your personal needs at the time.

3) Your portfolio is large enough that you can liquidate it at your leisure, pay whatever taxes are due, and invest the remaining funds in U.S. Treasury Bonds – the safest investment in the world.

The income that will be generated is more than enough to meet your financial needs. Thus, you are in a position where you have secure income every month, and the only work you need to do is open up mail, which contains checks, and deposit the money. This is the epitome of financial independence.

One might argue that when you do this you are reducing your return on investment, and making a sizeable contribution to Uncle Sam. This is a valid point, but you gain tremendous peace of mind knowing that your overall position is so strong that you never will have to worry about money. I am assuming here that the U.S. government will be around for awhile and that it will be honorable in making its debt payments.

4) Someone offers you a very high price for your property.

Neutral Circumstances

1) Real estate markets vary.

The Midwest has a history of stability, whereas investors who own property in the Phoenix area describe the market there as "boom or bust." I am surprised and dismayed to learn of home buyers who purchase their property one year, only to find out a few years later that the property's value has declined, and they don't even have any personal equity in their home. Having talked with other investors, I have learned that this situation has also occurred on the East and West coasts.

If you are a good tea-leaf reader, you may figure your market has topped out and it is time to sell. You sell, take your profit, hold your cash in conservative investments, and re-invest in real estate when the market is more favorable to the buyer. I've never done this, although I did feel that the Phoenix market was near bottom in 1993 and encouraged my cousin to buy there. It ended up being very good timing.

If you have a gut feeling that your market will decline and you don't want to go along for the ride, it's time to get out. I have put this into the neutral circumstances category because you are getting out of something rather than immediately improving your circumstances. You are in a holding pattern.

2) You've exhausted the depreciation allowance the government grants you and can no longer take the property as a tax deduction.

You therefore sell it and execute a 1031 deferred tax exchange to purchase a larger like-kind property where you can again take a depreciation deduction on your tax return.

3) You've syndicated a property to investors, and at the time of syndication, you committed to sell the property by a certain time in the future (e.g., in ten years).

To uphold the agreement, you must sell the property.

Unfortunate Circumstances

Charles Dickens' great novel, *A Tale of Two Cities*, begins with the line, "It was the best of times; it was the worst of times." Sometimes we, or our properties, fall into "the worst of times," and our best option may be to sell. Let's briefly consider some of these unfortunate situations that may put us or our heirs in a position where selling is the best option.

1) You die, and your heirs want nothing to do with ownership or management.

They want the money; estate taxes are due. In this situation, your properties are likely candidates for sale.

2) You become disabled and cannot operate the properties.

You've established a transition plan, and your spouse, domestic partner, or some other capable person knows how to take over management of the properties. Your heir-apparent, however, wants nothing to do with the properties and may choose to liquidate them. A second factor in the event of total disability concerns the kind of insurance you personally have. If you become disabled, hopefully you've purchased insurance to cover your personal expenses. Health insurance helps defray the costs of medical care, long-term disability insurance replaces the income you receive from the occupation you actively perform, and long-term care insurance helps pay the high cost of nursing home care (about $60,000 per year in metropolitan Chicago at the time of this writing) or home healthcare.

The financial burden of a disabling disease or injury could put you in the unfortunate position of having to sell your properties.

3) You determine that your location is deteriorating and values are declining.

As you recall, someone got angry at one of my tenants in December 1993 and burned down one of my Aurora properties. This thoughtless person could easily have killed ten people sleeping there at the time, plus killing or injuring the firefighters. I made a decision the next day to liquidate my property in that location over time, and redeploy the monies to a better location.

The crime rate in Aurora bothered me, also. I'd had another situation there around six months earlier, where a local gang member got into a dispute with members of a rival gang and kicked in the kitchen door of an apartment in my building. He told my terrified tenants to duck, and then started firing shots at the other gangbangers. I had to replace the door and placate my tenants. In my view, the location was getting worse, and I decided to sell and pay the long-term capital gains. The properties were profitable, but I didn't need the burden of worrying that someone in my building might meet a violent death. You should pay attention to your location.

4) Your property is losing money, and you see no hope for the future.

Your best option is to sell. If you unfortunately find yourself in this position, be prepared to sell at a loss or at least a minimal gain. No one I know is such an angel that he or she goes out looking for "loser" properties to buy in order to fulfill his or her life's purpose of bailing out needy owners. In this circumstance, you can only do the best you can.

I know of owners who have sold free and clear buildings for a dollar. A friend's dad owned a building in a deteriorating area in Chicago. One day an irate tenant complained about the lack of maintenance, and my friend's dad told him if he thought he could do a better job running the property, he could have it for one dollar. Sold American! The tenant lost the building about six months later; the negative cash flow ate up all the savings he had.

I would think twice about walking away from a building you cannot sell. If the property is foreclosed on by the lien holders, or is lost at a tax sale, this information will follow you whenever you try to get loans on new properties. With careful analysis, you won't be in a position of owning a permanent negative cash flow property.

5) You are tired of managing real estate and don't have confidence in management companies.

Your way out of management is to liquidate as noted above, then sell and exchange into less management-intensive properties such as industrial properties or buying a Walgreen's. Unfortunately, if you take the position, "I AM TIRED OF MANAGING AND MUST SELL," you are putting yourself in a weak position. You may not get as high a price as you'd hoped for.

251

6) You are forced to sell for legal reasons.

Regrettably, there are many such reasons:

- You declare bankruptcy and have to liquidate your assets

- To settle a debt, you must liquidate an asset in order to raise money

- You sell as part of a divorce settlement

- Government building inspectors shut your building down, and you don't have the resources to bring the property into compliance

- Foreclosure by your lender

- Other legal reasons

In the above situations, all you can do is to try to get the highest price you can. Under such circumstances, you sell, lick your wounds, and move on.

7) You don't get along with your partners, so you sell to gain peace of mind.

PART III

RUMINATIONS
FROM THE MIND OF
A MINI-MOGUL

17

How to Make Money in Real Estate: Let Me Count the Ways

Part III will focus on topics that didn't fit neatly into Parts I or II. These include a discussion of ways to make money in real estate, how the extensive reach of federal, state, and local government affects real estate investors, structuring partnerships, protecting your investment from major losses, environmental concerns, and several other thoughts and comments. Let's start with the good news: how to make money in real estate.

One of the wonderful things about real estate investing is that it offers so many different ways to make money. I have developed a list below describing several ways you can make money in real estate. Maybe you'll get a new idea from it.

I've been a conservative investor who has been very pedestrian along the path to becoming a mogul. I buy well-located buildings and plan to hold on to them forever. I learned most of what I know from books or from observing my fellow investors. The following list is from an investment perspective. It doesn't include other ways individuals make money by performing real estate services such as brokerage, legal services, insurance brokerage, mortgage lending, consulting, appraisal, architectural, or engineering services.

Ways to Make Money in Real Estate Investing

1) Buy at a discount from market and sell at a higher price.

The sale can be an immediate one (a flip), or it can be made shortly after you purchase. This includes putting an underpriced property under contract and assigning the contract to another buyer for a profit.

Many investors do this. You are looking for a real estate bargain here. The bargain might come from a foreclosure situation, an estate sale, an underpriced property, a HUD auction, a bankruptcy, an IRS sale, or a tax scavenger sale, to name a few possibilities. The key is to buy well under market, so you have room to sell at a higher price and put some money in your pocket.

2) Buy at market, fix the property up, and sell it at a profit.

A lot of investors I know do this. They seek out a well-located, run-down property and then judiciously upgrade it and raise its value. Sometimes they sell it, but most of the time they keep it for income and future appreciation. Some developers take this a step further. They purchase a property, tear it down, and build a new structure, which they then sell for a handsome profit. You obviously need to know what price the location will support before doing this.

3) Buy at market and then improve the property by better management.

You either increase income or reduce expenses. Rather than improving the property through structural or cosmetic changes as above, you increase the cash flow through better management. On the revenue side, you might simply increase rents, include laundry service and vending machines, or charge more for parking. On the expense side, you might find ways to decrease utility costs, repair costs, management costs, etc. The increased cash flow results in increased valuation.

With this approach, you are increasing both the cash flow and the value of the property.

4) Buy a winner.

Here you buy a property that produces an acceptable return on investment and appreciates over time. You make cash flow now and build equity for the future.

5) Buy at market value in a hot area or market and wait for increased cash flow and appreciation.

The four-unit I bought near De Paul University is an example of this. It lost money in the beginning, but appreciated well beyond my greatest expectations.

6) Convert an existing property to a higher and better use.

Some examples would include:
- Buy a large parcel of land at one price and then subdivide and sell it off in pieces adding up to a higher price, as Mr. W.D. did.
- Convert an apartment building into condominiums or into an office building.
- Convert a vacant industrial building into loft apartments.

7) Lease a property with an option to buy at a set price.

You then re-lease it and eventually sell it for a higher price than your option price.

8) Lease a property at one rent, re-lease it to someone at a higher rent, and pocket the difference.

One of my landlord cohorts is notorious for his low rents. He dreads vacancies, and will do almost anything to get his apartments rented. His rents are about 20% under-percentage under market. One day I offered to rent one of his apartments and told him I'd pay one year's rent in advance. I told him his rent was ridiculously low, and that I was willing to pay the whole year's rent up front in order to have the opportunity to lease it to someone else for a much higher rent. He mumbled to himself, but wouldn't rent it to me. He chose to give some tenant a bargain. Leasing at one rent and re-leasing at a higher rent can often be done with commercial properties.

9) Buy at a certain price with seller or assumable bank financing, and sell at the same price, but with a higher interest rate.

You make money on the interest difference. This can be referred to as a wraparound mortgage, or an all-inclusive deed or trust.

10) Buy delinquent property taxes.

Depending on the area and the laws of that jurisdiction, you can earn interest rates well above the norm, and have the opportunity to foreclose.

11) Develop.

Developers either build from the ground up, or do major renovations. If the developer sells, the developer makes a profit over and above his or her costs. Or the developer might opt to keep the property and make a positive cash flow and acceptable return on investment based on the revenues.

12) Make an agreement with an owner which gives you the option to purchase the property for a predetermined price.

You will typically have to give the seller "consideration" (a negotiated amount of money) to have the option to buy within a certain date. Hopefully you will be able to sell the property for a higher price than your option price, the consideration, and any other costs you may incur.

13) Become a syndicator.

You can put together deals where you and your investors purchase properties. There are many ways to make money as a syndicator, including acquisition fees, management fees, and gaining a percentage of the property in your role as the syndicator. Several of my properties have investors. More about this approach will be described later in this book.

14) Assemblage.

Using this approach, you quietly acquire several pieces of property which are located either near or adjacent to each other. You are in the process of acquiring a large parcel of property that could have a higher and better use. As an example, my sixty-seven-and seventy-seven-unit buildings are located in a very desirable area of Milwaukee which is prime for condominium development. Between these two buildings is a twenty-four unit property. One day the thought popped into my head that if I acquired the twenty-four unit building, I would control a major parcel of real estate in a very desirable location. A developer might pay a pretty sum to buy all three buildings, tear them down, and build a major condominium high-rise. But when I approached the owner of the twenty-four-unit, he wasn't at all interested in selling, and, in fact, was hoping I'd sell him my two buildings.

One legendary Chicago real estate investor, Arthur Rubloff, was a master of assemblage. Over several years, he quietly assembled pieces of real estate located on the far southwest side of Chicago. After gaining control of several acres, he developed Evergreen Plaza, a very successful shopping mall.

15) Buy real estate notes at a discount so that they produce high annual yields.

For example, let's say you find someone who sold a property and took back a first mortgage for $74,000 at 7% interest amortized over a twenty-five year period, with a ten-year balloon. After a couple of years, the note holder finds a nice retirement home and determines that he needs cash to make the down payment. Most banks won't use his note as the security for a loan, and so, in order to raise money, he has to sell the note at a discount. Let's say there's $72,000 left on the note. If he wants to sell it, he may have to discount it by $10,000 or $20,000 to liquidate the note.

The investor who buys the note for $55,000 has a stream of money payments coming in that will be well above a 7% return. If you get impatient, you can resell the note and hopefully make a profit at a higher price.

A second way to make money on notes is by brokering them. For example, let's say you are able to buy a note with $100,000 left on the loan for $70,000. You may be able to flip it to another note buyer for $80,000 and make a quick $10,000.

16) Substitute collateral.

As an offshoot of buying discounted notes, you could theoretically buy discounted notes or even bonds, and substitute them as part of your down payment when you acquire a property. For example, if you could find an $80,000 note to buy for $60,000, and then find a seller who is willing to accept the note as an $80,000 down payment (or part of a larger down payment), then you have just gained $20,000 of equity. However, I've never done this, and when I've approached sellers as to how responsive they'd be to this idea, they tell me they prefer cold, hard cash.

17) Lease or sell certain rights that you, as the owner, have on the property.

These could include water rights, air rights, oil rights, and the like.

18) Buy at a market price, but get a low interest rate.

A classic case is the five-unit building I purchased in Aurora, Illinois. I paid market price (about $70,000), but got 0% financing on the loan. This helped make the cash-on-cash return very high. To make this deal even better, Uncle Sam figured I overpaid for the property, and so the 0% loan was really an interest-bearing loan. Uncle Sam allowed me to impute the interest rate of 9% even though I wasn't paying any interest. Tax breaks are always welcome.

19) Take advantage of the many government-sponsored programs.

The government offers an array of goodies which can dramatically improve the figures when you perform a numerator/denominator analysis. These benefits include reduced property taxes, grants, loans that can be forgiven, dollar-for-dollar tax credits on your income taxes, and low-interest loans. All of these help improve your bottom line.

20) Buy out existing lien holders at a substantial discount and then purchase the property.

You can gain a lot of equity using this approach. I haven't personally done this, but I know others who have paid off contractors at great discounts so they would release their mechanic's liens on a property. They then turn around and purchase the property directly from the owner, but factor in the full value of the mechanic's liens.

21) Be a hard money lender.

If you have lots of spare cash sitting around, and you are concerned about getting a higher return on your money than what is offered by the banks or treasuries, you can become a hard money real estate lender. A hard money lender makes real estate loans using his or her own money. You are essentially operating like a bank. You can reap returns in line with existing lenders, or if you wish, you can target your loans to higher risk situations and earn higher returns. You can also make loans and ask for a piece of the future appreciation. In this case, you are an equity partner.

I personally follow Shakespeare's advice in Hamlet: "Neither a borrower nor a lender be" – at least in part. I'm a borrower who pays back loans on a timely basis. I have only taken back one note to sell a building. I have never actually loaned money directly to a real estate borrower. I'm not equipped to make loans the way a bank is. Nevertheless, lending money is one additional way an investor can make money in real estate.

This completes my list. Although I'm sure it's not comprehensive, it does give an overview of many money-making opportunities in real estate. With creative thought, I'm certain you could add more ideas. Real estate provides a wealth of opportunities.

18

My Personal Philosophy: Zen Buddhism and the Practice of Real Estate Investing

Over time, many friends and investors I know have asked me whether real estate investing is compatible with my being a Zen Buddhist. I suspect their perception is that real estate investors will stop at nothing to make a good deal, any sense of morality simply doesn't exist, and greed prevails. The Buddha himself was of princely birth and gave up all his wealth when he embarked on his spiritual journey toward self-realization. Many Buddhist monks, nuns, and teachers live ascetic lives in monastic settings with very few possessions.

Before addressing this question, let's consider some of the basic principles of Zen Buddhism.[6] From the viewpoint of Zen Buddhism, each of us has an inner self, called the "Buddha nature." The Buddha nature is manifested when you are "at one" or fully absorbed in whatever activity you are doing, such as eating, working, listening, and so forth. In this state, distractions do not cloud your mind from

---

[6]Very worthwhile books for those interested in learning more about Zen Buddhism are *The Three Pillars of Zen* by Philip Kapleau (Anchor Books, 1989) and *Zen Mind, Beginner's Mind* by Shunryu Suzuki (Weatherhill, 1973).

what you are doing. One of my first teachers in Zen described Buddhist practice as being in a state of compassionate love. Your attention is fully absorbed in the activity of the moment.

Our dilemma as human beings is that there are many impediments or distractions that block us from realizing our Buddha nature. Zen Buddhists refer to these distractions as "attachments" or desires. Buddhism talks of the Four Noble Truths:

Noble Truth #1: To live is to suffer.

We all experience suffering: birth is suffering; death is suffering; getting older is suffering; physical and mental pain is suffering. Suffering surrounds us.

Noble Truth #2: The cause of this suffering is our desires.

Our desires are rooted in our ego. Examples of these desires include excessive appetite for food, sensual pleasures, money and possessions, or power. These desires dominate our behavior and cause us pain.

Noble Truth #3: Eliminate these desires and you eliminate the suffering.

If one can cease the desires, the pain and suffering stop.

Noble Truth #4: The way to cessation of desire is by following the Eightfold Noble Path:

- Right understanding

- Right thinking

- Right speech

- Right action

- Right livelihood

- Right effort

- Right mindfulness

- Right concentration

As a student, here is my own perspective: The path to freedom from suffering is through following these eight ideals. The first two ideals relate to gaining wisdom or insight. The middle three relate to morality, and the last three relate to meditation.

So, to live a life following the path of the Buddha involves a great deal of time spent meditating to purify your mind, acting in a moral way toward the world around you, and gaining wisdom by following the teachings of the Buddha.

In addition to the Four Noble Truths, various precepts serve as guides to help the Buddhist in his or her effort to be at one with the Buddha nature:

- No intentional destruction of life

- No stealing from others

- No sexual misconduct

- No lying to others

- No alcohol

By following the Eightfold Path, especially the Buddhist meditation techniques, one can break free of the bonds or attachments that cause suffering, and can reach what Buddhists aspire to – the attainment of a state of enlightenment. When a person has an enlightenment experience or becomes awakened, that person feels at one with the world. The sense of separation between the self and others disappears. The person is totally absorbed in the activity of the moment. In the book, *The Three Pillars of Zen*, one of the practitioners describes his initial breakthrough this way: " I feel free as a fish swimming in an ocean of cool clear water after being stuck in a tank of glue."

While following each of the eight paths is important, the one that best applies to the real estate investor concerns "right livelihood." First and foremost, one's livelihood should be consistent with the precepts noted above. For instance, a drug dealer selling destructive substances isn't consistent with practicing right livelihood. Neither is anything that involves killing, such as being a hunter or a butcher.

I've attended numerous Zen lectures and have read a lot about "rightful livelihood," and I haven't found anything that has disparaged the building of wealth. What is important is one's attitude in acquiring and maintaining wealth. Following the precepts of honesty and consistency and having a responsive and helpful frame of mind with regard to others should be your focus.

Wealth can be a two-edged sword. On one hand, wealth can be a vehicle that provides an opportunity to be charitable and to help others in this lifetime. On the other hand, the wealthy person may find that possessions become a worldly "attachment" that propels the desire for more and impedes progress toward spiritual development. It's easy to get hooked on being rich and on the accouterments that accompany wealth. Essentially, your mindset about wealth and what you want to do with it is what's most important.

My initial interest in Buddhism was not based on a quest for spiritual growth, but rather was based upon a strong motivation to break free of the pain I felt. I hoped that through meditative practice I would develop peace of mind and feel more secure in the world.

My decision to become a real estate investor was based on my desire to become financially free, so that I would never have to count on a job for income. I've never aspired to own the ritziest house or car; the only jewelry I wear is my $200 wedding ring, and I don't have many indulgences. Having possessions to impress others or myself has never appealed to me.

It's often said that the most difficult aspect of Buddhist practice is not when you're quietly meditating in the meditation hall, but when you're involved in some outside activity such as working or interacting with another person. Real estate offers a practicing Buddhist many challenges.

I believe my Buddhist practice has helped me to be a better real estate investor and asset manager. I've tried to emanate Buddhist practice in many ways:

- I am honest when I am a buyer or seller of property.

- I keep my word.

- I don't cheat or take advantage of others.

- I treat others fairly and respect that they too have a Buddha nature.

- I do my best to listen to my tenants and employees.

- When a stressful situation arises (which it often does), I can concentrate on the situation without being deluged with distracting thoughts.

- I am respectful of all people and never intentionally try to be destructive toward another person (or even toward their pets, with which as a landlord I am not enamored). I try to allow each person to be themselves, which at times can be difficult because some tenants, vendors, or sellers have adversarial personalities.

- I do my best to maintain my properties and give all my tenants good, inhabitable housing, even if it costs me a lot.

- I have often tried to help people improve their life situation. This includes tenants employees, vendors, and other investors.

267

How does holding wealth affect me? I certainly sleep better at night, and I worry a little less about having the resources to meet my daily needs. I view myself as the steward of my assets. I have essentially received a gift, and my responsibility is to make the best use of it.

Thus I recognize that responsibility comes with the ownership of wealth, and I maintain my properties as best I can. How I specifically act out this responsibility continues to unfold as time passes.

In answer to the question whether Zen Buddhism and real estate investing are compatible, I'd respond, "Yes!"

19

UNCLE SAM GIVETH

They're everywhere: Uncle Sam and his relatives at the state, county, and local level! The government is your partner in everything you do in real estate. Each level of government can make loans, sell property, and give you tax breaks. Let's look at some of the benefits you can get from the government.

LENDING PROGRAMS

The government offers a wide array of programs to investors. These programs vary and may involve providing forgivable loans (like the one I received on the three-unit building), below-market interest rate loans, or low down payment or no down payment loans and loan guarantees. Some of the agencies that make these loans include: FHA, VA, GNMA, FNMA, just to name a few.

I've personally been involved with a couple of government loan programs. First, my partner and I received a $24,000 forgivable loan from the city of Milwaukee to rehabilitate the three-unit building. However, the city should not necessarily be viewed as the golden goose here. The loan was designed to provide an incentive to an investor or property owner to fix up a property in a target area (usually a low-income neighborhood) so that affordable housing was available and the neighborhood would improve. Milwaukee wanted to provide incentives to investors to create a better city. The money they lent wasn't really local money – it came from a federal grant. The officials liked us because my partner and I did a decent job rehabbing the property. They wanted to lend me more money to buy and rehab properties, but my focus was on the higher income neighborhoods. The city also had money set aside for the acquisition of real estate. This program wasn't an isolated one specific to the city of Milwaukee. Chicago had one, and I'm sure other cities had similar ones too.

At the time, Chicago offered loans with low down payments to first-time home buyers who agreed to live in the property for a certain number of years. In Chicago, I've lost tenants to these "first time buyer" loan programs offered by the city or some of the suburbs. My tenants figured why pay rent when they could own their home and pay a mortgage at about the same level as their rent.

Another government loan I took out was an FHA (Federal Housing Authority) loan for the three-unit building in Aurora. The interest rate was a little below market, and the seller had to pay a percentage of the loan amount (points) for me to get the loan. An FHA inspector examined the property and required that certain repairs be done before approving the loan. The loan was assumable. The inspector also conservatively appraised the property. I could have made a low down payment, but chose to put 20% down in order to avoid paying extra for private mortgage insurance (PMI). I saw a few advantages to the FHA loan: 1) it was assumable; 2) the seller was required to make certain repairs to meet FHA standards; and 3) the seller in my case had to pay the loan origination points. I don't believe the interest rate was very much lower than what conventional lenders were offering. I didn't really care about the low down payment, since my philosophy has always been to make a higher down payment.

My third government-sponsored loan was on one of the buildings in Phoenix, Arizona. My partner bought a sixty-four-unit building in Phoenix in 1993 and took out an FHA conduit loan. The good news was that the loan was available at all, because Phoenix in the early 1990s was in a bust cycle, and lenders offering permanent financing were scarce. However, the Resolution Trust Corporation owned many multi-unit buildings they wanted to liquidate at that time. The bad news was the loan contained a nonnegotiable yield maintenance prepayment penalty – something I recommended investors avoid in an earlier chapter. At one point, the penalty was about 10% of the outstanding loan balance.

The Wisconsin Housing and Economic Development Authority (WHEDA) offered me a low interest loan on the $24,000 we were going to spend on the three-unit low-income building. I opted to use cash to do the rehab.

Typically the government will offer below market loans to promote programs designed to help the welfare of Americans. The forgivable loan and the low interest WHEDA loan were part of an effort to upgrade what the city and state thought was a neighborhood at risk. FHA loans or Veteran's Administration (VA) loans are offered to encourage Americans to be proud homeowners, while the FHA section 223 loan was created to make money available to investors in multi-unit buildings.

Where can an investor or a home buyer learn about local government loan programs?

A very good place to start is your local phone book. You need to scan the government section for the city, county, state, and federal governments. Here are some places I'd call from my local phone book:

City Government

• Mayor's office

- Department on Aging

- Department of Buildings

- Economic Development Commission

- Department of Housing

- Human Relations Commissions

- Department of Planning and Development

County Government

- Office of the County Commissioner

- The Assessor's Office

- Building and Zoning Department

- Department of Economic Development

- Department of Planning and Development

State Government

- Department on Aging

- Department of Agriculture

- Capital Development Board

- Department of Commerce and Community Affairs

- Development Finance Authority

- Governor's Office

- Housing Development Authority

Federal Government

- Department of Agriculture

- Auction Hotlines

- Economic Development Administration

- Franchise/Business Opportunity

- Department of Housing and Urban Development

- Small Business Administration

Many of these government departments have Web sites that provide details on their programs. If you call them, they'll give you their Web site if you ask for it.

When you call, ask to talk to someone who can tell you about the various real estate loan programs that particular government agency offers. The key, in my experience, is locating someone "in the know." In general, the public servants I've dealt with have been most helpful, and with a little prodding will usually refer me to someone in another department or governmental agency that is offering a different program. I've also found meeting people face to face is especially helpful. It shows I care.

When I do this, government employees go far out of their way to get me to the right person. One problem in dealing with government agencies is their bureaucratic organizational structures.

Departments may have several divisions, and you might end up talking to many people in order to get a complete picture of what programs are available.

Taking advantage of the few government programs I have been involved with meant completing extensive applications and dealing with bureaucrats, which took great patience and persistence.

Overall, the government can be a very helpful resource if you wish to invest in one of the programs it is promoting, such as re-development of run-down neighborhoods.

GRANTS

Free money always sounds good to me. Whenever I visit my local bank to make a deposit, the seller always asks me, "Is there anything else we can do for you, Mr. Pockross?" My response is, "Do you have free samples?" The teller usually chuckles and I end up empty-handed. I've yet to get a free sample from a bank.

I have better luck with the government – it provides grants. I've been the recipient of many grants over the years. When I wanted to repair the sidewalk or re-side my property in Aurora, the city government was there to substantially cover the cost. When I recently needed replacement windows in Milwaukee, the city picked up about 80% of the tab. The government offers all kinds of grants to landlords or homeowners. Their agencies truly want to help. The way to learn about what's available is to contact the government agencies cited above.

RENT SUBSIDIES

In its efforts to help low-income individuals and families live in decent, affordable housing, the government has established rental subsidy programs for tenants. The program I am most familiar with is the HUD Section 8 program. Under this program, a government agency pays most of the tenant's rent. Prospective tenants apply to be in the Section 8 program, and, once approved, they begin searching for an acceptable place to live. I can't tell you the number of times I've answered the phone and listened to the words, "Do you take Section 8?"

I've had a fair number of Section 8 tenants. Typically, a prospective tenant looks at an apartment, expresses a desire to rent that apartment, and presents a Section 8 voucher. The government agency handling the Section 8 program then sends an inspector out to identify any repairs in the unit or building needed to meet their habitation standards. If you want to rent to the prospective tenant, you need to have the repairs done so the unit meets the standards. Once the repairs are made, the unit gets approved, the lease is signed, and the tenant moves in. In my experience, the government paid 70% of the rent and the tenant paid the balance. Even still, I've had to evict tenants for falling behind on their 30% share of rent. Most of the time, the government pays like clockwork, although receiving payment during the first few months is slow. Section 8 usually has a relatively low security deposit, but guarantees two times the rent to cover any damages the tenant might cause.

I have mixed thoughts about the Section 8 program. I appreciate that the government pays its share of rent on time, and makes my housing available to tenants who would otherwise not qualify. On the negative side, the approval process for a unit takes a long time. In addition, I, as the landlord, have to sign "their lease" rather than using my standard lease that I paid a lawyer to develop, and these leases are usually eight to ten pages long. Lastly, I've had some battles over acceptable rent levels. In one case, the government wouldn't allow a rent increase for a few years, and that tenant had the lowest rent in the building. My position was, "Pay my rent or the tenant moves." The tenant had been with me for years and was quite elderly. While I have compassion for the elderly, I felt my rental schedule would be compromised if I allowed a lower rent for this person. The Section 8 individual eventually came around and agreed to pay the higher rent.

If you want to pursue government-subsidized rental programs, you again will need to check with the agencies in your locale. Section 8 is only one program—many other special programs may be available in your area. For instance, Oak Park, Illinois wants to encourage landlords to own property in Oak Park, and so they offer incentives for adding security improvements such as intercom systems, locks and lighting, and low-interest rehab loans.

WHO WILL BUY?

If you are looking for a motivated seller, the government is a good place to start. When my partner and I bought the three-unit building in Milwaukee, it was being auctioned off in a HUD auction, after HUD had foreclosed on it. Other sources of real estate investment opportunities include IRS sales, tax scavenger sales, U.S. bankruptcy sales, VA foreclosures, and other special situations. When I was dealing with the city of Milwaukee to obtain the forgivable loan, the city had a long list of properties I could buy. In the early 1990s, real estate investors favored property offered by the Resolution Trust Corporation (RTC), because there were bargains available for the astute investor. As you recall, one of my partners bought a 124-unit property from the RTC for $2,225,000. Several brokers contacted him after the closing and urged him to list it for $3,300,000, saying they would find a buyer.

To learn about these investment opportunities, you can use a process similar to searching for a government-funded or guaranteed loan, as described above. Contact the appropriate government agency to learn about what it has for sale. In my case, HUD sent me brief listing sheets of multiunit properties available in my HUD region. A newspaper with general circulation *(Chicago Tribune, Chicago Sun-Times,* and *Chicago Daily Defender* in my area) frequently advertises HUD auction properties. In addition, various real estate brokers are authorized to deal in HUD properties. You can also call the Internal Revenue Service and the taxing authority that collects your local area property taxes. If you want to pursue tax scavenger sales, I highly recommend that you learn the laws and procedures for the county in which you wish to purchase.

Let the buyer beware. Just because a property is for sale doesn't mean it is a bargain or will provide you the return on investment you require. You need to conduct due diligence on these opportunities, just as with any other opportunity. Of special concern is whether the title of the property is clear. Are there any recorded claims against the property that must be dealt with before you can sell it? Perhaps the prior owner failed to pay some contractors, and a mechanic's lien has been placed against that property. Perhaps the property has a pending lien (lis pendens) soon to be claimed against it. The IRS might have a claim to back taxes. There could be building code violations in need of correcting before the property can be legally occupied on record. All of these things need to be checked. If you purchase a property at auction, it should be evaluated according to the standards you use to evaluate any other property: what does it cost to buy and fix up, and will you make the profit you expected?

While buying properties at government auctions isn't the path I've chosen, other investors I know have done well this way.

TAX BREAKS

When you own property, the government requires you to file an annual tax return regarding the operating performance of that property. The tax return will include any revenues you receive during the calendar or fiscal year, as well as all the expenses you incur. Unfortunately, capital expenses (repairs or improvements such as a new roof, carpet, appliances, boilers, etc. that last more than one year) cannot be fully deducted in the year the repair or capital improvement was done. Instead, they are allowed as deductions based on the expected life of the improvement. For example, if you pay $2000 to install new carpet and the carpet is expected to last five years, you can deduct $400 per year for each of the next five years.

The good news is that the Internal Revenue Service allows you to have an allowance for the natural wear and tear the building receives every year. In the IRS's view, the building depreciates in value and you can make an annual deduction for this.

For example, let's say you purchase a thirty-unit apartment building for $1,250,000 on January 1. Using a methodology you are able to justify to the IRS, you allocate $150,000 of the purchase to the value of the land and $1,100,000 as the value of the improvement – the actual building. (Talk to your accountant on how to make this allocation.) The IRS figures the building will last twenty-seven-and-a-half years under the current depreciation allowance and allows you to take an annual deduction of 1/27.5 of the $1,100,000 depreciation base, or $40,000 per year. This means that you get a tax loss for money you are not really spending. You cannot depreciate the land, because in the IRS's view that land does not receive any wear and tear.

Let's say the building produces $250,000 in total revenues per year. Let's further assume the total expenses for the building before depreciation expense is added are $220,000. The profit of the building is $30,000. You are then allowed to add your depreciation allowance – the $40,000 – to the expense side. By doing this, you have a $10,000 loss ($250,000 – $260,000). You don't have to pay any taxes on the $30,000 profit and, depending on your overall tax status, may be able to use the $10,000 tax loss.

The government has established depreciation schedules for various assets. For example, the depreciation schedule for the bricks and mortar of a residential apartment building is twenty-seven and one-half years, but commercial property is scheduled for thirty-nine years. In addition, the IRS has set time limits for carpets, autos, air conditioners, appliances, and so forth. An accountant or someone from the IRS can easily provide you with these schedules.

As an investor, you need to keep abreast of these depreciation schedules, since the IRS has a history of changing them. When I first started investing in 1982, the federal government allowed investors to use a special depreciation program named ACRS (Accelerated Cost Recovery System). Under this program, an investor could depreciate an apartment property using a fifteen-year base rather than the current twenty-seven-and-a-half. Not only was the depreciation life of the property shorter, the investor could elect to have higher deductions in the earlier years of ownership, so that the tax write-offs in the initial years of the investment would be higher. Investors could accelerate the depreciation schedule. One property I looked at had a seven-to-one tax write-off. If an investor made a $10,000 down payment, he or she would be able to deduct $70,000 in tax write-off in year number one. This program was intended to spur real estate economic activity. The government changed its tune in the mid-1980s and went to longer-term depreciation schedules, to the dismay of investors.

Nevertheless, depreciation expense is a legitimate deduction that can be very helpful on your tax returns. I know several investors who do quite well and don't have to pay income tax. Depreciation is not a total gift. When you sell a property, you have to pay a capital gains tax on the amount you have depreciated the property[7] (this can be avoided if you do a 1031 tax-deferred exchange – more on this shortly).

---

[7] Here's an example using current capital gains tax rates. You buy a building for $100,000. After owning it for twenty years, you depreciated it by $50,000 on your tax returns. You sell the building for $200,000. From Uncle Sam's perspective, your capital gain is $100,000 on the profit ($200,000 less $100,000) and the $50,000 you took as depreciation over the twenty years. The $100,000 is taxed at 15% under current tax law and the $50,000 is taxed at 25%. This is called recapturing the depreciation.

A second type of tax break is the housing tax credit. As you'll recall, when I purchased the three-unit building in a target area in Milwaukee, we were approved to receive dollar-to-dollar tax credits that we could take on our tax return. Let's say my tax liability to the IRS for a particular year was $10,000. If I had a $2000 low-income-housing tax credit, the IRS would let me deduct $2000 from my tax bill. I would be liable for $10,000 less $2000, totaling $8000.

The federal government's generosity doesn't come without strings. My units have to meet certain habitational standards. I have to rent the units to what the government defines as low-income tenants, and the rents charged cannot exceed certain maximums established by the Wisconsin Housing and Economic Development Authority (WHEDA). Before I accepted a tenant and allowed him or her to move in, I had to get written verification of his or her total income from all sources to make sure that tenant qualified as low-income. If the tenant renewed their one-year lease, I had to reverify his or her income, employment, etc. I had to keep detailed records of everything, as WHEDA had the right to audit my records and my units to make sure I was complying with the program's requirements. I was also required to provide quarterly status reports as to who was living in the building, their rent, their income, and so forth. The annual tax credit I received was a little over $2,100, and I was able to take this tax credit every year for ten years. Since the property was approved for the low-income housing tax credit in 1989, I had a fifteen-year compliance period where I could rent only to low-income tenants.

The federal government now requires a thirty-year compliance period. The IRS imposes penalties if you fail to comply and has established special rules that apply if you sell the property before the compliance period ends.

In addition to providing tax credits for low-income properties, the government also provides tax credits for senior-citizen housing. Tax credits were also available at one time for rehabbing older commercial buildings.

To learn what tax credits are currently available in your region, contact the proper governmental agency. I learned about low-income housing credits when the city of Milwaukee representative in the Housing Development and Rehabilitation Division told me about them and gave me the names and phone numbers of people to contact. My partner and I had to submit an extensive application in order to be awarded the tax credits. When we applied, Wisconsin had been allocated a specified dollar amount of credits for the year. Unfortunately, the demand for tax credits exceeded the supply, and WHEDA was put in the position of having to award the credits to some, but not all, applicants.

Overall, I liked getting the dollar-for-dollar tax credits. They helped a lot when I paid my taxes on April 15.

A third type of tax break available to investors is the 1031 like kind exchange. Under the provisions of a 1031 like kind exchange, you can sell your property and purchase a similar, or like kind, property. If you do so within specific time deadlines, you can defer paying the capital gains taxes until you sell the new property. If you sell the new property and buy a larger one within the set time limits, you can again defer paying all the capital gains taxes. This is known as *trading up*. In essence, you can defer paying any capital gains taxes for as long as you live, providing you comply with the IRS rules and never sell your latest acquisition.

Here's an example from my own experience. I purchased a four-unit building near De Paul University in Chicago in 1983. Because it increased in value, I was able to refinance it and use the proceeds to rehab the building and purchase more property. I sold the property in 1997 for $420,000, and at the time I owed about $230,000 on it. Two days after I sold it, I closed on a thirty-six-unit building at a price of $810,000. I took out a $645,000 note against the new building and put down $165,000.

For the mathematically inclined reader who is wondering why I didn't put $190,000 down rather than $165,000, let me now explain to you the concept of transaction costs. Broker commissions, legal fees, appraisal fees, and numerous other costs came to around $25,000 on this transaction. I was very careful to comply with the requirements of the IRS; my attorneys and accountant reviewed everything before I signed anything, and I used the services of a Deferred Exchange Corporation, which had all the necessary paperwork to meet the exchange requirements. The IRS referred to this as a 1031 like kind exchange. I complied with the requirements of the IRS in the following ways:

- I never actually handled the money from the sale of the four-unit building. Using "accountant-ese," I never took "constructive receipt" of the sale proceeds.

- I identified a potential property within forty-five days of the sale of the four-unit.

- I actually purchased (closed on) the thirty-six-unit building within 180 days of the sale of the four-unit.

- The thirty-six-unit building could be viewed as like kind property.

- The purchase price of the thirty-six-unit far exceeded the sale price of the four-unit.

- The note on the thirty-six-unit was much greater than the four-unit.

Thus, I deferred the capital gain tax on the sale of the four-unit.

The exchange I described above is frequently referred to as a "Starker exchange." Simply stated, you sell one property and purchase a like kind property within the set IRS time limits.

One of the new concepts in exchanges in recent years is the "Reverse Starker." With this approach, you buy the property you want and then sell your property. I myself have never done one of these, and I highly recommend that you talk to an experienced, competent attorney as well as an accountant before you attempt one. I also recommend that you check with lenders to find out if they will lend on a reverse Starker trade.

In my path toward mogul status, I have done 1031 exchanges and also one 1033 exchange (an involuntary conversion) on the fire-damaged property in Aurora. I certainly like the immediate tax implications of the 1031 exchange, as I can defer paying the capital gains tax indefinitely. Exchanges have some down sides that an owner must live with, however – the IRS requirements. I don't like having to identify a potential trade property with forty-five days and having to close on it within 180 days. That puts me in a difficult negotiating position. I've received numerous calls from desperate brokers and owners regarding recent sellers who have to identify and ultimately purchase like kind property asking me to "name my price." Since I have no desire to sell, I simply triple the market value of the property, knowing I would have to pay capital gains tax if I sell the property. More realistically, I have always identified and put under contract any property I've wanted in an exchange before ever putting my property on the market. I allow enough time in the contract to sell my property before closing on the new one. If my property doesn't sell in time, I have a way out of the contract or can negotiate a new contract.

One could argue that even with my approach I am in a weak position, having to sell my property with a tight deadline. This is true, and it is unrealistic to expect to get the maximum price when selling within the time frame established by the 1031 Exchange rules. My suspicion is that if I had a lot of time, I'd get a higher price. Fortunately, the markets in which I sold my buildings were strong sellers' markets, and I didn't suffer too badly. I had six offers on my six-unit and I was able to negotiate up. I had to weigh the benefits of the new property against the costs of selling the existing one, including the "less than maximum" price, but ultimately my decision was to proceed.

Exchanging is stressful because of the time deadlines. And in addition to meeting the requirements previously mentioned, you also need to have acceptable financing in place, and conduct complete due diligence on the new property.

In several cases, I simply sold my buildings and paid the capital gains taxes. As noted previously, I made the decision to sell all the Aurora properties after the fire in the three-unit.

Since the capital gains liability wasn't too large (probably in the $5000 to $10,000 per building range), I didn't think it was worth all the extra work to do a 1031 exchange. I simply sold those buildings at my own pace, paid the taxes, put whatever money was left in conservative, interest-bearing accounts, and eventually used the money to purchase properties in more desirable locations.

When engaging in an exchange, I follow several precautions to make sure that I am in compliance with IRS regulations. My accountant and attorney are involved every step of the way. While I incur some costs this way, I also avoid making a mistake that could disqualify the exchange and force a capital gains tax and potential interest and penalty assessments. The attorney and accountant I use have been involved with numerous like kind exchanges, so they know what pitfalls to avoid.

I also make use of a Deferred Exchange Corporation. Many title insurance companies have subsidiaries that specialize in exchanges, as do major banks. When the opportunity arose, I've called around to see who would give me the best deal. Often I've been able to get lower prices when I've used the same title insurance company and Deferred Exchange Corporation. (As an aside, I've come across title insurance companies who were willing to disregard their "rate sheets" and give me a lower price when purchasing title insurance. To get the discount, you have to call around and ask for it. Also make sure the title insurance company you use is reputable and is acceptable to your lender.)

In the end, the availability of like kind exchanges allows you to keep your equity intact and to take full advantage of it as you acquire larger properties. What I have written here about exchanges is just the tip of the iceberg. To learn more about the intricacies of exchanges, there are many informative books available on the subject. If you have an accountant or tax attorney, they will also be able to point you in the right direction for more detailed information.

OTHER GOVERNMENT GOODIES

If the government wants development or redevelopment to occur in a particular area, it certainly can become your friend. Here are a few of the other benefits government agencies can provide to investors:

- Elimination of property taxes for certain periods of time

- Reduction of property taxes for a specified period of time

- Approval of certain zoning changes and zoning variances, so you can build/rehab the physical structure and bring it to its highest and best use

- Expedited building permit approval

- Development of land near where you want to do your project. This could include new water and sewer lines, roadways, sidewalks, and so forth

- Providing favorable special loans

- Providing numerous other ways of encouraging private investors to take on special projects. This could involve measures to reduce an investor's expenses, to guarantee income, or to ease the development/redevelopment process.

How can you learn about such programs? By contacting the appropriate government representatives in various agencies. Be aware, though – obtaining benefits such as the elimination of property taxes for a long period will not be accomplished by a simple phone call or two. As an investor, you'll need to spend time with government officials, so they will support your project and approve your request. Remember, the government does not grant low-interest loans, building permits, zoning changes, or property tax abatement out of a sense of generosity; it grants these programs to improve communities. Be ready to discuss your project in detail and have appropriate documentation available.

20

UNCLE SAM TAKETH AWAY

Having learned some of the ways the government can help the investor, let's look at the flip side of the coin – how government can make things difficult for investors.

The reach of the government in real estate affairs is extensive. In essence, you need to factor in the impact of the government on virtually any real estate-related activity. Let's briefly consider some of the areas where government requirements and regulations affect your activities.

INCOME TAXATION

We're all familiar with income tax. It's imposed on us by the federal government, most state governments, and many counties and municipalities. Tax returns are necessary for your investment properties every year, whether you own them in your own name or as a legal entity such as a partnership, corporation, or LLC. Every dollar you take in needs to be accounted for, as does every expense.

As a general rule, I don't look forward to January. It's the heart of the winter in Chicago, and I spend countless hours assembling operating data for the prior calendar year for each building so I can give it to my accountant to process the returns on time. In addition, employee statements of earnings and taxes withheld must be

287

mailed by January 31, and 1099s for any independent contractors, federal payroll tax return for the quarter, reconciliation with the states of Wisconsin and Illinois between the W-2s and monthly withholding deposits, federal unemployment tax returns, Wisconsin and Illinois quarterly unemployment tax returns, Wisconsin quarterly sales tax returns, federal tax estimates, and monthly payroll tax deposits. To make matters worse, my annual low-income housing compliance report is due in January, and my Workers' Compensation insurance carrier insists on conducting its audit in January. Moguls may have accounting departments, but cost-conscious mini-moguls do their own tax reporting.

Last but not least, we're all familiar with fulfilling our patriotic duty by filing our own personal tax return, including payment of taxes due by April 15 unless you file for an extension.

The government taketh away money and time when it comes to taxation.

PROPERTY TAXES

For the right to own land and improvements on the land, state and local governments have come up with a creative way to bring in revenues – they assess and collect property taxes.

Property taxes are typically localized, and the taxing authority collects the taxes and distributes them to various entities. In Cook County, Illinois, where I live, property owners pay one tax bill to the county government, and the proceeds get divided among many tax districts, including public education, public health, and county and village governments. Real estate taxes account for a substantial portion of the property owner's expense budget – real estate taxes on my properties account for 15-20% of my revenues.

To make things worse, I have never known a public official anywhere I've paid taxes to announce that the government has too much money in the public coffers and so taxes must come down.

Typically, property taxes increase, and the government is quite inventive at finding new things to tax or transferring some of its operating expenses to the property owner and taxpayer. For example, I now pay fees for garbage collection and recycling. Obviously though, you do get something in return for taxes: police and fire departments, public health services, and many other government services.

The bottom line is that property taxes take a big bite out of the real estate investor's profits.

OTHER GOVERNMENT FEES AND FINES

One day, while compiling my annual data, I started thinking about all the fees and fines one might have to pay to the government. Consider this list:

- Annual fees to participate in the low-income housing credit program

- Fees charged when a city employee comes to the property to conduct the mandated annual property inspection. (I have to pay the inspector a fee so he can write up code violations where I have to pay a fine)

- Fees to take out building permits to do various projects. Not only must you pay a permit fee, but the permit has to be approved, which can take anywhere from a few hours to months, if it is approved

- Scavenger and recycling fees

- Fines for violating building code standards

- Fines for violating environmental regulations

- Court costs for initiating eviction procedures

289

- Annual fees for operating boilers

- Recording fees related to when you buy, sell, or are involved with some activity that must be recorded

- Government-mandated interest you pay to tenants on their security deposits

- The costs you incur to meet government requirements under regulations such as the American Disabilities Act or the Occupational Safety and Health Act

- Property registration fees

- Fines for having a messy garbage pickup area (The city doesn't seem to care that local scavengers tip the garbage cans over in their search for food, bottles, or cans. They just want the fine.)

Thus, the reach of the government in ownership and operating of a property is extensive, when viewed from a financial perspective. Unfortunately, the impact of government goes beyond the dollars-and-cents equation. Let's consider some other ways government agencies impact the investor.

ASSURING COMPLIANCE WITH REGULATIONS

Regulations affecting real estate owners are pervasive. Governments establish building code standards for almost everything imaginable. In newer construction, bedrooms have to meet certain minimum size requirements. Adequate parking has to be available. Standards exist regarding electrical capacity, fire prevention, accessibility for the handicapped, noise abatement, and so forth.

In many cities in which I've operated property, I've had to endure annual inspections to ensure that my property has met code. In addition, periodically an upset tenant (or, I'm sorry to say, a tenant looking for an angle to get out of a lease or not pay rent) will file a complaint with the appropriate department. I have dealt with numerous building inspectors over the years and found most of them to be reasonable human beings who are doing their job of promoting public health and safety, and I've always taken a bend-over-backwards, cooperative attitude with them. Unfortunately, I've had to deal with a few who are quite unreasonable and have made my life very unpleasant. My philosophy is to render unto Caesar what is Caesar's and do whatever it takes to come into compliance. At the same time, I will not be bullied, and I will use legal means to uphold my position when necessary.

Occasionally, I've hired attorneys to represent my interests in building matters dealing with local government. Over time, I have learned to live with the constant inspections.

ZONING

As a property owner, you are limited to using the land in the manner for which it is authorized, or zoned. For example, the house I live in is zoned for single family. If I wanted to tear it down and build a sixty-story high-rise, this would be against the zoning ordinance, and the village would stop me from pursuing that project. While this is an extreme example, it is very common for developers to want to change the zoning for a new land use. The developer requests a zoning change or variance from the appropriate government authority, such as the zoning board or the village trustees. If members of the board don't like the plan for whatever reason, the zoning request will be voted down, and the project will not go forward. In short, the government has the power to limit the development potential of a site through zoning regulations.

EMINENT DOMAIN

The government has the right to reclaim your property or a portion of it if it is needed for a public use. By law, the government is supposed to pay you a fair price for the property.

For example, when I lived in Pittsburgh, the Pennsylvania Department of Transportation wanted to build a highway next to the house I purchased (this was actually prior to my purchase of that property). Consequently, under the right of eminent domain, the government took possession of the five houses to the west of my property. All the houses were torn down and the Commonwealth of Pennsylvania built a highway on the land. Appraisers were hired by the Department of Transportation to establish values for the properties, and the owners were given a fair price, at least by the government's standards.

SPECIAL HEADACHES

One type of regulation I find particularly scary involves compliance with environmental standards. I know numerous owners who purchased properties in the 1960s or 1970s when little thought was given to asbestos insulation and tiles, radon, lead-based paint, or leaky underground storage tanks. Thirty years later, the presence of these items is a major headache for the owners, because the cleanup and disposal costs are staggering. These costs can exceed the market value of the property.

Fixing environmental problems can wreak havoc with the numerator/denominator approach to investing. The costs to correct an environmental problem such as soil contamination can easily create a negative return on your investment. You'd be better off investing your money in a passbook savings account.

The latest craze in recent years has been mold litigation. Tenants and homeowners are suing everybody in sight over the effects of molds (such as stachybotrus) on their health.

Property insurance policies may or may not cover mold issues. An investor I know who had a mold situation needed to hire a special attorney to fight with his insurance company about covering the mold claim. And my insurance policies have eliminated coverages for mold and fungus.

This puts investors in a difficult position. How can they protect themselves against environmental regulations? The first step is to be familiar with the regulations. Be able to recognize asbestos in your property or potential property. Learn where it was used. Be aware that there could be lead-based paint in a building. Some of my Aurora tenants were so convinced their children were eating lead-based paint chips from my building that they had the children's blood analyzed for this. Fortunately, no evidence of lead was found in their blood. You should check for long-term water infiltration and potential mold buildup as well.

If you are purchasing a property and don't want to pay for an environmental audit, you will still want to know the history of that property. Alarm bells should ring if a property was used by a dry cleaner, a gas station with underground tanks, or a manufacturer who may have leaked toxins into the ground. As part of your due diligence, you may need to take several soil samples to determine the cost of bringing the property into compliance (called remediation).

If you unfortunately find violations in a property you already own, you will need to bring it into compliance. A wide array of vendors are eager to help you comply with the regulations. In my experience, some of these were fly-by-night profiteers who gave me little confidence in what they did. Others seemed legit, and obviously they cost more. I've always used reputable environmental abatements companies, as I want the problem permanently solved, even if this does cost more.

Lenders are quite aware of the impact of environmental regulations on the buildings I buy or refinance. They typically request, at a minimum, a Phase 1 Environmental Audit (this costs approximately $1,500), and a signed and notarized affidavit from me disclosing anything I know about the property in question. It they don't like what's in the report or affidavit, they may very well pass on making the loan.

I sometimes worry about what the future holds. Will latex paint be found to be carcinogenic? Will specially treated lumber be found to emit toxins? Building materials commonly used today maybe prohibited in the future.

A second headache is pro-tenant legislation. Politicians want votes, and there are many more tenant voters than landlords voting. While I've been fortunate enough not to have invested in any rent-controlled areas, some locales do have controlled rents, where the government forces owners to set rent levels well below market. We've all heard about rent-controlled apartments in Manhattan where tenants get fantastic rental bargains, and many municipalities have a Tenant Bill of Rights.

In Chicago, landlords must make several disclosures to tenants, and tenants have many rights, such as the right to make repairs on the property and then deduct the cost of this from their rent. Landlords are required to keep tenant security deposits in a separate account at an institution domiciled in the state of Illinois, and tenants are entitled to an annual interest payment on their security deposit. Landlords who fail to maintain the security deposit in a separate account or who unknowingly fail to pay interest on a timely basis are excellent targets for class action lawsuits.

One of my landlord friends sent his tenant a letter documenting the interest the tenant was due and forgot to enclose the check for seventeen cents. The tenant said nothing and then sued the landlord. The tenant won in court and got treble damages – almost five thousand dollars – simply because the landlord didn't put a seventeen cent check in the envelope.

FUTURE REGULATIONS

Recent meetings at the Lincoln Park Builders Club have been quite instructive. Almost all the meetings have been devoted to the impact of regulations proposed by the Chicago City Council.

First on the agenda has been the Council's proposed set aside ordinance. Under this ordinance, anyone building or rehabilitating residential properties over twelve units would have to set aside 15% of the completed units as affordable housing. One member of the club estimated that this would cost him more than $100,000 per set aside unit, if he had to sell the unit as affordable housing.

The next issue we've been discussing is down zoning. Down zoning refers to the practice of reducing or restricting allowable development density in an area from its current level to some lower level of use. For example, you might have a four-unit building in a residential area zoned R-4. The property then gets down zoned to R-1, and if you replace the property (e.g., tear it down), the new zoning restricts you from building anything greater than a single family house.

Many developers in the group would prefer to buy a five-unit, tear it down, and build a three- or four-unit condominium. With down zoning, they can't do this.

The final agenda item lately has been landmarking. Landmarking refers to forcing an owner to preserve the facade of a property and possibly the interior as well. This discourages developers from purchasing a property and tearing it down so that the developer can redevelop the property. Such activity is prohibited if a building is landmarked.

As an investor, you need to be aware of any proposed regulations and, if necessary, be ready to oppose them.

Overall, government regulations can put a substantial dent in your pocketbook and can have a big impact on your way of conducting business. Nevertheless, virtually every investor I know has easily survived government regulation and has prospered anyway.

21

PROTECT THYSELF

Three aspects of real estate ownership scare me. The first is owning a property with a negative cash flow. The second is the impact of complying with environmental requirements, discussed in the last chapter. The third aspect is the potential for lawsuits. In our litigious society, the landlord is the prey. The thought of a child accidentally falling at one of the properties and becoming a quadriplegic concerns me not only on a personal level, but on a legal and financial level as well.

The property owner has multiple ways to protect him or herself, or to at least limit liability. The prudent investor should consider protective measures in order to sleep well at night. I use three general methods:

1) Operating the property to limit liability situations

2) Having adequate property and liability insurance to cover potential claims

3) Legally structuring the property to limit overall liability position

Let's consider these one at a time.

OPERATING THE PROPERTY
TO LIMIT LIABILITY SITUATIONS

As a concerned owner, I am always on the alert for liability hazards at a property that could cause injury to tenants, their guests, and my employees. Whenever I visit a property, I look for cracked sidewalks or broken steps. I check for the potential for falling ice in winter and icy walkways. I check hallway carpeting, especially on steps, to be sure there's no frayed carpet on which a tenant could catch a heel and fall. I look for holes in grassy areas that someone could step into and turn an ankle. I check for water leaks, strange odors, electrical problems, properly functioning boilers and air conditioning systems, elevators that stop perfectly level to each hallway floor, loose bannisters, and peeling paint. In short, my employees and I are on a constant vigil for physical situations in which a tenant, guest, or employee could be injured. I schedule immediate repairs when any hazards are found.

As an owner, your methods of operation are the first line of defense in a lawsuit. You don't want to be viewed as negligent in managing your property. I've only had one potential claim, where a tenant slipped on an icy step and landed on her coccyx bone, which cracked. For reasons unknown, she never even filed an insurance claim. An added service your property insurance agent should provide is doing a walk-through with you on the property to identify potential injury-causing hazards. The recommendations of an experienced outsider can be very helpful. For larger properties, risk management consultants can be hired to observe your operation and make recommendations on potential hazards.

A last method of operation to reduce your chances of a liability lawsuit comes from Basic Management 101 – good interpersonal skills with tenants, guests, and employees. This means having a cheerful demeanor and a responsive attitude toward tenants when they request repairs. I truly believe I have avoided a lawsuit or two because I try always to show a good attitude toward tenants. In one case a tenant slipped, fell, and broke her ankle on a wet marble step in a building vestibule. The water was there because another tenant had decided to shake off his wet umbrella on the steps after having just come in from the rain. The injured tenant mentioned to another tenant that she did not want to sue me because I was such a nice guy, and she realized that it wasn't my fault the other tenant shook water from his umbrella onto the steps. After this incident, I installed skid protectors on all the steps. In my view, a tenant is more likely to initiate a lawsuit against the "big, bad, rich landlord" if the landlord is indifferent or unpleasant.

HAVING ADEQUATE PROPERTY AND LIABILITY INSURANCE TO COVER POTENTIAL CLAIMS

As a second line of defense, you want to have the deep pockets of an insurance company to protect you in the event of a large property claim or liability loss.

Claims happen. I've had two major fires, a seriously injured employee covered by Workers Compensation insurance, and some smaller vandalism claims. None of the claims was the result of any negligence on my part as owner/manager. Nevertheless, they added up to hundreds of thousands of dollars in claim costs. Fortunately, for the most part I had adequate insurance coverage.

But I have seen instances where property owners did not have sufficient coverage. They may have ducked paying a few dollars on a Workers' Compensation policy, and then one of their employees became seriously injured and sued them. I've also seen claims where the owner did not have nearly enough property insurance to cover the replacement costs of the building damaged in a major fire. An insufficient limit of liability coverage can be a problem even without a fire.

Let's look at the basics of a property insurance policy. As an investor, I typically look for the best standard policy an insurer offers. As a property owner, you have several options to consider when selecting property coverage. The first concerns what perils (e.g., fire, vandalism, lightning, etc.) you want covered. I always choose the most comprehensive form – the Special Peril form. In addition, many companies offer additional coverage to enhance the policy over and above the Special Peril form. As an investor, you should check with your insurance agent about these.

A second decision for the investor concerns the valuation basis of the property. For buildings, there are three valuations: Replacement Cost (RC), Actual Cash Value (ACV), and Market Value (MV). The Replacement Cost is the cost to repair or replace the damaged structure with like kind and quality. The Actual Cash Value is the Replacement Cost less depreciation. The Market Value is what the property would sell for in the open market.

Let's consider an example: Your building is completely destroyed by fire. The Replacement Cost is $500,000. In our example, the building had an old roof and mechanicals and is depreciated at 35%. Therefore, the Actual Cash Value is $500,000 less $175,000 ($500,000 X 35% depreciation), or $325,000.

Let's now suppose the property sits next to a polluted dump and has a Market Value of $50,000. In summary, the property has a Replacement Cost of $500,000, an Actual Cash Value of $325,000, and a Market Value of $50,000.

Property insurance policies do not allow you to insure for Market Value. You have to insure the building on a Replacement Cost basis or an Actual Cash Value basis. If possible, choose Replacement Cost coverage and insure the building for the full replacement cost. If you can only insure the building on an Actual Cash

Value basis, then insure it for the Actual Cash Value limit of the building. The dollar amount of coverage should be reviewed with your agent to make sure you are fully protected.

As a vivid example, when I had the fire in the three-unit building in Aurora, I unfortunately had an ACV policy. I had insured the property with a $229,000 limit of coverage, but I had to take substantial depreciation reduction on the final settlement. Thus I was compensated only for the Actual Value of $154,000 for the total loss, rather than $229,000. I tried to follow my own advice, but I wasn't able to find an insurer who would issue a Replacement Cost policy on an eighty-year-old building. Like me, in some instances you may not have a choice; sometimes you may have to settle for an Actual Cash Value policy.

A third important feature to consider is making sure that you are covering an adequate dollar value of the property. One of my friends had a $450,000 fire loss but was insuring the building for only a couple hundred thousand. To rebuild the property, he had to dig deep into his own pockets. This could have been avoided if he had had adequate coverage when the policy was issued or renewed. If you have replacement coverage, be sure you insure for the replacement cost of the property.

Provide information on the type of construction and total square footage to your insurance agent, who can then determine the replacement value. If you are underinsured, property insurance policies have a coinsurance clause that can severely penalize you as the policy holder. Let's say you insure a building with a Replacement Cost of $1,000,000 for $750,000. From the point of view of the insurance company, you are underinsured by 25%. Unfortunately, if the building sustains a loss of $500,000 in damage from a fire, the insurance company would penalize the settlement by $125,000 (25% of $500,000) and would only pay out $375,000. With the proper limit ($1,000,000 in this example), the insurer would have paid the $125,000.

In addition to setting the proper limit, ask your agent for an Agreed Value endorsement. The Agreed Value endorsement eliminates the insurance company's ability to penalize you at claim time for under insuring.

It is often tempting to pay a lower premium and underinsure. Your lender will usually require coverage only up to the amount of its loan value, which may be too little insurance.

A second important type of coverage is loss-of-rent insurance, which protects you from business interruption and loss of income if you have a major loss. As an owner of residential property, I always have loss-of-rent coverage, in case tenants have to vacate after a property claim. Most of the insurers I've dealt with offer to cover the lost rent per unit for up to twelve months. When filing a claim, you must provide documentation as to the actual loss (e.g., existing leases, proof that the property is not habitable). I suggest that you get loss-of-rent coverage based on full occupancy at current rents and add a percentage for future rent increases. The coverage you have should be updated annually, so that you have adequate protection if your property is out of service for any length of time.

A third coverage that is an absolute necessity is liability insurance. Insurers typically offer this on an occurrence basis with an aggregate for all claims. For example, the insurer will provide a policy that will provide up to $1,000,000 in coverage to protect you for any single occurrence, but will cover no more that $3,000,000 in total (or in aggregate) for all occurrences. How much coverage you need is debatable. I have at a minimum $1,000,000 per occurrence and, for most properties, $2,000,000 per occurrence. One option that might be available to you is an umbrella policy that covers all your properties. In this case, you might have a $1,000,000 to $3,000,000 policy on each property, and then a $5,000,000 or $10,000,000 umbrella policy over all your properties, as a back-up for a major liability loss. In this case, you might actually have $11,000,000 of liability coverage protecting you. If you have more than one location on the policy, make sure you have a policy endorsement stating that you have the aggregate limit per location.

Another option is to package your properties under one policy. This is something to discuss this with your insurance agent, because the overall premium may be less.

Several other comments might be of interest in the area of property insurance:

- I typically have high deductibles to reduce my premiums, usually $5000 or $10,000 in the event of a casualty loss. I figure that my premium savings over the years have far exceeded the added premium for a lower deductible. Check the premiums for various deductibles when you review insurance proposals or your renewal.

- Several important types of coverage are available that your agent doesn't always tell you about. I know, because I paid a lot of money for not having them. The examples that come to mind are: 1) Building Ordinance and Law; 2) Increased Cost of Construction coverage; and 3) Demolition coverage. When the six-unit building in Aurora had a major fire, the city government was kind enough to let me rebuild (as opposed to forcing me to demolish it). However, the city fathers wanted the building to meet current construction standards, rather than the ones in effect when it was constructed decades earlier. Consequently, I had to spend $10,000 out of my own pocket to have a licensed electrician rewire the property to meet code. The insurance company would only cover the replacement of whatever existed at the time. Building Ordinance coverage combined with an Increased Cost of Construction endorsement would have paid this expense.

• Another area to watch out for related to Building Ordinance coverage is whether your property has been allowed to have a "Legal Non-Conforming Use." The six-unit building in Aurora was deemed Legal Non-Conforming, and in the event the fire destroyed 50% or more of the building, I would have been forced to demolish what was left and reconstruct it as a conforming four-unit building. I would have lost two units and much value. Building Ordinance and Law coverage coupled with Increased Cost of Construction coverage will protect you in this situation.

• Typically not included in a standard insurance plan is Equipment Breakdown coverage (previously known as Boiler Machinery policy). This covers all expenses resulting from boiler explosions, electrical system failures, etc. Standard policies do not provide this coverage. I didn't have to learn about it the hard way, since many of my lenders mandated this as a loan requirement.

• A third coverage often excluded pays for demolition costs. When I had the fire at the three-unit, the city wanted the property demolished at my expense. Out of curiosity, I took some bids and was startled to learn the high cost of demolition.

• My philosophy is to not nickel-and-dime a property insurance company with small claims. I want the company there when there is a large claim. Consequently, if I have a claim that is a few thousand above my deductible, I pay the repair cost myself. Here's an example of the benefits of this approach. I know a property owner who was unfortunate enough to have some awful tenants. These people were forced to move, but caused about $15,000 of damage in the process. The former tenants could not be found, and even if found, they probably would not have had the money to reimburse the owner for the damages. Therefore, the owner filed a legitimate claim and recouped $14,000 (he had a $1000 deductible). Unfortunately, when renewal time came, the insurer provided timely legal notice that their company would not renew the policy and the owner would need to look elsewhere for coverage. His timing was far from favorable. In the spring of 2002, insurers had been very cautious about taking on new risk, and he eventually had to settle for lesser coverage at five times the premium. To prevent this, he should have paid the repair costs and not bothered the insurance company.

- Watch out for policy limitations and exclusions. Most of these are standard. In recent years, I've noticed every one of my insurers excludes asbestos, mold, and fungus coverage, as well as coverage in the event of a terrorism loss.

- Use more than one agent when getting quotes. Agents licensed to sell property and casualty insurance typically have contracts with a few insurers authorizing them to sell a specific insurance company's products. The agent must meet production requirements to continue selling that company's insurance. Consequently, most property and casualty agents I know have strong relationships with two or three companies at most. In addition, some companies have what is called a "captive agent."

The agent can sell only that insurer's product line. Examples include Farmers, State Farm, and Allstate. From an investor's point of view, you want to get the best value. Check with several agents to get quotes from separate insurance companies. If agents #1 and #2 are both going to Insurers A, B, and C, it's a waste of time to have both agents quoting. A second benefit to having multiple agents quote is that you get several perspectives on how best to handle your insurance needs.

• Whenever I've had a large claim, the first person I call is a public insurance adjuster to advocate my position with the insurance company. I know they'll do a good job advocating for me and I'll come out ahead. Insurance adjusters charge for their services; I've paid around 10% of the insurance proceeds. I feel that their experience in dealing with insurance companies will net me more than if I handled the claim directly with the insurer.

In the event of a large loss, insurance companies, like other profit-driven organizations, will want to limit their loss. They will either use one of their own adjusters or hire an independent contractor who specializes in insurance losses to investigate the origin of the loss and to negotiate with the insured. Whoever is representing the insurance company is typically well-trained and experienced, and knows how to limit the insurer's loss.

In my case, I would be at a tremendous disadvantage in a negotiation. So I bring in a hired gun, the adjuster, to represent me and help me get the maximum settlement. Adjusters can be found in the Yellow Pages under "Public Adjusters."

- Beware of state-sponsored insurance plans. If at all possible, get a private policy.

- The property insurance market runs in cycles. Sometimes the insurers are eager to sell property and casualty insurance, and at other times they won't even quote on this. This describes the general insurance market today. In addition, each company has its own cycle of business. At first, companies are eager for new business. The next stage in the cycle involves pricing the product to keep current clients, but not take in new business. The third stage is pricing the product high relative to the market, where they will probably lose some business. Then the insurers decide they want more business and price their products accordingly.

This all underscores the importance of shopping the market every year. You always want to see if there's a better value available in the marketplace.

OTHER INSURANCE YOU NEED TO PROTECT YOUR INVESTMENT

In addition to the coverages described above, several other types of insurance to consider are:

- Workers' Compensation insurance. This covers employees for work-related injuries and illnesses. Many states mandate this coverage if you have employees. As an owner, you usually have the right to exclude yourself. A Workers' Compensation policy has two sections. The first is referred to as Section A and is coverage for your liability arising from the State Workers' Compensation Laws. Section A Workers' Compensation coverage

307

does not have a set dollar limit. The limit for Section A Workers Compensation coverage is statutory, meaning the insurance company will compensate the claimant for whatever the statute says is to be paid. The second section of the Workers' Compensation policy is referred to as Section B/Employers' Liability.

Section B Employers' Liability has a "standard limit" of $100,000 per occurrence. I usually increase this amount to $500,000. Employers' Liability coverage typically pays for Third Party overt actions. This would be best discussed with your agent, along with increasing the Employers' Liability limit. I have Workers' Compensation coverage for my employees as well as for independent contractors who cannot provide me with proof that they have their own Workers' Compensation coverage. By doing this, I am protected in case one of the contractor's employees is injured while doing the work. I report the payment to the contractor when the Workers' Comp insurer conducts its annual audit, and I factor the additional cost into the amount the contractor gets paid.

• As a point of protection, you should require certificates showing current insurance coverage by your contractors for both liability and Workers' Compensation coverage. You don't want to be held liable when a tuckpointer accidentally drops a brick six stories and it hits a passerby on the head. Nor do you want to be liable if the tuckpointer falls off the scaffold and is seriously injured. Please ask for the certificate.

• Have yourself included as an insured with all contractors who work on your premises. Require this in writing from the contractors and their insurers. In this way, their policies will pay for part or all of any claim arising out of their operations/work. This is a very standard practice and is usually done for no additional charge.

- If you have employees, consider an employee-dishonesty bond. It will protect you in the event an employee absconds with your money or goods.

- Another insurance to consider is Employment Practices Liability coverage. This protects you from your wrongful acts in dealing with your employees. Examples would be sexual discrimination, wrongful termination, etc.

- A few final coverages to consider include Non-Owned and Hired Automobile insurance, Director and Officers insurance, and Fire Legal Liability insurance. Ask your insurance agent to explain the coverages, the associated premiums, and whether you should obtain these coverages.

LEGAL ENTITIES THAT PROTECT YOU

The last line of protection for the real estate investor lies in how the investor holds ownership of the property. The majority of homeowners hold ownership (herewith called "hold title") in their own names. Most often, the ownership of a house is John Doe and Jane Doe, joint tenants. The asset is directly in the name of the actual owners. If someone slips and falls and files a lawsuit, Mr. and Mrs. Doe and their liability insurance policy are the direct targets of the lawsuit.

As an investor, you want to limit your liability in these situations. You have a wide range of options to protect yourself, including establishing corporations, limited liability companies, and limited partnerships.

My strong recommendation is that you should consult a competent attorney about how you will legally structure your holding before you make an acquisition. If you already own the property, you may want to reestablish how the title is held.

I hold each of my properties as its own limited liability company (LLC). If something happens at one of the properties, my liability is limited to the coverage of my insurance policy and the equity my investors and I have in that particular property. Since each property is its own legal entity, my other properties are separate from this property and are protected from a lawsuit. I am the managing member of each LLC, and any other investors are simply members. While each LLC has its own tax return, the profits or losses pass through to the member on a K-1 form. This is included in the individual member's personal tax return.

There are many views as to how to structure your holdings legally. While my approach is to hold each property as an LLC, other investors might place two or three holdings into one LLC.

If you invest in single-family houses, you may find it cost-prohibitive and a bit onerous to place each house into an LLC. Other owners have established S or C corporations for their holdings, while still others with investors create limited partnerships.

At one time, an investor and I held properties together in a C corporation. Therefore, we were shareholders in a corporation. I didn't especially favor this method of ownership, since we were taxed as a corporation and then taxed individually on any dividends that were distributed. In addition, it was costly to set up, we had to have at a minimum one annual meeting with minutes, and we had annual filing charges payable to the state where we incorporated. The last straw was when I made a court appearance to evict a delinquent tenant, and the judge postponed the case until I hired an attorney to represent the corporation. Since I was not licensed to practice law in Illinois (or anywhere else), I wasn't able to represent the corporation, even though I was the major shareholder. So the tenant got three more weeks of free rent, and I had to hire an attorney.

An attorney can help you establish an LLC. Some important points to consider are:

- It costs money to establish each LLC. My cost has typically been $500.

- You need to have an Operating Agreement. I paid an attorney to develop the first one, and I have used it as a boilerplate for all the other LLCs.

- You need to file an annual tax return for each LLC. While the LLC offers you protection on liability lawsuits, the profits or losses pass through it to the individual members, to be filed with their personal tax returns.

- Depending on the state in which you filed for the LLC, that state may require an annual fee to maintain the LLC. You may also have to conduct at least one annual meeting of the members.

- You will need the approval of your lender if you want to establish an LLC. If you are in the process of acquiring a property, then you should make clear to the lender that you want to take title as an LLC. If you are establishing an LLC on a property for which you already hold title, you need to contact the lender and obtain approval for the transfer of title. I've never found this to be a problem, as my investors and I personally guarantee the loans. The lenders' main concern is that they get paid on their loan.

- You'll need to change all your checking and savings accounts so they are in the name of the LLC.

In addition to having each property under an LLC, I have established a management corporation (an S corporation) under which all my employees are paid. Since the employees perform work at more than one property, I find it expeditious to have a corporation to handle this. The properties pay fees to the Management Corporation, which in turn pays the employees.

There is also an insurance policy protecting the management corporation, which in turn pays the employees. I have an insurance policy protecting the management corporation.

When this Corporation was established in the early 1990s, limited liability companies were not as prevalent as they are today. Many states did not even allow them at the time.

As a final comment, protecting your properties is a critical component of investing in real estate. I strongly encourage you to seek the counsel of a competent attorney familiar with corporations, LLCs, etc., as well as an accountant to make sure you establish your properties for the maximum tax benefit.

22

PARTNERS: YOU DON'T HAVE TO GO IT ALONE

As a real estate investor, you have some basic choices when acquiring properties: do you do it alone or should you bring in other investors? A third choice might be owning some properties on your own and some with investors. When I was starting out, I took in investors for three reasons: 1) to reduce my financial risk; 2) to acquire larger properties that I did not have the resources to acquire on my own; and 3) to help people I cared about financially. After a few decades of ownership, I lean toward doing deals on my own, but wouldn't overlook my investors if a great opportunity presented itself for which I did not have the resources. Let's look at the advantages and disadvantages to having investors.

ADVANTAGES OF HAVING INVESTORS

I've brought in investors for different reasons. First and foremost, I like other people and want to help them. While I lack the ability to be a great psychiatrist like Sigmund Freud, I believe I am helping my investors, at least in their financial affairs.

As a second factor, I prefer to invest with sizable down payments. My investors' cash helps me make a down payment and still have working capital. Stated differently, without the capital that came from investors, I wouldn't have been able to make some of my larger acquisitions.

Thirdly, I feel that with the backing of investors, I have resources to weather many storms, such as slow rental markets or the need for cash in the event of an untimely capital expenditure. With the financial support of investors behind me, I find it easy to get loans. My bankers frequently call me to ask if I need any money for something.

The financial rewards of having investors is the final advantage. As will be discussed later, there are many ways of structuring your compensation when you bring investors into the picture.

DISADVANTAGES OF HAVING INVESTORS

The first disadvantage to having investors is that you are giving up some of your potential profit. You work very hard to find good deals; why give up some of the profit?

Secondly, you are giving up some control over the investment. If you want to sell the property, refinance, or rehabilitate it, the decision is not yours alone to make. You need the approval of, at a minimum, a majority of the ownership. In addition, the investors may want to offer their opinion about the building on matters such as its appearance or how it is managed.

It isn't fun getting criticism from your investors when you're trying your best to operate the property efficiently. While control issues may not always be at the forefront, be aware that your investors do have certain powers and can limit your control over managing the asset.

Thirdly, coordinating with other investors can be a chore. Whenever my investors and I are in the process of refinancing a property or selling one, I spend days shuttling around getting notarized signatures on a multitude of documents. Needless to say, the lender or attorney never has one complete package together, so multiple trips are necessary. Information about the performance of the property and tax returns (K-1s) also have to be distributed to investors on a timely basis.

The next disadvantage relates to the fiduciary responsibility you bear as the syndicator. It's your responsibility to account for all funds and expenses. While this may sound simple, you have to take into account what is best for the investors every time you make a decision. For example, if you are thinking about raising rents, you must consider the investors as a whole. If it were your building alone, you might decide to be highly aggressive with a rent increase and risk vacancies. As a fiduciary, you might be more moderate in your rent increase.

Another disadvantage relates to the disclosure requirements of the syndicator. If you plan to offer the investment to a large number of investors, you probably will fall under the purview of the Securities Exchange Commission (SEC), as well as state regulators. In this case, you'll need to prepare a prospectus that fully discloses projected rents, expenses, all risks, your strategy, your fees, and your background. This takes substantial time and money. Even if your deal is exempt from SEC requirements, you'll still need to disclose fully to investors accurate information about the property so they can carefully consider whether the investment meets their objectives. This information will very likely be reviewed by their attorneys or accountants. None of this is necessary if you are buying a property without investors.

Another disadvantage becomes apparent to me each year when I get my accountant's bill on April 16. A tax return is necessary for each investment.

Disadvantage number seven relates to incompatible investment objectives a group of investors may develop over time. People's lives change, sometimes not for the better. Investors die or become disabled. People lose their jobs and need money. While I pride myself on good investor relations, I have had problems. My approach is to purchase a property, hold it, and pay off the note. After the property is paid off, I distribute the income. While the investors are informed of this prior to making their investment and agree to wait, some investors might want to sell the property and trade up for a better opportunity, while others want the income now. I find balancing the changing interests of the different investors challenging.

The final disadvantage relates to having an unhappy investor. Investments can go sour and not meet the rosy expectations of the investor the day he or she signed on. Unhappy investors can cause a lot of grief. They can sue you, tarnish your reputation, and in general be very difficult to deal with on partnership issues. The difficulty becomes even more intense if an unhappy investor is a close relative or friend. When it comes to investing, misery doesn't love company.

Given the pros and cons of syndicating investments, the question arises as to how the syndicator gets paid. This is a matter of negotiation. The syndicator is trying to get as much compensation as possible, whereas the passive investor is trying to maximize a high safe return.

Typically, the syndicator will disclose his or her compensation, and the investor will accept or reject it. In my experience, my investors ultimately want to see what their expected return on investment is. If I show them an expected return of 15%, while other investment alternatives (stocks, bonds, CDs) are yielding 2 to 10%, my investment looks promising.

Investors' standards vary, too. When the stock market was producing annual returns in excess of 20% in the late 1990s, everyone was an investment genius and thought my returns of 12-15% were mediocre. When stock prices significantly declined and interest rates dropped to forty-year lows, everyone started getting interested in real estate investing again.

As a syndicator, I favor just compensation, since syndicators do provide a lot of value through their knowledge about real estate and their work in finding worthwhile deals.

Let's consider some examples of the many ways a syndicator might be compensated. As a syndicator, you can be compensated when the investment is initially made (in the beginning), during the course of ownership (in the middle), or when the property is sold (at the end).

GETTING PAID IN THE BEGINNING

At the beginning of the investment, you might get paid some sort of fee, or get a "free piece" of the investment, or both. A second way you might be compensated early is to buy property in your name at an under-market value price and then resell it to investors.

As a syndicator, you have invested two important assets in the deal: 1) actual money that is part of the acquisition (legal fees, accounting fees, phone calls, travel, loan acquisition fees); and 2) the value of your time and knowledge. You should be compensated for these. At a minimum, you should be reimbursed for your acquisition-related expenses.

When it comes to setting an amount for the fee, I don't know of any formal guidelines. Every syndicator I've talked to has his or her own way of being compensated. Some syndicators who are not licensed as real estate agents might set a fee of 4-6% of the purchase price of the building. This is comparable to the commission a real estate broker might charge. Thus if you syndicate a $2,500,000 property, you might have a fee of $100,000 or $150,000. My friend Charley does all his deals this way.

A second approach might be to base the fee on the down payment. In the example above, if a down payment of $500,000 was made, you might set a fee of 10% or 12% of the down payment.

Another approach would be to use an arbitrary figure that sounds logical to you and see if your investors accept the figure. Again using the example above, you might set a fee of $200,000 and provide proof to your investors that the building is still a good deal for them because you bought it at under-market value and it was appraised for $3,000,000, and so you deserve the fee.

When you receive this fee is negotiable. You might ask for it as part of the investors' initial investment, or you can ask for it at a time of a future refinancing or a future sale. However, my recommendation would be to get your fee sooner rather than later.

From the investors' perspective, your fee, while justified, represents a dilution of their investment. If you want to raise $1,000,000 and plan to take a fee of $150,000 out of the $1,000,000, the pure investment that goes into the deal is $850,000. The $1,000,000 has been diluted by your $150,000 fee. If your investors are like mine, they will focus on what their expected return on investment is. After taking the fee into consideration, if the investors can expect a 15% annualized return, they may be happy to pay that fee.

Your informational package should spell out to investors all your fees and other ways you will be compensated.

A second approach to a syndicator's compensation relates to getting a "free piece." For example, let's say you've found a run-down thirty-unit apartment building in a desirable location that will increase substantially in value and cash flow with cosmetic improvements and better management. The price is $1,500,000 and the down payment is $375,000. You might raise $400,000 from investors and, as part of your compensation, you would own a 10% or 20% piece of the property. Thus, in the future you would be entitled to a percentage of the cash flow, the principal reduction, any tax advantages, and appreciation. I've done this on some of my deals.

Here's another example. You find a house at below market value in need of some improvements. You don't have any money for the down payment or the improvements. You find an investor and make the following deal: the investor provides the down payment. You split all profits on a 50/50 basis. You do everything from overseeing the rehab, managing the property, and selling it. If you buy a house for $90,000, put in $20,000 for improvements, and sell it for a net of $150,000, there would be a profit of $40,000. The profit would be split, with you and the investor each getting $20,000.

A third example: you find a 10,000-square-foot office building that will produce a very high return if rented with a 10% vacancy factor. You have only about one-third of the required down payment to go into the deal, but you feel it is too good a deal to pass up. You find an investor who has the other two-thirds of the down payment and make the following deal: the investor puts in two-thirds of the required money and you split the profits 50/50 after the acquisition. In this example, 50% of the cash flow, principal reduction, tax consequences, and future appreciation would be yours. As the syndicator, you would get a "free piece" equal to one-sixth of the building. You put in one-third of the down payment and got one-half of the building.

One thing I have never done but have seen others do is to shift more of the tax loss to the investors. In the example above, the investor might get two-thirds of the tax consequences (hopefully a loss) while getting 50% of the other three benefits. If you are considering syndicating a deal where investors receive more of the tax loss, I recommend you seek competent counsel from a qualified attorney and accountant before the deal is made.

Another approach some syndicators use is purchasing the property in their name and then selling it to a group of investors. The investors would evaluate the investment based on their expected return. To take this a step further, the syndicator might then lease the property back from the investors who now own the property, so the investors have a guaranteed return. The syndicator then subleases the property and ideally the rents collected equal or exceed the lease.

As an example, let's say a syndicator finds and purchases an undervalued retail shopping center for $1,800,000. Based on the appraisal, it's worth $2,250,000. After purchasing the property, the syndicator then resells it to a group of investors for $2,000,000. As part of the sale, the syndicator commits to leasing the property back from the investors for $325,000 the first year with annual adjustments based on the localized Consumer Price Index.

The syndicator provides projections of income and expenses over a period of years, which show that the investors can expect a 12% return. All the investors agree to participate. The syndicator then subleases the space (or honors the existing leases). In the event the first year rent revenues are less than $325,000, the syndicator must make up the difference. On the positive side, if the rental revenues are $350,000 in the first year, the syndicator can pocket the $25,000 overage. In this example, the syndicator has essentially made a $200,000 profit up front and potentially receives the rental overage every year for the time the investors own the property. (The rental overage could be viewed as "in the middle" compensation.)

In the previous examples, the syndicator might combine taking a smaller initial fee and getting a free piece, as well as receiving money "in the middle" or at the end.

BEING COMPENSATED IN THE MIDDLE

The syndicator has several ways to be compensated in the middle. One approach, described above, is when the syndicator leases the total property from the investors and then either subleases the space or honors the existing leases. The syndicator then pockets any excess revenue. A second approach is very basic: the syndicator manages the property for a fee, typically a percentage of the gross monthly income.

Let's say you purchase a fifty-unit apartment building and syndicate it to a group of investors. The monthly income, if fully occupied, is $50,000 ($1000 per unit). As the syndicator, you might offer to manage it for a fee of 5%, or $2500 per month. The $2500 would be a welcome addition to your monthly cash flow. You might also ask for a general contractor's fee of 10% for any major work, such as a total rehab. Acting as a general contractor isn't easy, however, since you have to identify projects to be done, solicit multiple bids, evaluate the bids, award them, and monitor the work the contractors perform. Be aware that acting as a general contractor takes time.

A third approach for the syndicator to receive compensation in the middle is to offer investors the opportunity to lend money to the investment and then give them a piece of the profit on the sale or refinancing of the property.

As an example, let's say the fifty-unit building is purchased for $3,600,000. You raise $900,000 from investors and make the following deal: you view the $900,000 as a loan and personally guarantee the investors a return of 10%, or $90,000 per year. When the property is sold, you will split the final profits with the investors on a 50/50 basis. The investors get a guaranteed above-market return plus a chance to participate in the appreciation of the building. The key aspect to consider as the syndicator is that the property produces at least $90,000 annual cash flow so you can meet your guarantee to the investors. Otherwise as the syndicator, you might have to ante up the shortfall so that the investors get their guaranteed return. Any prudent investor in this situation would look first at the investment itself and, equally important, at who the syndicator is. Is the syndicator honest, competent, and in possession of the financial resources to back up the guarantee?

A fourth approach to receiving a monthly portion of the investment income is to specify as part of the agreement with the investors that the syndicator will receive a percentage of the monthly cash flow. For instance, if the property exceeds 95% occupancy, the syndicator might receive a half a percentage point of the income for every percentage point in excess of 95% (e.g., at 100% occupancy, the syndicator would receive 2.5% of the gross rents). As a second example, the investor might take the position he or she gets 1% of the gross revenue. I have also seen some syndicators get an asset management fee. If the property is worth $3,600,000, the syndicator gets a fee of 1%, or $36,000 per year.

A final way to have income in the middle would be to earn interest from the investment. For example: let's say you purchase a thirty-unit apartment building for $1,000,000. You're able to assume an $800,000 loan at 6.5%. Your down payment is $200,000. You syndicate this to a group of investors for $1,200,000. You collect $250,000 up front, of which $50,000 is a syndicator's fee, and carry back a note for $1,000,000 at the currrent market rate of 7.5% interest. You have "wrapped around" your loan over the existing $800,000 loan at 6.5%. You are making 1% interest on the underlying loan of $800,000 and 7.5% on the additional loan of $200,000. You also manage the property for a 5% of the gross monthly income fee. In this example, as a syndicator, you have gotten an up front fee of $50,000, a monthly management fee, and monthly interest income.

BEING COMPENSATED AT THE END

The syndicator can be compensated at the end in two different ways: 1) by receiving a share of the profits when the property is sold; or 2) by receiving some of the refinancing proceeds. Let's consider some examples:

You purchase a well-located run-down house in foreclosure for $95,000. Using an investor's money, you make a down payment of $15,000, assume the existing financing from the lender, and put in an additional $20,000 from your investor to improve the property. You sell the property for a net sale price of $145,000. You split the profit of $30,000 with your investor on a 50/50 basis. Everyone is happy. The investor made $15,000 on the $35,000 investment in a short period of time, and as the syndicator, you made $15,000.

In a second example, a syndicator purchases a $3,000,000 apartment building. The syndicator raises $810,000 for the purchase, which includes a $60,000 fee. Then the syndicator agrees to manage the property for a 5% fee for the next ten years. The property produces an 8% annual return and is sold after ten years for $4,000,000. At the time of the sale, the syndicator receives 20% of the $1,000,000 profit, as stipulated in the original agreement. The syndicator was initially compensated with a $60,000 fee in the beginning, a 5% management fee in the middle, and then received $200,000 in the end. The investors are happy because they received an 8% return during the ten-year life of the investment and $800,000 when the property was sold (divided up based on the original amount of the investment). It's a matter of negotiation between the syndicator and the investor(s) what percentage of the profit the syndicator receives when the property is sold.

As a third example, let's say the syndicator puts a 124-unit garden complex under contract for $2,250,000 and then syndicates it to investors before closing. As part of the agreement with the investors, the syndicator agrees to take a $50,000 fee at acquisition, a 10% "free piece," a 4% management fee, and a fee of $100,000 at the time the property is sold or refinanced. The syndicator implements improved management, and the property operates well and throws off cash flow to the investors. Over the next five years the market heats up, as interest rates have fallen and the location has become desirable. Upon refinancing, the property appraises for $5,100,000 and the investors and the syndicator take out a refinance loan of $3,500,000. From the refinance proceeds, the syndicator returns to the investors their original investment, pays himself the $100,000 fee noted above, distributes some of the refinancing proceeds based on the percentage of ownership including the syndicator's 10% free piece, and retains the balance for future capital needs. Again, everyone is happy. The investors had a decent return before the refinancing and following the refinancing, they have their original investment back, plus some of the appreciation (tax free since it is from refinancing), and they still own the property. The syndicator is happy having collected $150,000 in fees, a portion of the appreciation, a management fee, and still owns 10% of the property.

A fourth possibility would compensate the syndicator totally based on the performance of the property. Let's say the syndicator decides to develop a shopping center and guarantees investors a 12% rate of return on their investment. If the performance of the property falls under the 12% level, the syndicator/developer makes up the difference. If the investment performs well, the syndicator and the investors split the profits 50/50 at or above the 12% level.

Some developers I know form joint ventures with other people, such as other developers or their lenders. I view this as an active partnership rather than a syndication with passive investors.

How a syndicator structures an investment depends on the needs of that syndicator. If he or she needs an influx of money quickly, the syndicator will most likely want to focus on receiving fees in the beginning. If monthly cash flow is important, the syndicator might structure the investment for monthly cash via a management fee, interest income, an asset management fee, or a percentage of the cash flow. On the other hand, if the syndicator has visions of rainbows in the future, he or she might seek a "free piece" and a percentage of the profit at sale or refinance. As a syndicator, I tend to focus on monthly cash flow and free pieces.

If you decide you want to put together a group of investors for an acquisition, it's important that the investors' objectives coincide with your own. For instance, if you are considering purchasing a half-vacant retail center, upgrading it, leasing it out for higher rents, and then selling it in two years, make sure all the investors agree to this plan. In my case, paying off the building so that it becomes "free and clear" is the objective. All investors are fully informed that they cannot expect any money from the investment until the loan on the property is paid. This could be anywhere from eight to twenty years. After the property is paid in full, they will receive their proportionate share of the monthly cash flow. If they can't afford to wait, then they don't invest. My investors have all agreed to this. If the property needs operating capital, the investors know they are at risk for this.

As a syndicator, you need to provide your investor(s) information about the potential property. This includes information on the investment, your compensation, expected investor returns, how you plan to structure the acquisition legally, and so forth. This information will likely be scrutinized by the investor, an accountant, and an attorney. In addition, when you syndicate you need to be in compliance with federal and state securities laws.

The federal compliance is monitored by the Securities Exchange Commission (SEC), and a number of rules affect syndications. You can request a helpful brochure called Q & A: Small

Businesses and the SEC by calling the SEC at 800-732-0330. If you are Internet savvy, you can get the brochure by going to www.sec.gov/info/smallbus.shtml. Next click on "Information for Small Business" and then select Q & A: Small Businesses and the SEC.

You will also need to check with the department in charge of monitoring securities at the state level (in Illinois, the Secretary of State).

If a complaint is filed against you for securities violations, it can cost you a stiff fine, as well as being on public record. When an investor considers making an investment with a syndicator, the investor will be evaluating two things: 1) the quality of the investment product; and 2) the quality of the syndicator. Investors want to have trust and confidence that their money is safely invested. Consequently, if an investor doesn't know you, he or she will want to know:

- your background

- your track record on real estate investments

- what assets you as syndicator have to support any guarantees

- references from other investors

- any disclosures that might be a flag, such as a bankruptcy, criminal record, or any foreclosures

- how much of your own money you are putting into the investment.

As noted earlier, I tend to be very picky about my investors.[8] I want an investor who is patient and in a financial position of strength so that this particular investment isn't critical to his or her

---

[8] In writing this book, I am in no way seeking new investors.

future. The last thing I want is a "pain in the brain" type who wants to get involved in every decision and second guess my every move. Life is too short for that.

Overall, incorporating passive investors in your path to real estate financial freedom enables you to grow more quickly than investing on your own.

23

Q & A

Over the years, many aspiring real estate investors have come to me for guidance. They typically have pages of questions, which I patiently answer. I have already addressed many of these questions. Here are a few others I am often asked:

Q. I'm married and have a family of four to feed and house. I hate my job (or my job is okay, but leading nowhere). I am so excited about real estate that I want to do deals full-time. When should I leave my job?

A. I wouldn't turn in my two weeks' notice just yet. Your job provides many benefits: predictable steady income; employee benefits, including health insurance and paid time off; contact with other human beings; and hopefully good performance on the job, which enhances one's sense of self-esteem.

Real estate offers some terrific benefits: income, wealth accumulation, total control of your time, enhanced self-esteem, potentially making the world a better place, and lots of fun. Each of us has to make our own decision based on our specific life situation and on our self-knowledge.

I would not leave a job except under the following conditions:

• Your real estate income after taxes is equal to the job income after taxes (be sure to include the cost of health insurance).

• Your real estate income after taxes isn't as much as you made from the job, but is enough to meet your living expenses.

• Your spouse works and willingly agrees to allow you to seek a real estate fortune, foregoing your paycheck. The working spouse in this situation might set a time frame for you to produce results. If this is the case, put your heart into your efforts. In my own experience, my hard-working wife was far from delighted when I reported to her the details of my work day. She didn't really like to hear how much I enjoyed my one-hour nap or my hour of thinking about the purpose of life when she'd had a tough day at the office. As an option, you might leave your job while your spouse works full-time, but bring in some income through part-time employment.

• You strongly believe and are totally confident that you could earn more money making real estate deals in a year than you could from your job. Ideally, you have enough money socked away that you could meet your living expenses for a long time. Incidentally, I view a job as an income-producing asset. If you earn $40,000 per year and anticipate that you could earn a 10% rate of return, an asset worth $400,000 producing $40,000 a year of income produces as much as your job. I'd rather have a real estate investment than a job. You could be in the unfortunate position of being unemployed and longing to do real estate, but a job provides you with predictable cash flow. If you are uncertain which direction to go, find a job for the time being and work toward eventually having enough real estate income to leave the job.

Q. I'm really excited about real estate and want to become a mogul. How do I get started?

A. Assuming you are starting at zero, I would build my strength and knowledge about real estate. More specifically:

- Read books to increase your knowledge.

- Save money for a down payment, or find other sources of money, such as investors or assets you own from which you might borrow

- Build your resource network by connecting with lenders, real estate agents, and other real estate owners.

- Decide on your strategy. Do you want to buy houses, small apartment buildings, larger buildings, retail and office buildings, or industrial property?

- Investigate potential geographic areas where you want to invest, so you can target certain neighborhoods or cities.

- Familiarize yourself with real estate prices. If you want to buy a brick three-bedroom, two-bathroom house in Area A, then start keeping an eye on what is for sale. Go to open houses of homes for sale.

As you are growing, you may not yet be totally self-confident about what you are doing. There will come a time, however, when you begin looking for a specific property that meets your parameters. At this point you've started.

Q. Speaking of acquisition strategies, I don't know what to do. What is a strategy, and how do I develop one?

A. Here are two examples:

1) I will buy one single-family house a year for the next twelve years.

2) I will purchase ten apartment units each year for the next ten years, so that I have one hundred units by the age of forty-five.

You, the investor, have to decide what your comfort zone is. If it's your first investment, you might want something small, like a single-family house or small apartment building. I wrestled for about a year with what direction to go in and finally chose apartments. Most investors I know started with smaller apartment buildings, and then bought larger ones. Some branched out into office buildings, retail centers, and industrial property. The key is that these investors decided what they wanted to do and just kept on making acquisitions. I don't know of any investors, myself included, who had a rigid, formal written-in-stone plan.

Q. With the price of real estate so high, it doesn't seem to make sense to buy anything. Is it still possible to succeed in real estate?

A. Absolutely. I believe today's prices will look like bargains in ten or twenty years. To succeed, an investor needs to be thorough in his/her acquisitions analysis, persistent, and patient – and it helps to have deep pockets when times get tough.

Q. I see advertisements in the newspaper and on television about tapes or seminars on how to become financially independent via real estate. Are these for real, and are they worth it?

A. As an investor, I've read countless books, attended one seminar (on equity sharing), listened to numerous tapes, subscribed to various newsletters, and gotten my hands on seminar notebooks other investors have loaned me. Collectively they've given me a lot of good ideas that I've incorporated into my deals or my management techniques. Other investors I know have also read books and gone to seminars and some, but not all, have succeeded. Lastly, some investors who are extremely successful may have read at most one book, and they laugh at the thought of forking out money to go to a seminar. When considering buying tapes or attending seminars, the questions I pose are: What does it cost? How much of my valuable time does it take? Does the content seem to be something I am interested in? Does it seem worthwhile? While I'm a cheapskate, I do value education. I honestly feel the books I've read were the most helpful, followed by the greatest teacher of them all: hands-on experience.

If you are planning to be a developer or specialize in commercial real estate, most of the garden-variety real estate seminars won't be for you. Quite often, law firms or consulting firms will hold educational seminars on topics of interest to you. If you are a neophyte who is likely to purchase distressed single-family houses and small apartment buildings, I suspect some of the seminars would be of value to you. I'd at least read a few books before attending so that the material the instructor goes over is somewhat familiar to you. I myself have not attended a seminar in over twenty years. What's most important is your determination to succeed.

Q. Are there any books or seminars you recommend?

A. Please see the Appendix for recommended reading. Also, check your local library or bookstore. I am always doing this, looking for new books and new approaches.

Q. What do you think of getting a real estate salesperson or broker's license?

A. Among the advantages would be having direct access to the MLS database (assuming you're licensed as a salesperson working under a broker who is a member of the MLS). You'd have quick access to what is listed, and you would get a piece of the commission in the event you purchase a listed property. Taking this one step further, if you become licensed as a broker and become a member of the board of Realtors that provides the multiple listing service, you'll be able to buy properties and make deals with sellers and get a price reduction by foregoing your share of the commission. This makes it easier to be a seller. You can list your own property and split the commission.

If you choose to get a license and not work actively as a salesperson, you can still work with a broker who serves inactive salespersons. As a licensed salesperson, you have to work under a broker's supervision. In Illinois, certain brokers will hold a salesperson's license so the salesperson complies with the law. The broker charges a small fee to hold your license. The benefit here is that when someone you know is buying or selling something, you can refer them to the broker and get a share of the commission.

The disadvantage of holding a license is that legally, you must disclose that you are a licensed salesperson or broker. If you run an ad or call potentially distressed sellers, you must inform them that you have a real estate license. The seller may feel uncomfortable that a commission is involved, or might feel that you as an agent know a lot more than they do about the value of the property and might take advantage of them. If you don't have a license, the seller knows there's no commission to pay and perceives it as a matter of two individuals making a deal.

I had a real estate salesperson's license for several years. The license was helpful because I'd typically get a couple of referral fees a year. Once I made the referral and the property had sold, I very much enjoyed depositing my commission check. I also got commissions when I listed my properties and had a knowledgeable, active agent sell my properties. I discontinued the license after I sold all my Illinois properties and when my insurance clientele started to grow. I simply didn't have time to meet the ongoing Continuing Education requirements.

Q. Should you time your buying and selling of real estate?

A. I am far from a genius when it comes to market timing. In my experience in the Midwest, residential real estate prices tend to rise or stay level. Currently, a lot of local condo developers sitting on newly built vacant units are keeping prices level, but they are offering more upgrades and very low-interest financing.

My perspective is a long-term perspective. I buy when an opportunity arises and plan to hold the property forever, unless I have a specific reason to sell – a better opportunity, savings in time and aggravation, deterioration of the neighborhood, etc. I don't time the market.

I do, however, pay attention to the economic climate. At present, the U.S. economy is in a very modest growth stage, but interest rates, while low compared to 1982, are steadily rising. On the buyer's side in terms of larger apartment buildings, prices are high, and I find it difficult to justify a purchase based on my financial analysis. Many of the stock market investors that have had sizable losses in recent years are now inquiring about becoming real estate investors. When that interest gets translated into actual real estate investments, it helps keep property values up.

Q. Can anyone do real estate?

A. NO! As the chapter on "having what it takes" describes, certain personality characteristics are necessary. Let's consider some characteristics that get in the way of becoming a successful investor:

- lack of interest in real estate

- lack of time to devote to studying about real estate as well as acquiring and managing real estate

- low energy

- ineffective "people skills"

- inability to handle stress that comes along with acquiring, managing, and selling real estate

- procrastination

- lack of commitment to succeed in real estate

- total lack of self-confidence – such that you cannot proceed at all. You feel overcome with fear at the thought of dealing with an angry tenant or other real estate matters

- not being a competent businessperson. Some people simply don't have the business savvy it takes to get into real estate

- having health problems that limit your ability to find, buy, manage, or sell real estate

- limited ability to add, subtract, multiply, and divide

- laziness

Q. From what you've accomplished in real estate investing, how much do you attribute to "luck" and how much is "skill"?

A. I really don't know. In Chicago, home to my first investments, investors have been blessed by a booming market over the past twenty-five years. I never dreamed that the four-unit near De Paul would be worth triple what I paid for it in a few years in what was a "nothing down" deal. That can also be said of the six-unit in Chicago (bought for $85,700; sold for $360,000), the Milwaukee condos (bought for $90,000; market value now $300,000), or the 124-unit in Phoenix I owned a small percentage of (bought for $2,225,000; brokers offered to list it at $3,300,000 after purchase consummated; recently sold for $4,600,000). I'd give my vote here to luck, and view the dramatic price appreciation as a gift. On the non-luck side of the ledger, however, I made the decision to purchase these properties in the first place, and to accept the benefit or downside risk the properties offered. At least I wasn't sitting on the sidelines thinking, "If I only would have..." I took action. All the other properties have gradually increased in value and income over the years (with some years being better than others). Their performance is in line with what I'd expect an investment to do over time – they have grown in value. I believed that would happen, and luck wasn't involved.

Q. I've been a real estate investor for around fifteen years. It's worked out well, as my monthly cash flow is about $12,000 per month and my net worth on paper is about $3 million. I can see my estate and my annual income growing into a sizable figure. I'm concerned about the legacy I will leave behind. More specifically, I have concerns about how much to leave to my children or to charity, and about how my real estate holdings will operate after I die. Do you have any thoughts?

A. You raise the question, "How do you plan for your estate when you pass on?" While I am not an attorney or an accountant, I can offer a few thoughts. If you do not have a will, I strongly urge you to make an appointment with an attorney and have one drawn up. Without a will (the legal term is being intestate), you are at the mercy of the state and federal laws legislating people who don't have wills. Your estate may be divided up far differently than you would want. In addition, many unnecessary fees might be levied. If you have a net worth of any magnitude, you should definitely find a competent attorney who specializes in estate planning and develop an estate plan now.

As a licensed insurance agent, I have prospected many of my well-to-do real estate cohorts hoping to sell them life insurance to protect their loved ones from estate taxes. Their lack of knowledge and lack of planning were startling. What I frequently saw was that many people plan to live forever and have great difficulty dealing with the thought of their own mortality. While I confess that I would have liked to make a sale and get a commission, I felt genuinely helpless to get them to do something that would not earn me even one cent of commission – see an attorney and put together an estate plan. (Note: for larger estates, you may need a team of advisors, including accountants, tax attorneys, estate attorneys, and financial consultants.) This takes work. You must decide how your assets get passed on, documents need to be drawn up, and your assets may have to be transferred out of your name. In my case, I had to transfer my membership interests in each of my LLCs into my living trusts. This made for a lot of time-consuming paperwork, but eventually it got done.

Estate planning isn't a "do it once and you're done for life" proposition. Periodically, you'll need to update your plan. While it's not fun to think about meeting up with the grim reaper and making succession plans, it is vitally necessary. Doing so can save your heirs a lot of money and aggravation. If you don't have an estate plan, or if yours is out of date, I strongly encourage you to develop one, or update what you have.

Finally, be sure to update your transition plan as to how your properties will operate in the event of your disability or death.

Q. What is the future of real estate?

A. I don't know. Over the past few decades, we have witnessed an astounding escalation of property values throughout the country. I believe this will continue, but not with the same robust increases we have seen. A recent meeting of the Lakeview Developers is telling. Commercial property owners on the north side of Chicago have been clobbered lately by a variety of economic forces:

- The rental market has been the worst anyone has ever seen (some members have been investors for thirty-plus years). Many landlords cut rents and offered move-in specials with up to three months free rent. A lot of renters have purchased houses and condos because interest rates have been so low.

- The triennial real estate assessments have been outrageously high. Some investors had reassessments that were up by 300 or 400%.

- Other costs such as property insurance premiums have been rising. In essence, these investors have been in a classic cash-flow crunch, with decreasing revenues and increasing expenses. Not one of them, however, was selling. Several hands in fact shot up when the club president raised the question, "Who's a buyer?"

My view is that well-located property will prove to be a profitable investment over time. Just be sure you have the "deep pockets" to weather the tough times.

24

NIRVANA: IS THE PURE LOTUS LAND SO FAR AWAY?

I remember attending a real estate seminar in 1980, observing ordinary people giving their "how I made a lot of money" testimonials, and thinking how fantastic it would be to have financial freedom. My thinking was that all my personal problems would be solved and I'd live a life of freedom in the style of a king.

Having enough money has always been important to me because I grew up poor. Feelings of scarcity have always pervaded my thoughts. I think about money every day. I've read enough books on money-related topics to fill a small library. My life's struggle has been about having enough money.

So what are my thoughts and observations after twenty-plus years of real estate investing and the better part of a lifetime devoted to the pursuit of money? Has real estate investing eliminated any personal problems and allowed me to live like a king?

The answer for me is somewhere between yes and no.

Real estate investing has helped me grow as a person. I am no longer fearful about dealing with a boss, because I don't have a boss in the traditional sense. My boss is the economy, my clients, my tenants, and my employees. In my journey, I have witnessed displays of human nature by my tenants and others that have been inspirational to me, while other actions by tenants, contractors, lenders, or other investors have been totally despicable. I have learned about such exciting topics as the breeding habits of cockroaches, eviction procedures, or how to read a credit report. On the day of my college graduation, I never could have imagined learning about such subjects. My self-confidence and interest in the world around me have greatly expanded.

At the same time, I don't feel a complete sense of financial freedom, and given my personality, I doubt that I ever will. I don't know if there will ever be "enough." My mindset is frugal. I don't own fancy cars or live in the Taj Pockross or dress like Mr. Fashion. If stores or advertisers are targeting "impulse buyers," I am not in their audience. I hold the record at the local muffler shop for most muffler replacements under their lifetime warrantee, and the Water Department in the town where I live couldn't believe our water usage was so low. They actually sent an investigator out to check up on us. He found nothing wrong and just left, shaking his head. My wife has given up any hope that I'll ever be able to "spend freely."

Any personality issues that I had prior to my becoming a real estate investor are still there. The cash flow from the real estate, however, affords me the time to explore my issues as well as pay for a therapist. My success as an investor hasn't caused me to view myself as "Mr. Fantastic." I never broadcast my success, and I try to see people around me as complete human beings, rather than as lawyers or doctors or failures in life.

Being driven, I still wake up at 5:45 A.M. every day and drag myself over to the gym for an hour of rigorous exercise. This isn't easy on cold, snowy winter mornings. My body is aging and doesn't seem to particularly care if I am a real estate mini-mogul or not.

From comments some of my investors and tenants have made, I believe I've made a positive difference in a few lives. I feel good about that, and I also hope this book will make a positive difference in your life. I am not aware of any negative impact I've had on any of my tenants' lives, though I'm sure some don't think highly of me.

OBSERVATIONS OF OTHERS

I've had the opportunity to meet and spend time with countless real estate millionaires. Most came from backgrounds similar to mine, while a few came from affluence. My general observation is that most of my cohorts keep acquiring though they have long ago met just about any person's definition of "enough." My perception is that different things motivate them. Some are born wheeler-dealers who love to bargain and do more deals. Some buy more because they get bored with their existing empire and want a new challenge. Some keep going because they don't know how to stop. Others are just plain greedy and want to be the richest person on the planet. Some investors I've come across seem to feel they have the Midas touch, and they venture into new arenas such as owning other businesses – restaurants, retail, or manufacturing. Unfortu-nately, however, most investors I've known who have strayed from real estate have not fared well.

The majority of moguls and mini-moguls I know are living the good life. They take exciting vacations, drive expensive cars, and live in beautifully decorated houses or condominiums in the best neighbor-hoods. Some have commented to me that they have so much money, it no longer means much to them. In a way, everything seems free.

When I look under the surface, though, I see the same pain I see in any other person. As described earlier, the first of the Four Noble Truths espoused by Shakymuni Buddha is, "To live is to suffer." The inner pain or suffering I see varies with the person. Some have personal health concerns. Others have angst about their children's welfare or the state of their marriages.

343

Still others are wealthy, but very lonely. They wonder if they've led a noble life. Some suffer from feelings of inadequacy, lack of self-esteem, depression, or guilt feelings about their good fortune.

The prosperity that real estate brings doesn't allow people to escape this pain. It does, however, help in a few ways. You don't have to worry about lack of money, and your money can buy you some very important resources: the time and services of other people. It's nice to have money. I don't know of any of my investor friends who have ever regretted getting involved in real estate. Most of them are very grateful for the rewards it has brought. I don't know any who would trade their life of prosperity for a life of poverty.

In the Buddhist tradition, one of the best-known historical figures was a layperson named Pong. Pong never aspired to monkhood. He became very wealthy and had many possessions. One day Pong, a devout Buddhist, met an enlightened master and came to the realization that his possessions were poisonous. They caused him to attach himself to the material world, and they brought out greed in others. Pong resolved to throw away all his worldly goods. He placed everything onboard a ship and went out to sea to throw the possessions overboard. Unfortunately, before he was able to make his gift to the sea, the ship was overtaken by 500 pirates, who were set on plundering it.

Pong received the pirates without fear. He told them that if they believed his possessions would benefit them, he would cheerfully give them everything. The pirates were shocked. They had never encountered someone like Pong.

The 500 pirates became enlightened, and all became Buddhist monks. Pong didn't jettison his possessions but returned to port and donated everything to the Buddhist temple. His wealth was used to help others.

Buddhist literature offers many variations on this story, and the morals are usually the same. Having money is neither good nor evil. The mindset behind how you use wealth is the most important thing. Pong had no attachment to his possessions and used them for the good of others. His thoughts and actions did not promote greed and in fact helped the 500 pirates to develop spiritually.

I try to follow Pong's example.

To me, the journey of becoming a real estate mini-mogul has been wonderful. I don't regret doing it.

Alas, here are my final thoughts:

- "Never, never, never give up."

- Real estate is a terrific means for reaching financial independence. It's available to almost everyone.

- Always keep your values and maintain your integrity.

- Do what you have a passion for. This may or may not be real estate. My observation is that the happiest people have a passion for something in life. Many of us don't have this. If you don't have a passion, keep searching and you will find one.

- Real estate can be a vehicle for making a positive difference in other people's lives. A recent experience brought this home to me. I am currently in the process of upgrading one of my buildings. The apartments hadn't been touched for about fifty years and the rents were low. Many of the tenants had been living there for ten or more years. Resistance to change was strong when I initiated the project a couple of years ago, but the tenants slowly climbed on the bandwagon, and over time they were excited to move back into their new, spiffy apartments. One tenant in particular was worrisome, however. He had the worst unit in the building and wouldn't even let my crew in periodically to paint the place. Painting would have been to little avail, as he had the unit so packed with possessions, I couldn't figure out how he even slept there. But as the building started changing, so did he. When it came time for his unit's rehab, he went along with it. Boxes and boxes of who knows what began to disappear from his apartment. We renovated it, and he moved back in. Soon delivery trucks started arriving with new furniture. The other tenants started commenting to the building manager that the tenant had really mellowed. He began taking pride in what he now called his "palace." I truly believe his life improved, as it did for those around him. Having done other rehabs with existing tenants staying on after the rehab, I have found that this wasn't at all an isolated experience. I believe the improved surroundings allowed the tenants to value themselves more.

I'm a Mr. "Let's Make the World Better" kind of guy, but I never imagined how investing in real estate would change me and those around me for the better when my journey began. But it did.

I hope it does it for you!

Happy investing!

APPENDIX

A LIST OF RESOURCES:

How I Turned $1000 into $5 Million in My Free Time, by William Nickerson. Published by Simon and Schuster, 1980. A classic rehab and trade-up approach strategy is described in this book. It is a book many of my rehabber friends first read when getting started.

How to Become Financially Independent by Investing in Real Estate in Your Free Time, by Albert J. Lowry. Published by Simon and Schuster, 1977.

Nothing Down (or his later book, *Nothing Down for the 90s*), by Robert G. Allen. Published by Simon and Schuster, 1990. This book was a best seller. It is well written and provides clear examples of various financial techniques.

Real Estate Investments and How to Make Them, 3rd edition, by Milt Tanzer. Published by Prentice Hall, 1997. This is a basic book describing how real estate investments work. I developed my numerator/denominator approach from this book.

Anything written by John T. Reed. I like his writing because he is thorough, entertaining, and thought-provoking. I especially liked his *How to Buy Real Estate for at Least 20% Below Market Value, How to Manage Residential Property for Maximum Cash Flow and Resale Value*, and *Residential Property Acquisition Handbook*. They are all published by John T. Reed, 342 Bryan Drive, Alamo, CA 94507.

Double Your Money in Real Estate Every Two Years, by Dave Glubetich. Published by Impact Publishing, 1981.

..commend several books on personal finance. Look for titles written by Suze Orman, Terry Savage, Jane Bryant Quinn, Maria Nemeth, or the Kiplinger Organization.

Modern Real Estate Practice, 17th edition, by Fillmore Gilaty, Wellington Allaway, and Robert Kyle. Published by Dearborn Real Estate Education, 2006. This has up-to-date information on state laws affecting real estate.

Landlording: a Handy Manual for Scrupulous Landlords and Landladies Who Do It Themselves, by Leigh Robinson. Published by Ex Press, 1988.

Practical Apartment Management, by Edward N. Kelley. Published by Institute of Real Estate Management (IREM), 2004.

The Ultimate Secrets of Total Self Confidence, by Dr. Robert Anthony. Published by Berkley Books, 1979.

Success Through a Positive Mental Attitude, by Napoleon Hill and W. Clement Stone. Published by Prentice Hall, 1960.

Discovering Your Soul's Purpose, by Mark Thurston. Published by A.R.E. Press, 1984.

If you are interested in purchasing a Real Estate Investment Trust (REIT), an informative book is *Investing in REITS – Real Estate Investment Trusts,* by Ralph L. Block and Veronica J. McDavid, published by Bloomberg Personal Bookshelf, 1998.

The one book on negotiation that comes closest to my principles of negotiation is *Getting to Yes: Negotiating Agreement Without Giving In,* by William L. Ury and Roger Fisher, published by Penguin Books, 1983.

ACKNOWLEDGMENTS

Thank you all for all your marvelous advice in the creation of this book from an idea to a finished product. This book wouldn't exist without each of you being there.

Margaret Burka, my faithful assistant who has been with me through every twist and turn in the book creation process.

David Wood, Appraisal Services, for appraisal advisement. Rest in peace.

Moneybags, for ongoing encouragement, support, and friendship.

Mr. Wheeler-Dealer, for all your help and for making the world a better place to live.

Steve Cain of Washington Mutual, for all your numerous, very helpful comments on the manuscript.

Gary Szpara, North Shore Bank, for content comments on financing.

Les Rubin, CPA, Rubin and Associates, for your thorough review related to accounting issues.

Thomas J. Masterson, property and casualty insurance broker – for advisement regarding property and casualty insurance.

Joey Lansing, Syndicated Equities – for advisement regarding syndication of properties.

Ilyse Friedman, wise friend – for helpful comments and support regarding the manuscript.

Laurie Rosin, The Book Editor – for editorial services.

Claudia Volkman – for creative editing and typesetting services.

Alan Gadney and Carolyn Porter for cover design and production services

Marlene Goodman – for producing wonderful illustrations.

Bruce Tate, Associated Bank – for helpful comments regarding financing.

Jack Lawlor, attorney, Sonnenschien, Nath and Rosenthal – for ongoing support and helpful advisement regarding legal issues and Buddhism.

Mark Burka, senior vice president and portfolio manager, Ziegler Capital Management LLC, subsidiary of Ziegler Companies, Inc. – for helpful advisement regarding investments.

Lila McClelland, friend, for constructive comments regarding the manuscript.

Michele Pockross, spouse, for putting up with me for the past quarter century.

Stanford Gass, attorney, Gass and Lewis, Ltd., for helpful advisement concerning legal issues.

Thomas Duggan, attorney, DeWitt, Ross and Stevens, for helpful comments concerning legal issues.

Phil Pappas, friend, for ongoing support and advisement during the writing of the book.

ABOUT THE AUTHOR

James S. Pockross has been a real estate investor for twenty-five years. He has put together numerous deals and currently controls approximately 270 rental units. He belongs to several organizations and has served as the president of the of the Lakeview Developers Association and also as an officer of the Lincoln Park Builders Club of Chicago. The City of Aurora selected one of his properties for its annual Excellence in Property Improvement awards.

Mr. Pockross received a Bachelor of Science Degree in psychology from the University of Illinois, where he was awarded a Phi Beta Kappa key. He also earned a Master's in Business Administration Degree with specialization in finance and hospital administration from the University of Chicago, where he graduated with honors.

A hospital administrator by training, Mr. Pockross has worked as a hospital administrator and as a policy analyst for a hospital trade association.

He is licensed to sell life, accident, and health insurance and owns an insurance agency specializing in health insurance for small companies.

Mr. Pockross' interests include basketball, football, baseball (he is a very long suffering Chicago Cubs fan), the stock market, contract bridge, and travel. He has visited all fifty states and many countries.

Mr. Pockross is married and claims that the boss of his household is their pet cat, Mimi.

INDEX

A

actual cash value 300, 301
adjustable mortgage 26, 53
Allaway, Wellington 348
Allen, Robert G. 347
amortize 21, 80
Anthony, Robert 348
appraiser 44, 53, 145, 159, 160, 161, 162, 163, 164, 165, 166, 167, 171, 179
appreciation 13, 60, 97, 139, 141, 142, 143, 147, 150, 151, 157, 199, 207,
        209, 256, 257, 262, 319, 321, 324, 337
arithmetic 21, 80, 141, 142, 159, 169, 171, 172, 246
assemblage 259
auctions 70, 71, 73, 133-135, 164, 256, 276-277
Aurora 3, 55, 56, 57, 58, 59, 60, 61, 62, 64, 66, 67, 68, 69, 70, 77, 79, 80, 85,
        87, 88, 91, 93, 94, 95, 111, 129, 163, 171, 173, 197, 250, 261, 270, 274,
        283, 284, 293, 301, 303, 304, 351

B

balloon payment 91, 96, 190, 203, 212
bill collectors 61, 197
Block, Ralph L. 348
building-code violations. 47, 51, 58
building inspector 29, 51, 52
building inspectors 64
Building Ordinance coverage 303, 304
Building Owners and Management Association 175
buy at market 157

C

C.B. Richard Ellis 127
canvassing 127, 129
capital expenses 96, 277
capital gains tax 68, 106, 279, 283, 284
capital improvement and replacement reserves 178
capital improvements 79, 139, 140
capitalization rate 145, 159, 164-167, 172, 247
Chicago Tribune 26, 70, 124, 276
Churchill, Sir Winston 12

351

QUICK ORDER FORM

FAX Orders: 1-419-281-6883

Telephone Orders: 1-800-BOOKLOG (800-266-5564)

Email Orders: orders@atlasbooks.com

Web Orders: www.samsonpub.com

Postal Orders: Atlas Books Distribution
                        30 Amberwood Parkway
                        Ashland, OH 44805

Please send _____ copy (copies) of
Confessions of a Real Estate Mini-Mogul
I understand that I may return this order for a full refund
for any reason, no questions asked.

Name: _____

Address: _____

City: _____ State _____ Zip_____

Telephone: _____

Email: _____

PRICE OF BOOK: $19.95   ISBN: 978-0-9796951-0-0

SALES TAX: Please add 8.00% for products shipped to Illinois addresses.
Please add 7.25% for products shipped to Ohio addresses.

SHIPPING & HANDLING: U.S. – $5.50 for 1st book; $2.00 for each additional book.
                     INTERNATIONAL – $9.00 USD for 1st book;
                                     $5.00 USD for each additional
                                     book (estimate)

PAYMENT: Check _____
          Credit Card ____
          Visa _____ MasterCard _____ Discover _____ American Express _____
          Card Number: _____
          Name on Card: _____
          Exp. Date: _____ 3-Digit Code: _____

To contact Jim Pockross or Samson Publishing, Inc.
please email samsonpublishing@comcast.net or call 847-256-2399